Emily Post's

WEDDINGS

OTHER BOOKS FROM THE EMILY POST INSTITUTE:

Emily Post's Etiquette

16TH EDITION

Emily Post's Wedding Planner

3RD EDITION

Emily Post's Entertaining

WEDDINGS

THIRD EDITION

PEGGY POST

HarperPerennial
A Division of HarperCollinsPublishers

HarperCollins books may be purchased for educational, business, or
sales promotional use. For information please write:
Special Markets Department, HarperCollins Publishers, Inc.,
10 East 53rd Street, New York, NY 10022.

DESIGN BY BTD

ILLUSTRATIONS © LAURA HARTMAN MAESTRO

PHOTOS © ANDREA SPERLING

LIBRARY OF CONGRESS CATALOGING-IN-PUBLICATION DATA

Post, Peggy,
        Emily Post's weddings / Peggy Post. -- 3rd ed.
            p.   cm.
        ISBN 0-06-270227–0
        1. Wedding etiquette.   I. Title.
        BJ2051.P62 1999
        395.2'2--dc21   98-42646

---

99 00 01 02 03 ❖/RRD 10 9 8 7 6 5 4 3 2 1

Contents

INTRODUCTION

Y ou're engaged! As the couple of the moment, you're in the throes of rejoicing with your parents and friends, picturing a life of married bliss. With all the excitement comes another wish—that of a perfect wedding. But what does "perfect" mean? For one thing, it no longer describes only the storybook formal event with six bridesmaids and yards of white tulle. (Simple weddings are some of the most beautiful.) In truth, the ideal is a wedding that personalizes style, dress, and surroundings to reflect who you are, and that at the same time runs smoothly for all concerned—you, your family, your wedding party, your guests. The same applies to your suppliers and contractors, whether they include the all-purpose caterers and musicians that come with an elaborate event, or the florist and stationer who alone satisfy the needs of a smaller informal wedding.

For my own wedding, my husband and I put on a casual clambake reception—complete with seafood and corn on the cob—because we decided it just "felt right" for us. But what, you might wonder, would my great-grandmother-in-law, Emily Post, have made of our choice? That's easy: She'd have been there with bells on. She was one to change with the times, understanding that "etiquette" is first and foremost about making people feel comfortable with one another, whether going about the business of their daily lives or readying a wedding ceremony. Also, she knew that the magic of a wedding lay less in the details than in the tender quality of the occasion and the radiance of the bride—*and* the groom. "The radiance of a truly happy bride is so beautifying that even a plain girl is made pretty, and a pretty one, divine," she wrote in *Etiquette* (1922). "She and the groom both look as though there were sunlight behind their eyes, as though their mouths irresistibly turned to smiles."

While that sentiment has stayed the same, weddings themselves haven't. Changes in society, from a more culturally diverse population to the redefinition of the family, have revolutionized the rite, giving rise to more informal ceremonies, a revival of ethnic customs, and a more active role for the groom. Beyond that, weddings have become more adventurous and imaginative, with destination weddings and theme weddings part of the evolution.

It goes without saying that these changes can be confusing and stressful to sort through—a truth that was driven home to me when I took on the monthly "Etiquette for Today" column in *Good Housekeeping* magazine in 1995 and found wedding questions from all quarters—brides, grooms, attendants, guests, contractors—that were very much of the present, reflecting changing family structures and the relaxation of traditional rules. One future bride wondered, "Which of my fathers can walk me down the aisle? And can my mother?" Another, deciding on gift registries, asked, "Is it okay for us to register at a camping goods store?"

The flood of questions also pointed to the need for an update of the Emily Post wedding book, which was last revised in 1991. This new edition of *Emily Post's Weddings* is not only updated but arrives in conjuction with *Emily Post's Wedding Planner,* references to which you'll see in the following pages. The separate planner helps you keep track of every detail, providing space for jotting down notes on cost estimates, appointments, gift lists, and more—needs that apply to weddings of any kind.

The differences in weddings today? First, they are more personal, with brides and grooms bending tradition to suit their backgrounds, preferences, and tastes. Second, today's two-career couples take a different attitude about how expenses should be divided and who will foot the bills. Third, the groom, and sometimes his parents, are more involved in the planning and organization than ever before. (Happily, the old saying, "A man never knows how unimportant he is until he attends his own wedding," has mostly fallen by the wayside.) Finally, the changes in family structure pose a host of complicated questions: When parents are divorced and remarry and family trees branch out in all directions, who is responsible for what and who is seated with whom—and who keeps track of it all while making sure everybody stays happy?

Other questions—some new, others that have always arisen—can be answered with a simple yes or no. Is it all right to have a cash bar at your reception? Although some hotel and club managers will tell you otherwise, the answer is a definite no. Does an engagement have a time limit? Again, no. Can you avoid hurt feelings when discouraging the attendance of children at the ceremony? Yes. Do guests who are invited to the ceremony and reception have an obligation to send a gift, even if they're not attending? Generally, yes.

Whatever questions and challenges come your way, I hope this book will give you guidance relevant to today. I also hope you'll have *fun,* whether your wedding is small and informal or grand and traditional. Really, all that's needed for the "perfect" wedding is the bride and groom's love for each other, the confidence to make decisions, and making sure everyone involved is treated with courtesy. A sense of humor comes in handy, too, helping you to negotiate any unexpected bumps along the way.

The date is set, the time is nigh, and it's time to get busy. As the two of you approach one of the most important days of your lives, just remember to keep the details in perspective and your happiness and joy in the forefront. May it all turn out beautifully—the perfect wedding for *you.*

PEGGY POST
January 1999

Emily Post's

WEDDINGS

CHAPTER 1

THE ENGAGEMENT

Your engagement represents a time of euphoria, joy, and often, over-whelming detail. Whether the time between your engagement and your wedding is six weeks or six months, every now and then you should take time off from organizing the wedding to enjoy the fun and happiness your engagement brings.

Engagements require only a few simple guidelines. First, there are no papers to sign or tests to take to become engaged. You have only to say yes for an engagement to become official. Second, there is no mandated length of time for an engagement. Some people might consider six months a long engagement; others take their time and stretch it out to three years. The third guideline, for those re-entering marriage, is not to become officially engaged until you are officially divorced. Many a couple has jumped the gun and announced their engagement when a divorce is still in process. Even if an annulment or divorce is imminent, an engagement to another person should not be announced until it is final.

The engagement period is a time to make sure that this is the right decision for both of you, to think through potential obstacles to your happiness and how you plan to deal with them. It is a time to cement your love and commitment to each other. It is not a good idea to become engaged on a whim. While there is potentially less pain for all concerned in the breaking of an engagement than in the ending of a marriage, there is nonetheless a sense of loss. Once family and friends are told of your plans to remarry, your commitment becomes real.

THE LENGTH OF THE ENGAGEMENT

There is no correct length of time for an engagement. It may be as brief or as long as the couple requires to make their arrangements, save for their life

In the mid-nineteenth-century South, informing every relative of an engagement and wedding plans was done in person. The new bride and her mother would travel to the many households of family members by carriage, making their "engagement rounds," telling and retelling the news.

together, or complete schooling, work, or a period of mourning. The average length for an engagement in the United States is 14 months.

Ideally, the shorter the time span between the engagement and the wedding day, the less stress on all parties. A long engagement usually means a prolonged period of planning and organizing. Indeed, in some regions this is a necessity, as ceremony and reception sites can be booked a year or more in advance. If your engagement is a prolonged one, be sure to make time for each other, for your families, and for yourself to relax. Organizing a wedding should not be a chore; rather, it should be a time of expectation and joy. The more time you have, the more you can personalize your wedding, whether this means writing your own vows, making your own gown, or finding perfect, meaningful gifts for your attendants.

TELLING THE FAMILIES AND CLOSE FRIENDS

A certain protocol should be followed in getting the news out about your betrothal, even in these modern times. When sharing your engagement plans with families and friends, there are certain family members and close friends who should hear the news first. The guidelines of when, how, and to whom the news is spread have to do with people's feelings; let thoughtfulness be your guide.

OLD WAYS, NEW WAYS

Historically, if the marriage had not been arranged by the two families in the first place, it was up to the groom to ask the young woman's father for permission to propose. Of course, doing so was generally contingent on the positive signals he had received from the young woman during their courtship. If her father declined to grant his permission, that was that—unless of course the couple was defiant enough to run off and be married without the requisite blessings. If permission was granted, however, the groom would then, on bended knee, formally propose. Then he would head home to inform his parents.

Today, in most cultures, things are very different. The bride and groom themselves make the decision to marry. They then inform their families but do not necessarily ask for their permission. Generally, parents are the first to get the news, and in most cases the bride tells her parents and the groom tells his. But sometimes they do this together, sharing the news as a couple. It is to be hoped that the news doesn't come as a shock to the engaged couples' loved ones. If, during the courtship, the couple feels their relationship is becoming serious, it's a good idea for each to become acquainted with the other's loved ones and close friends. If this is impossible because they live on opposite coasts or separate continents, then the couple should be sure to mention their special relationship in phone conversations, letters, or e-mail before announcing their engagement.

Although it may seem old-fashioned, it is still courteous for the prospective groom to explain his plans and his prospects to the bride's parents, as evidence of his respect for them.

Telling Children

When one or both members of the engaged couple has children from a previous marriage, the children should always be the first people to hear the news, told to them by their parent alone, without the future stepparent present. Children of any age need time to adjust to the idea.

Telling Other Relatives and Friends

Once parents and children have been told the news—and not before—the happy bride and groom will want to share their engagement plans with other relatives and friends. They can do so by making telephone calls, writing notes, or sending faxes or e-mail. Or they might wait and surprise everyone with an announcement at an engagement party. Regardless, there are certain people other than parents and children who should hear the news first, and who would be hurt to read of the engagement in the newspaper or hear of it from someone other than the couple. These include grandparents, siblings, favorite aunts and uncles, and close friends. Always include them as special people who deserve to know before the rest of the immediate world finds out.

Telling Ex-Spouses

An ex-spouse should also be notified of the impending marriage—especially if children are involved. It is particularly important to let an ex-spouse know before the children announce it. This courtesy allows an ex to better deal with the news and help the children deal with it. Even if there are no children, it is a discourtesy to let an ex-spouse hear this news from anyone other than the former husband or wife.

WHEN FAMILIES DISAPPROVE

When parents disapprove of the relationship, an engaged couple faces a dilemma. If they decide to marry in spite of this disapproval, they should simply tell their parents when and where the wedding will take place and that they hope the parents can be there. Parents who care about their future relationship with their children will put aside their misgivings and attend. They gain nothing, and possibly lose a child for good, if they refuse.

Often, parental disapproval stems from anxiety. If the disapproval is over an age difference, parents may worry about the health and longevity of the older person. They may also think the age gap means no grandchildren. In these instances, it is wise for the bride and groom to discuss any concerns directly (and alone) with their own parents in an effort to allay any apprehensions.

If parents disapprove because of a socioeconomic divide between the bride and groom, the problem may simply resolve with time. The more-affluent parents may worry that their child is being taken advantage of. If this is the one obstacle to receiving enthusiastic approval from parents, the couple can consider a premarital agreement (see chapter 4). If they prefer not to do this, then in time the obvious affection and commitment of the couple and a lasting marriage should eventually alleviate their parents' fears.

If it is your own parents who show disapproval, it is important to remain calm and not react with anger. Show that you are willing to listen to their concerns, but reiterate your allegiance to your mate-to-be. When you take a calm and confident position, it is likely that they will take you seriously. With all the tact you possess, let them know that you are not rejecting *them*, and even though you disagree with their opinions or concerns, you truly hope they will change their position over time.

If your children disapprove of the engagement, the dilemma is even greater, and family relationships can become quite strained. If time and communication cannot bridge the gap and basic civility and politeness have been abandoned, then professional counseling could be initiated to help the entire family understand one anothers' feelings.

WHEN OTHERS DISAPPROVE

Times have changed dramatically since the days of Emily Post. One of the biggest changes is the almost 3.5 million households composed of couples living openly together "without benefit of marriage." When one such couple decides to marry, they may be surprised to find disapproval—not of the marriage itself but of any planned celebrations.

There is no arguing with people's moral standards or beliefs. There also may be some people who are unenthusiastic about your upcoming marriage for other reasons. If there are people in your life who object to your plans—whatever the reason—simply try to be gracious and forgiving.

DIPLOMACY AND A DIFFICULT FAMILY

In these complex times there often exist difficult family situations that a wedding can bring to light. The bride's mother, for example, may announce that she will not attend a single wedding party or the wedding itself if her ex-husband is going to be there. The groom's mother may insist that she will not participate if the groom's father's mother (her mother-in-law) is invited. Children in the custody of their other parent may refuse to attend the wedding out of fear that their custodial parent will be upset or angry with them. Ambassadorial-level diplomacy is called for in these situations, preferably coming from the member of the couple who is related to the difficult family member. Although the couple should discuss what to do, it is wise not to involve each other in family disputes at this point in the relationship—for if the problem is not smoothed over, it is often the outsider who is blamed for interfering.

WELCOME TO THE FAMILY

A betrothal is not just the joining together of two people in wedded matrimony; it is also the joining together of two—and sometimes more—families. For the sake of the happy couple, this is the time for the parents of both to put their best faces forward and greet their new family with warmth and open hearts.

GETTING TO KNOW YOU

When parents of the bride and groom live near enough to meet one another before the wedding, tradition has it that the groom's family calls the bride's family to introduce themselves, express their happiness, and extend an invitation for a meeting. If for any reason the groom's family does not contact the parents of the bride, however, her father and mother should not stand on ceremony and wait for them to get in touch. Instead, they should make the first move themselves. This is a time of joy for the couple, and both sets of parents should act with spontaneity and in the spirit of friendship, regardless of who makes the first contact. If it is impossible for them to meet, they should attempt to call or write so that an initial introduction is established.

A LETTER OF WELCOME

When it is not possible for a mother to meet her son's fiancée, and if they have not spoken on the phone, the mother should write a letter, using the following as a guide:

> *Dear Brittany,*
>
> *Robert has just told us of his great happiness, which, of course, makes us very happy, too. Our one regret is that we are so far away that we cannot immediately meet you.*
>
> *We do, however, send you our love and hope that we shall see you very soon so that we can officially welcome you to the family.*
>
>

Affectionately,

Janet Parkington
>

The bride's mother could send a similar letter to her daughter's fiancé. When a divorced person with children is remarrying, the older children could write to their mother's fiancé or their father's fiancée.

WHEN PARENTS ARE DIVORCED

When the bride's parents are divorced, the groom's parents should get in touch with each of the bride's parents separately, calling first the one with whom the bride has been living or to whom she is the closest. They should arrange separate meetings with each parent so that the groom's parents can meet both the bride's parents and their spouses, if any.

When the groom's parents are divorced, the one with whom he is closest should contact the bride's parents. Otherwise, the bride's parents should initiate the introduction. If the groom's other parent and the bride's parents fail to continue the introduction process, the couple ideally steps in at this point to make sure that they do meet.

When all the parents are divorced, the groom's parent most inclined to begin the process of having the families meet should, in consultation with the bride and groom, contact first whichever of the bride's parents that she suggests.

Under no circumstances should the bride or the groom force their own divorced parents into social situations that have the potential to make them—and others—feel uncomfortable. As much as they want to have their parents reunite as an intact family in honor of their own wedding, it is often an unrealistic expectation.

WHAT TO CALL THE FUTURE IN-LAWS

You should continue to call each other's parents exactly what you have been calling them up to the moment of your engagement. If you have called them Mr. and Mrs., just continue to do so until they suggest otherwise. If they want you to call them Mom and Dad, it's fine to do so if you feel comfortable. Most married couples refer to their in-laws by their first names. If, after you are married, your in-laws have not suggested a less formal address, you may then ask them what they would like you to call them.

SPREADING THE NEWS

In addition to calling and writing family members and friends, a couple often chooses to submit an engagement announcement to their hometown newspapers. It is inappropriate to send printed engagement announcements, so many couples make their announcement public through the newspaper. Most newspaper engagement announcements appear approximately two to three months before the wedding day, even if wedding plans have not been firmed up. But there are no hard and fast rules: An announcement may appear up to a year before the wedding date or as little as a week before. An engagement announcement should never be made if either member is still legally married to someone else. Nor is a public announcement appropriate when there has recently been a death in either family or when a member of the immediate family is desperately ill.

The announcement of the engagement is generally made by the bride's parents or her immediate family, often using a standard form provided by the newspaper. Be sure to include a telephone number so that the information can be verified by the newspaper, if necessary. The bride's parents should ask the groom's parents if they would like the announcement to appear in their hometown papers as well. If so, the bride's parents can send it to those papers at the same time that they send it to their own.

Although each newspaper may have its own format, the information included and the basic content is as follows:

Mr. and Mrs. William Smith of Evanston, Illinois, announce the engagement of their daughter, Miss Christine Nicole Smith, to Mr. John Paul Rapaglia, son of Mr. and Mrs. Joseph Rapaglia of Monroe, Connecticut. An October wedding is planned.

Miss Smith was graduated from the University of Richmond and is a human resources assistant at Consolidated Advertising in New York City. Mr. Rapaglia was graduated from Mary Washington University. He is at present a member of the New York Yankees baseball team.

In a small-town newspaper, additional information about the bride and groom's parents may be used, but information about schools and employment remains the same. Following are some situations that require variations in wording of the basic announcement shown above. Wording can be pulled from various formats to construct the proper announcement for even the most complex situations.

When One of the Bride's Parents Is Deceased

> *Mrs. [Mr.] Gerald Robert Havlin announces the engagement of her [his] daughter, Miss Caroline Joan Havlin, to Mr. Anthony Vellone. Miss Havlin is also the daughter of the late Gerald Robert [Carol Putnam] Havlin. . . .*

When One of the Groom's Parents Is Deceased

> *Mr. and Mrs. William Francis Venable announce the engagement of their daughter, Miss Linda Barnes Venable, to Mr. Jonathan Huntington, son of Mrs. [Mr.] Robert Huntington and the late Robert [Eleanore Johnson] Huntington. . . .*

When the Bride's Parents Are Divorced
The mother of the bride usually makes the announcement, but as in the case of a deceased parent, the name of the other parent must be included.

> *Mrs. Donald Pico announces the engagement of her daughter, Miss Nancy Sasso. . . . Miss Sasso is also the daughter of Mr. Victor Sasso of Providence, Rhode Island. . . .*

When the Groom's Parents Are Divorced
The announcement presents the groom's parents separately, noting their places of residence, if different, but never pairing them as a couple even if they live in the same town.

> *Mr. and Mrs. Charles Cernek announce the engagement of their daughter, Miss Kathleen Mary Cernek, to Mr. Marvin Emil Henk, son of Mrs. Jeralyn Hughes Henk [of Palo Alto, California] and Mr. Michael Henk [of Sarasota, Florida]. . . .*

When Divorced Parents Are Friendly

When divorced parents remain friendly, they may both wish to announce the engagement, together.

> *Mrs. Walter Murphy of Palm Beach, Florida, and Mr. Timothy O'Neill of Philadelphia, Pennsylvania, announce the engagement of their daughter, Miss Linda O'Neill. . .*

When one or both parents have remarried, all parties may wish to participate in the announcement.

> *Mr. and Mrs. Walter Murphy of Palm Beach, Florida, and Mr. and Mrs. Timothy O'Neill of Philadelphia, Pennsylvania, announce the engagement of Mrs. Murphy's and Mr. O'Neill's daughter, Miss Linda O'Neill. . .*

When the Bride Is Adopted

If the bride was adopted in infancy or childhood, there is no reason to mention the fact that she is adopted. If she joined the family later in life, however, and has retained her own name, it is proper to say:

> *Mr. and Mrs. Archibald Penn announce the engagement of their adopted daughter, Miss Beth Cook, daughter of the late Mr. and Mrs. Thomas Cook. . .*

When the Bride Is an Orphan

The engagement of a bride with no parents is announced by her nearest relative, a godparent, or a very dear friend. She may also announce her own engagement, in the third person.

> *The engagement of Miss Hope Lee (daughter of the late Mr. and Mrs. George DeWitt Lee) is announced, to Mr. Jared Adam Tobin. . .*

When the Bride Is a Widow

The parents of a young widow would announce her engagement in the same way as they did the first time she was married, using her current name.

Mr. and Mrs. Paul Jensen announce the engagement of their daughter,
Mrs. Frederick Jensen Goldsmith [or Bonnie Jensen Goldsmith]. . .

An older widow may announce her own engagement, using the name by which she is known. If she has grown children, they may wish to announce the engagement:

Mrs. Joseph Carter, Ms. Gabrielle Berhnt, and Mr. Guy Berhnt
announce the engagement of their mother, Mrs. David Berhnt to Mr.
Curtis Palmer. . .

When the Bride Is a Divorcée

Similarly, the parents of a young divorcée would announce her engagement, using her former husband's last name if she continues to use his name, or her maiden name if she has changed her name back following a divorce.

Mr. and Mrs. Wilson W. Ahearn III announce the engagement of their
daughter, Mrs. Caroline Howell [or Caroline Ahearn Howell] [or
Caroline Elizabeth Ahearn], to. . .

When the divorcée is an older woman or independent of her parents, she may choose to announce her own engagement:

The engagement of Mrs. Patricia Hughes to Mr. Vincent Toppel is
announced. . .

When a First-Time Bride Is an Older Woman

An older woman marrying for the first time may announce her own engagement.

The engagement of Miss [or Ms.] Dolores Nutant to Mr. Jared Green
has been announced. . .

When the Couple Announce Their Own Engagement

For any number of reasons, the couple may choose to announce their own engagement.

Ms. Victoria Ann Farrington and Mr. Benjamin Dodd are pleased to announce their engagement. . .

Or they may choose to choose to announce it in a third-party format:

The engagement of Ms. Victoria Ann Farrington to Mr. Benjamin Dodd has been announced. . .

When the Groom's Parents Announce the Engagement

Occasionally a situation arises in which the parents of the groom would like to announce the engagement. This could happen when the bride is from another country and it would be difficult for her parents to put an announcement in the paper in his hometown. Rather than announce it in their own name, the groom's parents should word the notice as follows.

The engagement of Miss Natalie Coleman, daughter of Mr. and Mrs. Clay Coleman of Munich, Germany, to Mr. John Evans, son of Mr. and Mrs. Walter Evans of Chicago, is announced. . .

TIMING OF AN ANNOUNCEMENT

If an engagement party is planned, the announcement may appear before or after it takes place. If the couple hopes to surprise their guests at a party, the party should be held just before the news appears in the paper. If surprise is not a factor, then the party may take place soon or even weeks after the announcement is printed in the paper.

THE ENGAGEMENT RING

Engagement rings are steeped in centuries of tradition and have taken many forms. Throughout the years, rings have been made of woven grasses and tri-colored bands and have contained birthstones or stones with special meaning. In recent decades, the myth that the groom should spend the equivalent of one, or even two, month's salary on a diamond ring has grown to epic proportions.

A bride-to-be does *not* need a ring to make her engagement official. If she does have a ring, it does not need to be the largest diamond the groom can find.

Many couples prefer to use the money that would be spent on a ring toward the practicalities of building their lives together. Some couples postpone the purchase of an engagement ring until years after their wedding, when their finances enable them to buy the special ring they've envisioned.

RING ORIGINS

The engagement ring of modern times is simply a symbol of betrothal, but its roots are steeped in a potpourri of traditions. In ancient Africa, custom required that the bride's and groom's wrists were tied together with circlets of grass during the ceremony, and metal rings were sometimes given as partial payment when grooms purchased brides. During the prehistoric period, a man would tie braided grass rings around the wrists and ankles of his bride. It was believed that this would protect her from any evil spirits that might be waiting in the wings, as well as keep her own spirits from escaping. In ancient Egypt, well before coins were used as money, gold rings were the currency. An Egyptian husband would place a gold ring on his wife's finger to demonstrate that he trusted her with his money.

FINDING A REPUTABLE JEWELER

These days, the bride is often involved in selecting the engagement ring; in fact, only 30 percent of men do so alone. Although you needn't break the bank to buy an engagement ring, the cost can still be significant. Accordingly, you'll want to deal with a reputable jeweler who will do the best and most honest job to find you what you want. Shop around before you buy, but ask your friends and family for references when you decide to get serious. Generally, it is a good idea to do business with someone who comes highly recommended, who has been in the business a good while, and who is a member of the American Gem Society or the Jewelers of America. Beware of jewelers who advertise "wholesale to the public"; this is usually a falsehood. And once you have selected a ring, make the sale contingent on an independent appraisal. If the jeweler declines, take your business elsewhere.

RENAISSANCE ENGAGEMENTS

Gimmel rings, from the Latin "geminius" (twin), were double or triple interlocking bands that were popular engagement rings during the Renaissance. One piece was given to the prospective bride and one piece to the groom, to be reunited at the time of the wedding ceremony.

The Engagement

SELECTING A RING

Your engagement ring should be exactly right for you and the groom. You will be the one wearing it, so you'll want to make sure the fit is comfortable and flattering. And even though it is purchased as a token of love, an engagement ring is also an investment. The more you as a couple know, the wiser the investment. Following are a few facets of ring buying to help you make the best choice.

DIAMONDS: THE FOUR C'S AND MORE

Diamonds, the traditional gemstones for engagement rings, are the emblems of love and engagement. Knowing the four C's allows you to converse comfortably with jewelers when you are shopping for a diamond engagement ring.

Carat

Carat is the measure of the weight of a diamond. One carat is one-fifth of a gram (200 milligrams). There are 142 carats to an ounce. One carat also has 100 points. This system of measuring diamond weight began in India and was based on the weight of the seeds of the carob tree, which were used to balance scales.

Clarity

Diamonds are rated on the basis of blemishes (or inclusions) that occur in nature, such as inner cracks, bubbles, and specks that are hard to detect by the naked eye. The size and placement of the blemishes determine a diamond's clarity rating, which ranges from flawless to varying degrees of small inclusions to the least desirable rating: "imperfect." When a diamond is rated flawless (FL), it is given the highest clarity rating; a flawless diamond is rare.

Cut

The way a diamond is cut determines its brilliance. In fact, cut is generally considered the most important of the four C's. When cut, a diamond is faceted in a series of flat, angled surfaces that reflect light off one another. This is what causes the stone to sparkle.

RINGS OF FAITH

Fede rings, so named for the Roman word for faith, seem to have originated in the early 1600s. These rings, still seen today, were constructed with two small gold hands encircling either side of the ring and clasping the other at the ring's center. Some fede rings are detachable, and the prospective bride and groom each keep one piece until they are married. Sometimes, a small heart lies hidden beneath the hands.

Color

Another criterion for determining the value of diamonds is color. Diamonds are rated on a color grade scale from D (the highest) all the way down to Z. Those that are clear and colorless are rated D, while progressively lower ratings indicate stones with traces of earthy colors such as brown, yellow, or gray.

More C's

A fifth C for diamonds is certification. This is the written proof of a diamond's weight, grade, and identifying characteristics from the International Gemological Institute and should come with your ring.

The sixth and seventh C's for any stone and ring choice are cost and care. Cost depends on your personal budget, but care is an important consideration for everyone. The hardness of a diamond makes it easy to clean and the most durable of stones. Other gemstones are softer and more susceptible to damage and therefore require more care. The setting of the stone is also a care concern, particularly for brides who use their hands in their work. A raised or elaborate setting that can get caught easily or get in the way may not be as good a choice as a more protective setting. One such setting is called a bezel, where the band hugs the middle section of the stone. Another protective setting is a channel setting, where the stones are set between two strips of the band so that they are held at both top and bottom.

The last C is comfort. Whatever the shape or size of the ring you choose, it should be comfortable, allowing your finger and hand to feel unencumbered. It should not be an annoyance nor should you even be aware that you are wearing it; otherwise, the temptation will be to take it off—and then what's the point of having it?

GEMSTONES

Instead of a diamond, many couples prefer a gemstone—a perfectly acceptable choice—for the engagement ring. Gemstones are classified as "precious" and "semiprecious," with precious stones being emeralds, rubies, and sapphires. Long prized as symbols of mystical powers, gemstones were also graced with symbolic meaning during Victorian times, when they became especially popular in engagement rings. Some examples of symbols given to gemstones:

AMETHYST	*power*
AQUAMARINE	*happy marriage*
BLOODSTONE	*bravery and wisdom*
DIAMOND	*purity and innocence*
EMERALD	*honesty and intelligence*
GARNET	*constancy and fidelity*
JADE	*good fortune*
LAPIS LAZULI	*good health*
OPAL	*consistency and fearlessness*
PEARL	*good health and beauty*
RUBY	*clarity of the heart*
SAPPHIRE	*faithfulness*
SARDONYX	*marital happiness*
TOPAZ	*cheerfulness and strength*
TURQUOISE	*prosperity and success*

Some couples select gemstones for engagement rings based on the birthstones of the bride or the groom or both. If you want your ring to symbolize something besides your engagement, you can choose the stone representing your birth months.

JANUARY	*garnet or zircon*
FEBRUARY	*amethyst*
MARCH	*aquamarine or bloodstone*
APRIL	*diamond*
MAY	*emerald*
JUNE	*pearl*
JULY	*ruby*
AUGUST	*sardonyx or carnelian*
SEPTEMBER	*sapphire*
OCTOBER	*opal or moonstone*
NOVEMBER	*topaz*
DECEMBER	*lapis lazuli or turquoise*

SETTINGS

The setting of a ring is defined as the way the stone or stones are arranged within the metal of the ring itself. Two of the most popular settings are 1) the traditional Tiffany setting, where a single diamond perches high on the band, and 2) the illusion setting, which is usually a group of smaller stones surrounding a larger one.

Two terms often used in describing stones within settings are *baguette* and *pavé*. Baguettes are smaller stones, usually rectangular with square corners, set on both sides of a larger, centered stone. Pavé diamonds are small stones that are fitted into tapered holes placed very close together, forming a continuous surface.

STONE SHAPES

Just as you try on clothes to ensure a comfortable, flattering fit, you should try on rings to find the settings and stone shapes that best fit and flatter your hand. Less traditional shapes include heart-shape stones and "fancy cuts." The shapes shown here are the most traditional shapes.

- **MARQUISE** shapes are oblong with pointed ends. This cut is named after Marquise de Pompadour, the mistress of Louis XV.

- **ROUND** shapes are the most popular, probably because their many facets allow them to reflect more light—hence their other name, "brilliant."

- **OVAL** shapes are adapted from the round-cut diamond.

- **EMERALD CUT** diamonds are rectangular with levels, or steps, from base to top.

- **PEAR** diamonds are round on one end and pointed on the other. The round end is worn toward the hand, the pointed end toward the fingertip.

KARATS VERSUS CARATS

The metal used for the ring itself should always be harmonious with the other elements of the ring. Platinum is a popular choice—it is extremely durable and doesn't wear away as easily as gold. Gold becomes more durable as higher amounts of other metals are blended into it. The amount of gold is defined by karats, listed by a number, up to 24. The purest gold, and therefore the softest and most likely to bend, is 24 karat gold. An 18 karat gold ring is 18 parts gold and 6 parts another metal. A 14 karat gold ring, the most popular, is 14 parts gold and 10 parts another metal. Ask your jeweler's advice when choosing which metal is best for your setting and stone.

WEARING YOUR RING

A bride may wear her ring as soon as she receives it—that is, unless she or the groom-to-be is still married to someone else and awaiting a divorce. If an engagement party is planned where a surprise announcement will be made, she may want to wait to wear it so as not to spoil the surprise. The bride wears the ring on the fourth finger (next to the little finger) of her left hand. In some countries it is worn on the fourth finger of the right hand. Regardless, it is removed before the marriage ceremony and replaced by the wedding ring, which is worn closest to the heart. The engagement ring is then placed above (closer to the fingertip) the wedding ring.

Naturally, no one should wear an engagement ring given by someone who is still married, no matter how close the divorce or annulment may be.

A RING FROM A PREVIOUS MARRIAGE

When a widow becomes engaged to marry again, she should stop wearing her rings from her previous marriage, whether or not she receives a new engagement ring. When deciding what to do with her first engagement ring, she may want to consider keeping it for a son to use as an engagement ring for his future bride. Or she might have the stone or stones reset into another piece of jewelry for herself or her daughters.

A divorcée does not continue to wear the engagement ring from her previous marriage. She may, if she wishes, have the stone or stones from that ring reset in another piece of jewelry. She does not need to return the ring to her ex-husband when she becomes engaged again.

HEIRLOOM RINGS

The bride-to-be who is presented with a family heirloom ring as an engagement ring has the choice of simply sizing the ring to her finger or having it reset by a jeweler. On the other hand, she may feel uncomfortable taking the ring, in which case she needn't accept it. No matter how many generations it may have been in the family, an heirloom ring should never be one from the previous marriage of a bride or groom, passed along just because it exists.

CHOOSING WEDDING RINGS

Wedding rings may be selected at the same time as the engagement ring, but often they are not. Many times they are selected and ordered during the engagement period, when the bride and groom can take the time to find what will be a meaningful, serious purchase. Even if the groom has selected the engagement ring as a surprise for his intended, both should participate in the selection of the wedding ring or rings.

The bridegroom may or may not choose to wear a wedding ring. If he does, you'll then need to decide whether you want matching rings. If so, his will generally be a little wider and heavier than the bride's wedding ring. Otherwise, it may be any type of ring he prefers—as long as it is one you are able to afford. In the United States, the man's wedding ring, like the woman's, is traditionally worn on the fourth finger of the left hand.

TYPES OF WEDDING BANDS

Wedding bands are designed in platinum or yellow or white gold and come in a variety of finishes. If the bride is going to wear her engagement ring with her wedding band, the two should preferably be of the same metal and work well together.

As with engagement rings, bands should be chosen with an eye to the shape of the bride's hand. If her hands are small, a narrow band looks best. Larger hands with longer fingers can wear wider and more elaborate rings.

L.O.V.E.

Victorians sometimes used gemstones to spell out messages or their names on rings, more often on wedding rings than on engagement rings. A ring spelling "regard," for example, would contain stones in the following order: Ruby, Emerald, Garnet, Amethyst, Ruby, Diamond. A ring for "Margaret" would have even more stones, which might be Moonstone, Aquamarine, Ruby, Garnet, Amethyst, Ruby, Emerald, and Topaz. And "love"? Lapis lazuli, Opal, Verde antique (a green-veined marble), and Emerald.

For both the bride and the groom, comfort is of the utmost importance. A ring that is too wide or heavy or that gets in the way is not the right ring.

ENGRAVING

Wedding bands may be engraved with designs on the outside or they may be plain. The inside is usually engraved with words, initials, or simply the date. The engraved words may be a message that is a sentiment known only to the bride and groom. Before finalizing your purchase, ask the jeweler how many letters may be engraved on the inside of your wedding bands so that you can write out the inscription to be fit inside the ring.

THE ENGAGEMENT PARTY

If there is an engagement party for the couple, anyone may host it. Usually, however, it is the bride's parents who do so. It may be any type of party but is most often a cocktail party or a dinner. The host, usually the bride's father, makes the engagement official by proposing a toast to the couple when all the guests have assembled.

At a very large party, if the announcement is not a surprise, the bride's fiancé stands with her and her mother and is introduced as the guests arrive.

THE GUEST LIST

The majority of engagement parties are restricted to relatives and good friends of both families, but you may invite anyone you choose. The people invited to the engagement party are often those who will be your top-priority wedding guests. Occasionally, the engagement party is a large open house or reception.

STRAIGHT TO THE HEART

Does love travel to the heart from the finger? Ancients thought so, as they were certain that the direct route was in the vein of the third finger of the left hand—the only finger, it was believed, with a vein that made the connection to the heart.

THE MATTER OF GIFTS

Engagement gifts have never been obligatory and are not expected from casual friends and acquaintances. They are, however, becoming customary in some parts of the country, usually given to the couple by family members and close friends. Often, inviting guests specifically to an engagement party carries with it the implication that a gift is expected. If the bride and groom choose not to receive engagement

A RING FOR HIM

Although European grooms have worn wedding bands for centuries, the rings became more widely worn and more popular in America during and directly after World War II, when men in the military sought to carry with them a token of home.

gifts or don't want to burden others with an abundance of wedding-related costs, they may simply surprise all (or most) of the party guests with the announcement of their engagement. Their big news is then treated as a celebration, not as a gift-giving event.

Some guests who know of the surprise ahead of time might bring gifts. In this case, the couple sets the gifts aside and does not open them during the party. If the gifts were opened in front of all, those who did not bring a gift would feel uncomfortable.

If the party is a small dinner for very close friends and family, gifts may or may not be brought by guests, depending on the particular geographical, ethnic, and family customs. Those closest to the couple who want to give a gift should do so in private and not at the party. A good guideline for anyone who is attending a small party but isn't sure: Ask the hosts of the party for their guidance. A guest might then take a small gift as a token of his or her love and affection. If everyone brings a gift and there is time, the bride and groom may open their gifts and give thanks in person. A follow-up thank-you note is therefore not mandatory—but it is always an excellent idea.

Gifts that are sent after an announcement appears or after a party must always be acknowledged with a thank-you note.

A BROKEN ENGAGEMENT

If an engagement is broken, the bride should immediately return the ring unless it is an heirloom from her own family. There is some debate over whether the ring should be returned if the engagement was broken by the man rather than

The Engagement

by the bride or mutual agreement. It makes more sense to return it; why have bad memories of the end of an engagement just to be spiteful? It's better to take the high road—and move on.

The bride should also return any other presents of any value that her fiancé has given her, and he returns her gifts to her as well. Wedding and shower gifts, as well as any engagement gifts, should also be returned to the givers. If it is too difficult to return them in person, they may be returned by mail, accompanied by an explanatory note:

Dear Rachel,

I am sorry to have to tell you that Ed and I have broken our engagement. Therefore, I am returning the lovely tray that you were so kind to send me.

Love,

Sara

If the engagement was announced in the paper, a notice may appear announcing that the marriage will not take place. The notice need say no more than "the engagement of Miss Sara Brown and Mr. James Forster has been broken by mutual consent."

Should the groom pass away before the wedding takes place, however, the bride may keep her engagement ring unless it is a family heirloom, in which case she should offer to return it to the family. She can keep any gifts given by relatives and friends but may prefer to return them—especially if they are constant reminders of her loss.

CHAPTER 2

THE BIG DECISIONS

The engagement is on; you and your loved ones are thrilled; the future is bright with hope and possibility. Now is the time for the two of you to sit down and have a serious discussion. Simply put: Now is the time to talk about the kind of wedding you both envision. If you've always dreamed of floating up the aisle in a long white gown and your mate thinks a casual clambake on the beach would suffice, don't let that deter either of you. Keep talking.

Differing ideas are just that: ideas. Wedding planning starts with ideas. Being part of a twosome means working together to make the both of you content and happy.

It is also time for a reality check. Two of the biggest factors influencing the major decisions of your wedding plans are money and convenience.

Whether you have a long or a short time to plan your wedding, start out by separating your primary decisions from less important ones. You'll find that once you've made the big decisions, the secondary decisions will fall into place. Think of the primary decisions as the foundation for every other choice you make.

Before you start debating the merits of a large-versus-small wedding or a formal-versus-informal one, both of you should make a list of all the qualities you admire about weddings you've attended or you see as important to your own wedding. Use descriptive words such as:

grand	*old-fashioned*
intimate	*spiritual*
luxurious	*secular*
elegant	*musical*
dramatic	*colorful*
casual	*friendly*
contemporary	*romantic*

Now pare the list down until you are left with the five or so qualities that you consider most important. What kind of affair do these words describe? A gathering of those nearest and dearest to you in your parents' backyard? A grand ballroom with everyone in evening clothes? The beach where you spent every summer of your life and pledge to always return to? The church where you were confirmed? The synagogue where your bar mitzvah took place? The chapel on the edge of the woods by your grandmother's house?

Let the qualities you have chosen as most important guide your decisions. The personal touches that will make it uniquely your own will evolve as you continue to plan.

THE TOP-PRIORITY DECISIONS

Your initial decisions will be based on the following:

- The GUEST LIST
- The BUDGET
- The DATE: time of year, day of the week, and time of day
- The STYLE of your wedding (formal vs. informal; religious or civil)
- The availability of your wedding OFFICIANT
- The LOCATIONS for both the ceremony and the reception

THE GUEST LIST

While your available budget is certainly *the* determining factor for your wedding, your guest list has everything to do with how the money is spent. If neither of you can imagine celebrating your nuptials without your mutually large families in attendance, the guest list will by necessity be a big one. If your guest list is large and your budget small, you may have to forego a big, formal, sit-down dinner reception. Otherwise, paring your guest list down may allow it. *Narrowing the guest list is the easiest way to cut costs.*

Ask your families to come up with a maximum guest list, in priority order, with an asterisk by those who absolutely must be there. Explain that you can't make any final decisions about the kind of wedding you are having until you have some idea of the size of the guest list. For more on guest lists, please refer to Chapter 5, Guests and Guest Lists.

THE BUDGET

If your parents are paying for the wedding or contributing to it, now is the time to discuss finances. Be realistic about your expenses, and be appreciative of whatever your parents can contribute. If your parents have given you a figure that is the most they can spend, it is up to you to work with that amount or combine your resources with theirs. Then tally the projected costs for your wedding, and compare it against your resources. For fairly formal weddings, 50 to 60 percent of the costs generally go toward the per-person reception fees. Some caterers suggest making a budget for the reception and then reducing it by 25 percent to cover any overruns. That doesn't mean, however, that you should cut quality to save costs. There are many ways of cutting corners without cutting quality.

If you are paying for your own wedding, you will have a good idea from the beginning what kind of event you can realistically afford. If your budget is limited, you will have to decide what takes priority: a big, glamorous wedding with a shorter guest list, or a larger guest list and a more toned-down reception. This is the time to find compromises by shortening the guest list, by choosing a time of year or time of day when costs are less, by choosing an affordable reception site, or by foregoing a big wedding party. The variations, as you can see, are endless. For more on wedding expenses, see Chapter 3, Expenses.

THE DATE AND TIME

Time of Year

The time of year for your wedding is a key consideration, for three reasons. First, the favorite months for weddings are June, September, August, May, October, and July. Accordingly, the most popular wedding sites will be at a premium during those months, in terms of both availability and cost. If budget is a concern, you will do better to select a month when rates and fees are lower. In general, the best budget months of the year are January, February, and March. Of course, if you plan a destination wedding or honeymoon in the Caribbean in February, you'll be paying peak prices.

If time is a factor and you are looking ahead only a few months, you will have a more difficult time finding clubs, wedding sites, bands, and photographers that are not already booked.

A PROPER TIME TO MARRY

There is an old folk saying that says "Choose not alone a proper mate, but a proper time to marry." If you don't need to contemplate practical considerations in choosing the month you will marry, there is folklore, myth, and tradition to guide you!

The Victorians loved attributing meaning to everything, and many paid close attention to the wedding rhymes that suggested certain results from certain wedding dates.

JANUARY—Marry when the year is new, he'll be loving, kind and true.

FEBRUARY—When February birds do mate, you wed nor dread your fate.

MARCH—If you wed when March winds blow, joy and sorrow both you'll know.

APRIL—Marry in April if you can, joy for maiden and for man.

MAY—Marry in the month of May, you will surely rue the day.

JUNE—Marry when June roses grow and over land and sea you'll go.

JULY—Those who in July do wed must labor for their daily bread.

AUGUST—Whoever wed in August be, many a change is sure to see.

SEPTEMBER—Marry in September's shine so that your life is rich and fine.

OCTOBER—If in October you do marry, love will come but riches tarry.

NOVEMBER—If you wed in bleak November, only joys will come, remember!

DECEMBER—When December's snows fall fast, marry, and your love will last.

Actually, these rhymes had a foundation that went beyond the fanciful. For example, the dire predictions for May weddings came from the custom of observing the Feast of the Dead during this month, when everyone worked hard to appease the souls of the departed. Queen Victoria took this so seriously that she permitted no royal weddings in the month of May. What made January a sure bet for a marriage to the ancient Greeks? This month was dedicated to Hera, defender of women and wife of Zeus. Anyone marrying in January received an extra blessing under Hera's power, and a plus on top of that—this was the time for fertility rites, the results of which just might be passed on to the January bride. Fertility recommended September, too, because of the benefits of the full harvest moon. If love mattered most, then April was the month to marry, for it was the favored month of Venus, the Roman goddess of love.

Still undecided about when to be married? There is always the Victorian assurance that the luckiest time of all to be married was on the same day of the week that the groom was born, regardless of fertility rites, harvest moons, or when the goddess of love might be looking in. It was better yet to marry on his birthday, perhaps so he'd always remember his anniversary.

Time of year is also a factor for a weekend wedding at a travel destination, whether Disney World or Bermuda. The off-season might be a better bet. Check with your travel agent before making any decisions.

Second, if your vision involves the outdoors in some component of your wedding, you will be limited to warm-weather months, unless you are planning a reception at a ski resort. Even then, a winter ski resort may also be fully booked well in advance.

Third, some religions have restrictions on weddings taking place during such holy days as Lent or Passover. If you are hoping for an early spring wedding, check the calendar—and then check with your priest, minister, or rabbi.

Fourth, consider not only availability in choosing the time of year you marry but also the effect it will have on family and friends. Think about any hardships your wedding may cause guests who do not live close by. Generally, major holidays such as Thanksgiving, Christmas and the Fourth of July are not recommended as wedding dates. Those are prime family vacation times, when people have long-time traditions and plans. Secondary holiday weekends, such as Memorial Day and Labor Day, may be more convenient but can be difficult for families with children who are still in school or will be starting school the next day.

On the other hand, having your wedding on a holiday weekend may be a smart choice; guests who have to travel will have an automatic three-day weekend and won't have to take an extra day off from work.

Day of the Week

Most weddings are held on weekends, and for good reason: Weekend days are the customary days off from work. Within the weekends, Christians don't usually wed on a Sunday, their Sabbath, and Jews don't usually wed on a Saturday, because it is their Sabbath day of prayer and rest. Historically, Christian weddings were almost always held on Sundays because the work week extended from Monday through Saturday—and who could afford to miss a day of work? An old English rhyme gave advice about good and not-so-good days to marry if the customary Sunday wasn't chosen:

Monday for wealth
Tuesday for health
Wednesday the best day of all
Thursday for crosses
Friday for losses
Saturday no luck at all

Old English logic aside, a weekday wedding can reap the benefit of lower prices and certain availability of ceremony and reception sites and vendor and supplier access. A weekday wedding, particularly in the late afternoon or evening on a Thursday, is also a logical consideration for a destination wedding. It provides an entire weekend for guests to fit in a mini vacation along with the festivities.

Time of Day

The time of day your wedding takes place can also make a big difference in your budget. A late afternoon or early evening wedding is generally more expensive than a morning or early- to mid-afternoon wedding. Reception costs are affected as well—if you plan a reception in the middle of the day or anytime from 4 P.M. to 8 P.M., your guests will expect to be served a meal. Moreover, the later the wedding, the more formal it is likely to be. The time of day and the wedding's formality, however, aren't necessarily indications of how elegant a wedding will be. Just because you are being married in the morning doesn't mean your semiformal or informal wedding will be any less elegant than one held at night. Because there are so many variations, it is smart to clearly communicate to your officiant, reception site manager, and other service providers exactly what you mean by formal, semiformal, or informal.

If you are planning to be married during the wedding high season when most sites may already be booked, consider switching your celebrations to a less frequently booked time of day. The most popular booking times are, in order of popularity, Saturday afternoon, Saturday morning, Friday evening, and Sunday afternoon.

THE STYLE OF YOUR WEDDING

There are three categories of weddings—formal, semiformal, and informal. The formality is related to the location of the ceremony and reception, the size of the wedding party, the number of guests, and the time of day. While the style of a wedding in a church or synagogue may be formal or informal, a home wedding generally lends itself to informality—unless, of course, the home is a mansion. The variations on each style are endless, but there are a few basic differences in the three categories.

The Formal Wedding

The formal wedding ceremony usually takes place in a house of worship or in a large home or garden. The bride and her attendants (usually from four to 10 bridesmaids) wear long gowns in formal fabrics, and the groom and his attendants (usually from four to 10 ushers) wear cutaways or tailcoats. Female guests wear street-length dressy clothing for a daytime wedding and usually floor-length gowns or cocktail dresses for an evening wedding. Male guests wear dark suits and ties for a daytime wedding and tuxedos for an evening wedding. An evening formal wedding that requires white tie is the most formal of all.

The formal reception is usually a sit-down or semi-buffet meal. Invitations are engraved, decorations can be elaborate, transportation for the wedding party is usually provided by limousines, and music (if the reception includes dancing) is often provided by an orchestra or full band.

The Semiformal Wedding

For a semiformal wedding, the bride and her attendants (usually from two to six bridesmaids) may wear long, ballerina, or tea-length gowns, usually made of simpler fabrics than those for a formal wedding. The groom and his attendants (usually from two to six ushers) wear gray or black strollers with striped trousers or a formal suit for a daytime semiformal wedding and a dinner jacket with black trousers or a formal suit for an evening wedding. Female guests wear street-length tailored or semi-dressy dresses for a daytime wedding and cocktail dresses for an evening wedding. Male guests wear dark suits for both.

The ceremony can take place in a house of worship, chapel, hotel, club, home, or garden, and the reception is generally a buffet or a cocktail buffet later in the afternoon with a small band or orchestra or a DJ.

The Informal Wedding

At an informal wedding, the bride and her attendants (usually from one to three bridesmaids) wear simple white or pastel floor-length gowns or ballerina, tea-length, or street-length dresses. The groom and his attendants (usually from one to three ushers) wear suits or sport jackets and slacks. Female guests wear what is appropriate to the location—usually street-length dresses. Male guests wear sport jackets and slacks.

The ceremony can take place in a house of worship, chapel, or rectory. It can also be held in a home or garden with a justice of the peace presiding. The reception can take place in a restaurant or at a home with a caterer and/or friends providing refreshments—usually a breakfast, brunch, or lunch in the morning or early afternoon and an informal buffet or simple hors d'oeuvres and wedding cake for an afternoon reception. Music may come from a single musician or background tapes.

Religious or Civil

Now is the time to decide whether to marry in a house of worship or a secular location. You might want to speak to several different potential ceremony officiants as you make your decision.

Color Schemes

Your overall color scheme can start coming into focus at this time. Your wedding style includes your color choices, whether based on time of year, seasonal flowers, the bridesmaids' dresses, the locale, the formality of the occasion, or simply your own personal preferences.

THE AVAILABILITY OF YOUR OFFICIANT

If you place great importance on who performs your ceremony and wouldn't consider getting married without having him or her officiate, check on availability before making *any* decisions about the date of your wedding.

SACRED SPACES

Is it necessary to get married in a church or synagogue? Ancients believed the most sacred space for a wedding was one created by nature, such as a hilltop where heaven and earth meet, because it possessed the spirituality of the ongoing cycle of life. As they gradually came to believe in one deity and built houses of worship, sacred spaces became temples, synagogues, and churches.

CEREMONY LOCATION

If you plan to marry in a house of worship, try to briefly reserve a few dates pending your final decision to be sure the church or synagogue will be available once you have confirmed your reception location.

Otherwise, you will want to consider alternative possibilities, whether indoors or outdoors, in a hotel or wedding hall, at home or at City Hall. Do you want a private ceremony with only a few close friends and family members attending? That, too, will influence your choice of ceremony.

For a further look at selecting ceremony sites, turn to Chapter 10, Planning the Ceremony.

RECEPTION LOCATION

Your choice of reception site will affect the type of food you serve, beverages, service, formality level, entertainment, and reception hours. By the time you have counted your guest list and determined a date and time for your wedding, you can then focus on the kind of reception you want and your location preferences. Begin checking out sites immediately in terms of approximate cost and availability, since in some parts of the country reception sites are booked at least a year in advance.

Consider the pluses and minuses of the different kinds of reception sites. Keep in mind that hotels and private clubs are experienced in handling large parties and can do much of the organizing for you. Reception halls with in-house caterers may cost more but may be worth it, considering the ease of service. If you're considering a reception at home or at a site where a tent will be used, remember that everything—from the lighting to the flooring to the decorations—will have to be delivered and assembled and then disassembled once the party's over. It can be costly to transform a tent into a ballroom.

Sites that are bare will require more attention, in terms of decor. A wedding at a historical site or rental facility, such as a botanical garden or mansion, may require less decorating work but may also require that you use the facility's in-house catering staff or else find a caterer who can work with the facility and provide seamless service.

If the idea of a destination wedding appeals to you, remember that friends and relatives able to take the time off to get there and afford the additional costs will be few. If the cost proves prohibitive for many guests, you might think about being married with the few close relatives and friends who can make the trip in attendance and then having a reception when you return home from the honeymoon.

For a further look at selecting reception sites, turn to Chapter 12, Planning the Reception.

One-Stop Wedding Locations

Locations do exist that offer everything under one roof—ceremony and reception area, food, decor, flowers, and more—and a wedding coordinator to orchestrate the whole thing. This can certainly translate into ease of service. The pluses of these "one-stop" sites are obvious: For busy couples with a short engagement time, they couldn't make things easier. Minuses are the lack of choices and ways to personalize the wedding.

IS A WEDDING CONSULTANT FOR YOU?

More and more couples have full-time careers and a limited amount of time to devote to wedding organization. For busy people with hectic schedules, hiring a wedding coordinator or consultant is a smart alternative to trying to do it all. Wedding consultants indeed can be of great service: They can scout sites and oversee the budget, the caterer, the band, the florist, and any number of service providers. They can snag discounts and bargains from vendors. In short, they can lift the load from your shoulders when you are feeling burdened, simply because they have encountered and solved the same problems you may be facing in hundreds of ways. Their purpose is not to take over your wedding but to help make your dreams come true and your plans a reality. Plus, wedding consultants can save you money in the long run.

Think about what kind of help you need before making a decision. There are many different levels of service and types of consultants. A full-fledged bridal consultant can do anything and everything for you. A wedding-day coordinator springs into action on the day of the wedding, making sure everything goes according to schedule. A wedding-day director might be provided by the ceremony site to supervise all the details of the ceremony only and to make sure church or synagogue rules are followed. There are consultants and coordinators who handle varying responsibilities in between.

When you are working and living on one side of the country and will be married where you grew up—which happens to be on the other side of the country—it is likely that your mother or a wedding consultant is overseeing most of the details. One way to keep current with each other's progress is to exchange computer disks of lists, questions, and information. Faster yet is to send an e-mail and attach any lists you need to share. Use websites to do research, but don't agree to something you haven't seen or that your mother or consultant hasn't seen on your behalf, be it a reception locale, flowers, or anything else.

Wedding consulting is a relatively new industry—and the only way to find out the extent of the capability of someone you are considering hiring is to seek out recommendations and ask questions. Trained, full-time professionals are usually members of the Association of Bridal Consultants, a national organization, and are independent consultants, meaning that they are not associated with a vendor, such as a department store or florist.

THE COST OF A CONSULTANT

When an independent wedding consultant or coordinator is hired from the start to oversee most of your wedding plans, she tends to work on a fee basis, generally 10 to 20 percent of the total wedding costs. Others charge a flat fee, depending on the services they provide. Once you have a budget in mind, calculate what the cost of a consultant will be and weigh that against the value of your time. Keep in mind that a successful consultant will be able to pass along enough savings to defray most of her fee—and that time can be just as important a commodity to you as money.

Be truthful and up-front with the consultant right away on any budget limitations so that she can capably act on your behalf. Make it clear that even if you have a large budget, the sky is not the limit. Part of her job is to find the best price for whatever service or element she is seeking. But to be effective, she must first know what her parameters are.

The Big Decisions

What to Expect From a Wedding Consultant

In general, a bridal consultant can provide the following services:

- Help you decide on ceremony and reception sites.
- Help you select all the suppliers and vendors you will hire, such as the florist, the caterer, musicians, the photographer, and the videographer.
- Coordinate communication between and among vendors, suppliers, and sites so that, for example, the florist knows when and how to obtain access to the ceremony site to decorate.
- Serve as a referee, friend, budget advisor and watcher, etiquette expert, shopper, detail manager, and organizer.
- Coordinate your rehearsal with the officiant.
- Supervise all the last-minute details of your wedding day.

Questions to Ask Wedding Consultants

When interviewing consultants, have a list of questions prepared that will help you evaluate what you can expect of them, and at what cost. These questions include:

- Are you a member of a professional consultant organization?
- Are you affiliated with any service providers?
- How many weddings have you coordinated?
- How long have you been in business?
- Can you provide client references?
- How much of the wedding planning can you supervise?
- Do you delegate any of the responsibilities you take on to others? If so, which ones?
- Will you be on hand to help on our wedding day?
- Will you provide a one-time consulting session to help me get organized if I decide that's all the help I need?
- Can you provide a list of your services at their individual prices?

THEME WEDDINGS

Theme weddings are becoming more and more popular. The theme of the wedding may be carried over into every aspect of the celebration: from the attire to the food to the decorations.

The theme may be simply an homage to a long-ago era. If you are planning to wear your grandmother's Victorian wedding gown, you may want the festivities to complement the outfit. Victorian brides and their attendants often carried tussy mussies (nosegay bouquets inserted in a silver, cone-shape holder), so have your florist make these instead of traditional bouquets. Add lace to pew decorations and centerpieces. Decorate with rose petals; use candles and fans. Plan a Victorian menu.

A theme could also be connected to your first date. It could revolve around a holiday. A nautical theme makes sense for a couple who met on a sailboat and who loves to sail: Use nautical colors and signal flags for decorations and have a seafood menu at a yacht club.

Another kind of theme is the cultural or ethnic one. If you have strong ties to an ethnic community or want to honor your roots and family ties, incorporate into your celebrations some of the symbols and traditions that have special meaning for you. Do your homework: Plan clothing, decorations, menus, music, and events to add special meaning to your ceremony and reception. When planning, think about all the ways you can use the theme you have chosen, beginning with your invitations. Not only will you find unique ways to personalize your wedding, but you will also find new connections to your own heritage.

Keep in mind that while a theme wedding is fun to plan, it can be an imposition on guests if you expect them to dress to fit the theme—which often means they will have to buy something in order to comply. Instead of issuing directives to guests about the style or color of clothes, it's more thoughtful to let guests wear whatever they wish, confining your clothing theme to you and your attendants.

WEDDING DETECTIVES

In West Africa, family members including aunts and cousins serve as "wedding consultants" involved in all the details of the wedding, from the courtship to the ceremony. They also serve as wedding "detectives," making sure that the intended spouse has a good reputation, excellent health, sufficient means, suitable family heritage, and good future prospects. Once a couple passes inspection, family elders sit the bride and groom down for serious counseling while the "consultants" proceed with organizing wedding details.

DESTINATION WEDDINGS

Also increasingly popular are destination weddings—choosing a dream location to marry, celebrate, and even spend your honeymoon. A destination wedding is ideal for the couple who wants to get away with a few close friends and family for a combined celebration and vacation. It also is a smart solution for the couple who wants both a wonderful honeymoon and a lavish wedding but has to choose one over the other. Unless you have the wherewithal to charter a plane for a slew of guests and rent rooms for all of them (customarily, these expenses are the guests' responsibility), you can't expect all of your invited guests to be able to afford to attend. Still, by letting your guests in on your plans well in advance, you may find some able to come.

A destination wedding can be as formal or casual as you like; there is no set guideline. The guest list will often be shorter than a wedding set in a traditional location, simply because of the logistics and expense of a destination wedding; again, there is no absolute rule.

Cruise ships are entering the wedding industry with gusto, building chapels and hiring wedding consultants to accommodate the growing number of couples who wish to marry aboard ship. Traditionally, in order to be recognized as legal in the United States, maritime marriages were held in U.S. ports of call. Nowadays international cruise lines are finding ways to perform at-sea weddings that are legally recognized in the United States and give captains the legal authority to perform the ceremony. Before you make any wedding plans, confirm that the cruise line you choose has the legal authority to perform shipboard marriage ceremonies.

If your dream is to be married at a popular travel spot, plan early. Find a travel agent who specializes in destination weddings and related components—finding officiants, florists, bands, photographers, and caterers. You'll want a travel agent who will spend the time to find the best airline rates and who can advise you on the difference between peak-season and off-season costs at your destination—often the price dif-

AGE VERSUS FORMALITY

The younger the bride, the more formal the wedding. It seems that 51 percent of brides from the age of 18 to 25 prefer formal weddings, in comparison with just 14 percent of brides over 35. That doesn't rule out an elegant formal wedding for an older woman; it just seems that informal and less traditional celebrations are the preferred choices for the over–35 crowd, many of whom have been married before in formal occasions.

ferences can be considerable. Or find a wedding consultant or on-site resort planner who has planned weddings at a chosen destination, and let her take care of contracting the services you will need. It may be worth the fee to spare yourself the long-distance calls and difficulty in communicating in another language.

THE SECOND LEVEL OF DECISIONS

Once you have settled the who, where, and when of your wedding, it is time to start shopping, interviewing, and booking vendors, suppliers, and services. Because each of these next steps generally requires considerable advance time, there is no time like the present to start:

- Shop for and make decisions about clothing and accessories—for the bride, groom, and attendants.
- Visit stores and list gifts you wish to receive with bridal registries.
- Begin reviewing reception menus.
- Interview and listen to bands or DJs, or start listing songs you would put on tapes for the reception.
- Interview and talk to florists.
- Interview and look at the portfolios of photographers and videographers.
- Order invitations, enclosures, announcements, and other printed material.

THE THIRD LEVEL OF DECISIONS

With all your outside resources in order, you now can turn your attention to the details that will make your wedding day personal and unique. You might do the following:

- Listen to and choose music for your ceremony.
- Select readings for your ceremony.
- Make lists of music choices for your reception.
- Plan special events you want to include, such as your first dance at the reception, a bouquet toss, or a party for your attendants.
- Select gifts for your attendants, perhaps parents, and each other.
- Begin to chart seating arrangements for your reception.
- Incorporate family and cultural traditions into your wedding.

PLANNING THE HONEYMOON

Many couples consider making honeymoon plans a top-priority decision, particularly if they plan to marry and vacation during a peak season or travel to a popular honeymoon or travel destination. In many instances, couples will make their other top-level decisions around their honeymoon plans. At the very least, the newly betrothed should make some preliminary choices regarding the honeymoon date, location, transportation, accommodations, and length of stay.

Honeymoons need to be planned up front because of budget considerations as well. In the frenzy of planning the wedding and reception, couples often forget to compute into their total expenses the cost of a honeymoon. The expenses of a honeymoon trip are greater than just that of transportation and lodging—the honeymoon budget must include meals, transfers, souvenirs, sightseeing and sports-related costs, tips, taxes, and the little luxuries, such as a massage or poolside charges for lounge chairs and towels. On a cruise, a number of attendants will expect tips. Always ask whether a gratuity is included in the final bill.

Because the honeymoon is as much the groom's vacation as it is the bride's, the planning should be shared by both of you. That includes doing research, meeting with travel agents, talking to resort planners, and making reservations.

THE FINE ART OF DELEGATING

If you don't plan to use a bridal consultant, you may have friends and family willing to help you out. If yours is an elaborate wedding and you have a hectic personal schedule, consider delegating certain tasks and even major responsibilities to those who have generously offered to take them on. Delegate gracefully, however. Don't turn into a drill sergeant, barking orders at those who are helping you. Your family and friends are not your staff; they are your support team.

Begin by examining your priorities. If you love music and want the time to listen to and interview every musician or DJ yourself, then delegate something else. Let a friend or relative who loves flowers make them her project, providing you with pictures, ideas, and choices. Never exclude the groom. Even if he couldn't care less about the color of the table linens, he *will* care more about things in his areas of interest. Find out what they are, and delegate them to him.

Once you have relinquished a responsibility, don't dwell on it. Don't second-guess yourself or others. Don't micromanage. When you've put someone in charge, let others know. Tell the florist your sister is in charge of flowers so that he contacts her and not you. Call the tent supplier to let him know that your future spouse is in charge of tent details—and give him his telephone number.

Your wedding day may be the most important time to delegate tasks. It is the time for you to focus on your ceremony and enjoy the reception afterward. That's what honor attendants are for. They don't sign on just to look great in tuxedos or long dresses; they are also there to be your two right arms.

STAYING ORGANIZED

It doesn't take long for chaos to reign if you don't begin with a system of organization. Whether you use *Emily Post's Wedding Planner,* set up files on your computer, or devote a separate briefcase just to wedding-related papers, you will find everything is easier to manage when you can find it in a snap. A few tips from the most efficient brides and grooms include:

- Create a master to-do list, preferably in time sequence.
- Carry fabric swatches, photos of gowns, photos of locations, and table measurements at all times.
- Design a contact list with the names and numbers of everyone you're working with. Those numbers might include telephone, address, fax, and e-mail.
- Carry a calendar with all your appointments highlighted.
- Create a folder for all contracts, or staple them to the appropriate page in your planner. Don't leave home without them in case you have to check details from one supplier when working with another.
- Keep important papers you will need (birth certificate, divorce papers, driver's license) in one envelope or folder.
- Check off completed to-do's as you accomplish them. You'll feel great as you see the number of check marks grow.

SURVIVAL TACTICS FOR
THE BRIDE AND GROOM

The two of you are going to have to be a solid front—a team—and, most important, each other's support amid a barrage of wedding advice as you labor over the big decisions. Although the advice is well-meant, it can also be confusing and tiresome. As you sift through the advice, your fortitude will have to come from yourselves and each other.

You will probably come across a wealth of articles and books detailing the entire process of getting married, with assurances that the solution to any conflict is having your own way. This just isn't true; it's not that simple. It *is* your wedding, but you are each connected to a family and to others who care about you and want to remain important in your lives. This connectedness is what mandates the three C's of wedding planning:

- COMPROMISE
- COMMUNICATION
- CONSIDERATION

With this in mind, practice with your partner as you work toward achieving a shared vision of your wedding. How you end up handling your wedding plans can foretell how you will handle the other major decisions of your life together. This is the time to develop a way of reaching accord together in the future. But remember that, along with the stress that can accompany both the big decisions and the little details, there should be a sense of adventure and fun. You are celebrating one of the most joyous milestones in your lives.

STAYING CALM

As you plan your wedding, don't let stress and anxiety send you into an emotional tailspin. It is indeed an emotional time; you are going through a rite of passage—even if you've lived together for 10 years or are an older couple with grown children. Don't let the details bog you down. When things get tough, keep reminding yourself that it is the *marriage,* not the wedding, that is important. To help keep things on an even keel:

- INCLUDE, DON'T EXCLUDE. Even if you're doing everything your-selves, keep others—your mothers, children, or friends—in the loop. Don't let them feel left out. Ask their advice every once in a while. Don't, however, ask their advice about things you have already decided on. You would then either have to reject their advice or change your plans and give up something you really wanted to do.
- DELEGATE. Surely, others will want to help. And what bride and groom couldn't use some help?
- BE FORGIVING. When things get touchy between you and your family, be the first to apologize. Remember, pride goeth before a fall. In other words, what possible difference does it make to you to apologize first? You see your-self as adding to your family. Your family feels they are giving you up. Give them extra attention.
- STOP REACTING. Take a deep breath. Think about what might be moti-vating someone to be so difficult. Is he feeling left out of your life? Is she wor-ried about what your relationship will be with her once you're married? If you can't figure it out, take another deep breath.

To keep yourselves intact and calm as all around you lose their heads, take care of yourselves:

- Eat right—you need the energy.
- Exercise—you need the release.
- Get enough sleep—you can cope much better when you're rested.
- Go on dates—the two of you need time alone together.
- Find beauty in everything—and where you can't, find humor.

CHAPTER 3

EXPENSES

Whatever the size or style of wedding you plan, the end result will depend not on how much money you spend but on how you spend it. A wedding is an important milestone and should be a time of special indulgences—but that doesn't mean mortgaging the farm to do so. There are many ways to save without stinting.

These days, a large, elaborate wedding can cost tens of thousands of dollars. In fact, the average wedding in the United States today costs close to $19,000. Excess does not necessarily equal success. A simpler, less elaborate wedding can be equally elegant and memorable. Remember: Your relationship is what is important, not the extravagance of your celebration.

The list of budget categories in this chapter is intended merely to explain the traditional division of expenses and give you a structure for planning. Keep in mind that any of these items may be omitted entirely without making your wedding any less beautiful or meaningful. Use these pages as a guide—and make your own adjustments.

There are many variations not only in ways to save but also in how costs are divided. Traditionally, the bride's family foots the bill for almost every expense, but today they are often helped out to some extent by the groom's family and even the newlyweds themselves. Forty percent of today's couples pay their own wedding costs, particularly if the wedding is a second one. But traditions are long-standing: It is still not correct for the bride's family to ask the groom's family to pay any of the wedding costs. If, however, his family *offers* to pay a share, it is quite acceptable for the bride's parents to accept.

WHO PAYS?

The answer to the question of who pays the wedding expenses is based on cultural tradition. In Mexico and some Latin American countries, for example, the bride and groom must find as many as 15 couples to be their sponsors, called *padrinos* and *madrinas*. These couples are responsible for a variety of the financial demands of the wedding. They may pay for the bride's bouquet or for the music at the reception. In fact, there is a *padrino* for almost all wedding categories so that the costs will be divided among them. The groom pays for the wedding dress; the sponsors pay for almost everything else. This custom is practiced in the United States by some families of Mexican and Latin American ancestry, particularly in the Southwestern states that border Mexico.

In Egypt, the groom pays a bridal price to the bride and her family, but part of it is used to pay for the costs of the wedding. Additionally, the groom and his family customarily pay for the couple's apartment, appliances, kitchen furniture, lighting, and the bride's dress.

It is never correct to ask others to sponsor your wedding costs unless doing so is customary in your culture. In any culture, the bride and groom must accept any budget shortfalls with grace and good humor and scale back their plans. If their parents don't offer to make up the difference, they should graciously accept this fact.

Who Pays, Traditionally

Traditionally, the bride's family assumes the burden of most wedding costs, a custom most likely translated from the ancient custom of providing a large dowry to attract a good husband. The dowry was eventually replaced in Victorian times by the provision of a settlement from the bride's family to the groom's family, along with a substantial trousseau—usually a year's worth of clothing and household items. The bride's family has continued to foot the bill for the majority of the wedding costs not, we presume, for the purpose of attracting a husband but because that's the way it has always been done—until recently.

Who Pays, Nontraditionally

Today it is not uncommon for both the bride's and the groom's families to share the costs of the celebration, or for the bride and the groom to pay for all or part of the expenses themselves. Modern couples are older and usually employed and independent by the time they get married, enabling them to not only plan their own weddings but also pay for them as well.

When families are willing to share the costs, the bride and groom should think about the range of possibilities ahead of time and be certain that they are in agreement with each other before sitting down with their parents to discuss the budget. If they want financial help, they must be willing to compromise. Any conversation about money should be both dignified and candid.

TRADITIONAL DIVISION OF COSTS

If age-old tradition is ruling the financial structure of your wedding, the following lists of traditional expense responsibilities should help—*all variable, depending upon your particular circumstances.*

TRADITIONAL EXPENSES OF THE BRIDE AND HER FAMILY

- Services of bridal consultant
- Invitations, enclosures, and announcements
- Bride's wedding gown and accessories
- Floral decorations for ceremony and reception, bridesmaids' flowers, and bride's bouquet
- Formal wedding photographs and candid pictures
- Videotape recording of wedding
- Music for church and reception
- Transportation of bridal party to and from ceremony
- All reception expenses
- Bride's gifts to her attendants
- Bride's gift to groom
- Groom's wedding ring
- Rental of awning for ceremony entrance and carpet for aisle
- Fee for services performed by sexton
- Cost of soloists
- A traffic officer, if necessary
- Transportation of bridal party to reception
- Transportation and lodging expenses for officiant if from another town and if invited to officiate by bride's family
- Accommodations for bride's attendants
- Bridesmaids' luncheon

TRADITIONAL EXPENSES OF THE GROOM AND HIS FAMILY

- Bride's engagement and wedding rings
- Groom's gift to bride
- Groom's attire
- Groom's gifts to his attendants
- Ties and gloves for groom's attendants, if not part of their clothing rental package
- Bride's bouquet (only in those regions where it is local custom for groom to pay for it)
- Bride's going-away corsage
- Boutonnieres for groom's attendants
- Corsages for immediate members of both families (unless bride has included them in her florist order)
- Officiant's fee or donation
- Transportation and lodging expenses for officiant, if from another town and if invited to officiate by groom's family
- Marriage license
- Transportation for groom and best man to ceremony
- Expenses of honeymoon
- All costs of rehearsal dinner
- Accommodations for groom's attendants
- Bachelor dinner, if he wishes to give one
- Transportation and lodging expenses for groom's family

BRIDESMAIDS' AND HONOR ATTENDANT'S EXPENSES

- Purchase of apparel and all accessories
- Transportation to and from city where wedding takes place
- Contribution to gift from all bridesmaids to bride
- Individual gift to the couple (if being in wedding is not the gift)
- Optionally, shower or luncheon for bride

USHERS' AND BEST MAN'S EXPENSES

- Rental of wedding attire
- Transportation to and from city where wedding takes place
- Contribution to gift from all groom's attendants to groom
- Individual gift to the couple (if being in wedding is not the gift)
- Bachelor dinner, if given by groom's attendants

- Transportation to and from wedding
- Lodging expenses
- Wedding gift

DETERMINING A BUDGET

A carefully prepared budget can spare you the nightmare of falling prey to impractical plans or running up unnecessary debts. Whether you plan an elaborate wedding with 300 guests or a simple ceremony with 30 friends in your own home, a realistic budget will help make your preparations more stress-free. If money becomes a source of tension, simply cut the guest list and adjust your plans accordingly.

Simply put: Base your budget on what you or your parents can afford. A budget for a large wedding should include allotments for each of the expenses listed below. The budget for a simple wedding should include the items that you cannot provide yourself and intend to purchase, as well as the things you plan to do either on your own or with the help of friends and family. For example, your Uncle Robert has offered to take the reception photographs as his wedding gift. And Aunt Deborah is baking the wedding cake as her gift to you, which spares another expense.

With imagination and good planning, a beautiful wedding can be held within any limits. Whatever you plan, stick to your budget; otherwise, the worry and insecurity may carry over to your relationship and get your marriage off to a stressful start.

Begin by determining the amount you can spend on your wedding. Do this before you sign a single contract or make a firm commitment with any vendor. If you have $5,000 to spend and the reception site you're hoping for will cost $3,500, you are probably not leaving enough money to cover other costs—accommodations for your attendants, fees, a band or DJ, wedding attire, and so on—unless some of those items will be paid for by someone else or given as a wedding gift. If necessary, reconsider and find a reception location that is not as costly. Choose a public garden, perhaps, or a friend's beautiful backyard. Or have a morning wedding followed by a brunch or an afternoon cocktail reception instead of a seated dinner. The variations are endless. With creativity and imagination and a willingness to be flexible, your wedding plans can fit your budget and result in a wonderful day.

The best way to plan is to begin with your absolute fixed costs, such as the minister's or rabbi's fee, the postage required for the wedding invitations, and the marriage license. Then add in the expected costs of your essential wedding expenses, such as the wedding dress, wedding rings, and gifts for the attendants. Subtract that total from your available funds and see what amount you have left to work with. This will give you a guide as to how much you have left for variable costs, such as flowers, limousines, a videographer, and the rehearsal dinner and reception. If there are more categories than dollars, set your priorities. Is gourmet food more important than expensive flowers? If so, adjust again. Costs that are not finite tend to grow with the guest list, so you should start there to make your adjustments.

COMPUTERIZE YOUR FINANCES

Consider investing in a financial spreadsheet for your computer to keep track of budget planning. Take notes in your planner as you research and obtain competitive bids, and then enter data by category. The software's ability to automatically add and subtract saves time and ensures greater accuracy. As you complete a category and finalize vendors and suppliers, print out pages of the spreadsheet and staple them in the appropriate section of your planner.

BUDGET CATEGORIES

The following list includes traditional costs associated with a wedding. Some are mandatory, such as marriage license fees; others are optional, such as limousines and a videographer. Whether an optional category is mandatory to you is *your* decision. For example, if it is important to you to arrive at the ceremony in a white stretch limousine, then this becomes a mandatory cost in your budget. But it is also an adjustable one: If you must have a stretch limo, call more than one car service to get the best value.

Don't forget the little costs that fall under each category. These items add up quickly. Besides shoes and jewelry, such items as stockings and lingerie are considered "bride's accessories." Be as thorough as you can to get the most realistic picture.

ITEM	MANDATORY/ OPTIONAL	COST (ESTIMATED)	COST (ACTUAL)
ATTENDANTS			
ACCOMMODATIONS			
BRIDESMAIDS LUNCHEON			
TIES AND GLOVES			
SUBTOTAL			
CEREMONY FEES			
OFFICIANT'S FEE			
CHURCH OR SYNAGOGUE FEE			
ORGANIST'S FEE			
CANTOR/VOCALIST/ INSTRUMENTALIST FEE(S)			
SEXTON'S FEE			
AWNING/AISLE CARPET RENTAL			
SUBTOTAL			
FLOWERS			
CEREMONY			
RECEPTION			
BRIDAL BOUQUET			
BRIDAL ATTENDANTS' FLOWERS			
CORSAGES			
BOUTONNIERES			
SUBTOTAL			
GIFTS			
BRIDE'S GIFTS FOR ATTENDANTS			
GROOM'S GIFTS FOR ATTENDANTS			
BRIDE'S GIFT FOR GROOM			
GROOM'S GIFT FOR BRIDE			
HONEYMOON COSTS			
SUBTOTAL			
LEGALITIES			
MARRIAGE LICENSE			
HEALTH/PHYSICAL/BLOOD TEST FEES			

(CONTINUED)

ITEM	MANDATORY/ OPTIONAL	COST (ESTIMATED)	COST (ACTUAL)
MUSIC FOR RECEPTION			
SUBTOTAL			
PHOTOGRAPHY			
ENGAGEMENT PHOTOGRAPHS			
PHOTOGRAPHER			
VIDEOGRAPHER			
SUBTOTAL			
PRINTED MATERIALS			
ANNOUNCEMENTS			
STATIONERY FOR THANK-YOU NOTES			
CALLIGRAPHY			
POSTAGE			
CEREMONY PROGRAM			
SUBTOTAL			
RECEPTION			
SITE RENTAL/SETUP			
SITE DECORATIONS			
FOOD/BEVERAGE EXPENSES (PER-PERSON COST)			
RECEPTION FAVORS (PER-PERSON COST)			
WEDDING CAKE			
SUBTOTAL			
TRANSPORTATION/PARKING			
LIMOUSINES FOR BRIDAL PARTY			
TRAFFIC OFFICIALS AT CEREMONY AT, RECEPTION			
VALET PARKING			
TRAVEL COSTS FOR CEREMONY OFFICIANT, IF NECESSARY			
TRIPS HOME DURING PLANNING IF YOU LIVE AWAY			
SUBTOTAL			

(CONTINUED)

ITEM	MANDATORY/ OPTIONAL	COST (ESTIMATED)	COST (ACTUAL)
WEDDING ATTIRE			
BRIDAL GOWN			
BRIDAL ACCESSORIES			
GROOM'S OUTFIT			
BRIDE'S RINGS			
GROOM'S RING			
BEAUTY COSTS (HAIR, NAILS, MAKEUP)			
SUBTOTAL			
WEDDING CONSULTANT FEES			
SUBTOTAL			
MISCELLANEOUS:			
TELEPHONE BILLS RELATED TO PLANNING			
WARDROBE COSTS FOR WEDDING-RELATED EVENTS			
TIPS (IF NOT INCLUDED IN ABOVE COSTS)			
TAXES (IF NOT INCLUDED IN ABOVE COSTS)			
NONFLORAL CHURCH DECORATION			
SUBTOTAL			
TOTAL			

ECONOMY VERSUS VALUE

When comparison shopping, know the difference between economy and value. You can achieve economy if you plan well and give yourself the time to shop around and compare costs. Know exactly what you want and seek out promising resources. Look everywhere, from wedding websites to local suppliers. Value is really knowing precisely what you want and what you are willing to pay for. In this way you can satisfy your expectations for quality and service. If you find yourself paying for extras you don't want, you're not getting good value. For example, a band that charges for a master of ceremonies when you don't *want* a master of ceremonies is no value to you, just as a reception package that includes printed napkins and matchbooks has less value if you don't care about these incidentals.

SECRETS TO SAVING

There are endless ways to save on wedding expenditures without looking as though you are having a bargain basement wedding. Almost every component of your wedding has a wide range of choices and costs. Decide which components you consider important enough to splurge on; then find ways to economize with style and flair on the other areas.

What are the best ways to economize on big-ticket items? Cut your guest list, find a smaller but no less elegant reception site, and choose a time of year, day of the week, and time of day when prices are not at a premium.

Another way to chip away at your costs is to let friends help, with the understanding that their service is their wedding gift to you. If your attendants can stay with friends and family, this saves your having to pay expensive hotel or motel costs. If your cousin has studied millinery design and would love to create your headpiece and/or those of your attendants, shop with her and pay for the materials and thank her profusely for such a wonderful gift.

Below are three examples of essential wedding components and some creative ways to pare your expenditures on them.

Wedding Gowns

Read bridal magazines and check Internet websites for discount or wholesale bridal services that order gowns from designers for about 25 percent less than they cost at bridal salons. The drawbacks: You'll have to find your own seamstress to do alterations, and you won't have salon service. The pluses: You'll save money and/or be able to have the dream gown that you might not otherwise be able to afford.

Investigate renting a bridal gown. Rental gowns have usually only been worn once, and you can find a more expensive gown than you'd want to buy at literally a fraction of the cost. The drawbacks: You might not want to wear a previously worn gown, and you won't have a wedding gown to pass on to your own daughter, an almost moot point since only 4 percent of brides today wear their mother's wedding gown. The pluses: You won't have to devote precious storage space to keeping a gown you'll probably never wear again anyway. And, of course, you've spent less.

Other thrifty alternatives:

- Buy a once-used bridal gown at a secondhand or vintage clothing store. You can find real gems at these stores, one-of-a-kind designer and vintage gowns that have been worn only once.
- Make your own gown or have a seamstress relative or friend make it for you. Bridal sewing patterns are as up-to-date as the latest looks.
- Choose less traditional attire, such as a simple tea-length evening dress or a white suit.

Flowers

If flowers are your passion and therefore a key element of your wedding, then the florist's bill becomes a necessary expense. But you can save on flowers in any number of ways, including the following.

- Don't book your wedding around Valentine's Day or Mother's Day, times that flower costs are at an all-time high.
- Take advantage of existing floral decorations by having your wedding in December, when the church is already decorated with wreaths and poinsettias.
- Choose a botanical garden for your reception.
- Instead of investing in formal, expensive bouquets, have your wedding party carry free-form, loose bouquets of flowers from a local garden, tied prettily with a satin ribbon.
- Use silk flowers for the top of the cake, for your and attendants' hair, and for the flower girl to carry.

FORGO THE FORMAL

Instead of holding a formal rehearsal dinner at a club or restaurant where costs are high and your guest list is by necessity limited, have a rehearsal picnic, clambake, or barbecue where informality reigns and more guests can be included. It's a way to save money and celebrate in a relaxed, fun atmosphere. Or maybe you will decide to have an informal wedding reception; many couples report happy memories of their own picnic or beach-party receptions.

Photography

Photography for many couples is one of the most important expenses of the wedding. As such, it may not be the item to scrimp on. There are, however, ways to pare photography expenses. Of course, having a photographer in the family who offers his or her services as a wedding gift is one happy alternative. Having a professional photographer take the wedding ceremony pictures and a couple of friends photograph the reception is another. (In both cases, you should offer to pay for the film.) A third alternative is to use a professional for formal portraits, then buy disposable cameras for each table and ask guests if they mind taking candids during the reception. Be sure to provide a basket for them to drop the cameras into before they leave, or delegate the responsibility for collecting them to a friend or attendant. You may not have professional-quality results, but you will have candid recorded memories. A note of caution: Because your guests will be focusing on the festivities and not the camera, these "candid" shots may be of little use in truly capturing the people at your reception.

THE IMPORTANCE OF COMPARISON SHOPPING

One of the values of using a wedding consultant is that she often has access to quality services at the best prices from vendors and suppliers. She may also receive frequent-user discounts from suppliers. Without a consultant you probably won't get a frequency discount, but you can hunt for quality at the best prices—as long as you have ample time to comparison shop. If, for example, you know absolutely nothing about limousine services, don't just hire the first one you find in the telephone book. Ask about services of any kind before you sign any contract. By the time you have interviewed three or more companies, you will have a pretty good idea of what you need to know to make your decision.

Comparison shopping is also important when searching out a reception site. If getting married in November instead of October allows you to have the kind of reception you want for a third of the cost, consider it. Generally, prices are at their highest on Saturdays and in the late afternoon and evening. Reduce expenses by having a Saturday morning wedding instead of a Saturday evening one. This frees up moneys you've allocated for reception costs—often a whopping 50 to 60 percent of a wedding budget.

If you are making long-distance plans, comparison shopping is much more difficult. You can, however, delegate duties to your mother or a close friend who lives in the area if they are willing to take on the work for you.

CEREMONY FEES

Fees for the ceremony site, the officiant, the organist, and the soloist are not tips but should be delivered as you would tips, in a sealed envelope, addressed to each person, with your thanks included.

TIPS ON TIPPING

Many wedding professionals, from bridal consultants to photographers, are tipped only for extra-special service. If your florist arrived to decorate the ceremony site only to find a locked door, which caused him to wait an extra hour, a tip would be an extra thank-you for his professionalism, patience, and diligence. While you might set aside an extra 15 percent as an unexpected tip fund, you needn't anticipate tips for the consultant, club manager or caterer, florist, photographer or videographer. Often a caterer's gratuities are included in the total costs; many hotels include a service charge for the wait staff. Always ask whether gratuities are included before signing any contract.

You should plan a gratuity budget for the following:

- valet parking
- coat check
- powder-room attendants
- delivery truck drivers
- chauffeurs
- wait staff
- bartenders
- table captains

You should tip parking lot, coat check, and powder-room attendants ahead of time so that your guests have no obligation to do so. A general guideline is to give the site manager a flat fee based on 50 cents to a dollar per guest, to be distributed among the staff. Ask a friend to make sure that there are no tip dishes or baskets (which might make guests feel obligated to tip) sitting on the coat-check counter or the powder-room shelf.

In the case of limousine drivers and the catering staff, you can request that gratuities be included in the total bill; you don't want to be pulling out your calculator to figure out what you should give the bartender at the end of the reception. (Make sure there are no tip receptacles on the bar making guests wonder whether they should leave a tip.) Some reception sites request that all tips be paid in cash in advance. Check your contract and take care of this detail beforehand so that no one has to settle a bill during or after the event. If gratuities are to be given after the wedding or are not included in the final bill, they should still be counted out and put in sealed envelopes beforehand so that they can be distributed easily at the end of the reception.

When a tip is spontaneous and given to a vendor who has done an extraordinary service, it can be given at the end of the reception or the next day, with a note of thanks included.

ALL ABOUT CONTRACTS

You should expect to sign a contract with every supplier, from the stationer to the florist to the limousine service to the wedding consultant. *Every single detail* should be covered in writing in the contract, including taxes, gratuities, dates, delivery schedules, payment plans, cancellation fees, and refund policies. Take the time to read everything thoroughly; if you don't understand something, ask questions until you do. Never sign a contract under pressure. If you're still unclear about some aspect of the contract, take a copy of it to a friend who has experience in contractual agreements. Be sure you are clear on how and when bills are to be paid—and make sure there are clauses in the contract that ensure proper restitution in the event of a snafu that is clearly the vendor's responsibility.

SAVE THOSE RECEIPTS!

Save all of your receipts. Staple them into your planner under the appropriate category or put them into an empty shoe box marked "Wedding Receipts." That way they won't accumulate on your desk or get lost in your pockets; keeping track of receipts allows you to more easily monitor your budget.

Expenses

57

Staple your copy of each contract to the appropriate section of your wedding planner or keep contacts together in a notebook or file that travels with you. You never know when you are going to need to confirm a detail or check an arrangement.

HIDDEN COSTS

Even deciphering the fine print on a contract can leave you with unanswered questions. Know exactly what you need up front so that you can ferret out hidden, unanticipated costs. For example, make sure that alterations to your gown are included in the service and price in the contract with a bridal salon. If they are not, ask what the general costs are. Very often, a manufacturer's or designer's gown is ordered by the salon in a size larger than you need so that there is extra fabric when alterations are required. This can be a plus, but if you need few alterations to the size you usually wear, you are paying for charges you aren't expecting. Does the salon charge extra to press your gown after alterations? If so, how much extra? Would it be less expensive for you to take the gown to a reputable and experienced dry cleaner for pressing?

The contract for a reception site is based on the length of time your reception lasts, along with all other related costs. Find out what overtime really means before signing the contract. For example, if your reception is planned from two to five in the afternoon, does that mean the bar closes at five and the band goes home and that guests should be gone within half an hour, or does it mean that you have to end the reception by four-thirty to ensure that everyone is out by five? In the latter case, you may be incurring overtime costs if you think that the reception literally lasts until five o'clock.

Don't forget taxes and gratuities, which can add a significant amount to the total bill—especially in states that have a high sales tax. It's a good idea to make sure that taxes and tips are included in the total price. And inquire about any unfamiliar terms in the contract that would have hidden costs, such as "plate charges" in your invitation order.

Costs such as these can be well hidden in the prices you are charged. You are entitled to know exactly what is included—and what is not—before agreeing to the service. If the service provider or contractor is unwilling to give you a detailed listing or breakdown of costs, consider looking elsewhere.

CHAPTER 4
LEGALITIES AND OTHER MATTERS

Along with the romance, fun, and excitement of a wedding come the absolutes—the legally required paperwork and "to-do's" without which a marriage cannot take place. In order to be married in the eyes of the law, a couple must live up to the letter of the law—and the law can vary, not just from country to country but from state to state and even city to city. For example, you might find that Michigan requires a blood test, counseling, and witnesses for a marriage to take place (or a 60-day waiting period for couples who ignore the counseling requirement), while Ohio requires none of these. You certainly don't need to go so far as to hire an attorney to get married, but it is a good idea to check, in advance, what is required—whether you are getting married in your hometown or on an exotic locale on another continent.

Where do you start? Write or call the County Clerk's office or the Office of the Registrar in the town or county you are to be married. They may simply mail or fax you a list of legal requirements for acquiring a marriage license. Some states require that you register in the same state and even county where the ceremony will be performed, and some ask that you do so in person. The most important point is, start your research well in advance of the ceremony so that, come your wedding day, all will be legal and above board.

THE WHO, WHERE, AND WHEN OF GETTING MARRIED

LEGAL FACTORS

Age

Age is a factor in who is permitted to marry. In fact, in most states the age at which one may be married is much younger than the age at which one may legally drive, drink, vote, or apply for a credit card. A word of caution: While the following age restrictions hold true in most states, they do not hold true in all. For example, the minimum age for marriage in the state of Virginia is 16 unless special circumstances prevail, such when an underage bride-to-be is pregnant.

The age restrictions are, in general:

- If either applicant is under 14 years of age, a marriage license cannot be issued.
- If either applicant is 14 or 15 years of age, he or she must present the written approval and consent of a justice of the Supreme Court or a judge of the Family Court having jurisdiction over the town or city in which the application is made.
- If either applicant is 16 or 17 years of age, he or she must present the written consent of both of his or her parents.
- If both applicants are 18 years of age or older, no parental or legal consent is required.

If the consent of both parents is required, there are some qualifiers. One parent alone may consent if the other parent has been missing for one year; if the parents are divorced and the consenting parent has sole custody; if the other parent has been judged incompetent; or, naturally, if the other parent is deceased.

Parents or guardians who consent to the marriage of a minor must personally appear and sign the required documentation in the presence of the town or city clerk or other authorized official. It is best to do this in the town or city where the application is made—if a notarized affidavit originated another city or state, it must be accompanied by a certificate of authentication.

No one may legally take your word for it that you are actually the age you say you are. In most states, you may be required to submit documentary proof of age. Generally, one or more of the following documents showing proof of age is required and acceptable.

- birth certificate
- baptismal record
- passport
- driver's license
- life insurance policy
- employment certificate

- school record
- immigration record
- naturalization record
- court record

Familial Restrictions

A marriage may not take place in the United States between those with the following relationships, regardless of whether they are legitimate or illegitimate offspring.

- An ancestor and descendant (parent, grandparent, great-grandparent, child, grandchild, great-grandchild)
- Brother and sister (full or half-blood)
- Uncle and niece
- Aunt and nephew

In most but not all states, marriage between family members closer than first cousins is prohibited. If this is an issue, it is important to check with the town or city clerk or the marriage license bureau in the town where the marriage will take place.

Capacity to Consent

It is the law that marriage requires two consenting people. If either person cannot or does not understand what it means to be married because of mental illness, drugs, alcohol, or other factors affecting judgment, then that person does not have the capacity to consent, and the marriage is not valid. If fraud or coercion are involved, the marriage also may be invalidated.

Gender

Generally, couples must be of the opposite sex to form a valid marriage. Religions have their own gender regulations, but there is a growing trend among clergy to bless same-sex unions. Most states do not allow same-sex marriages, but in Hawaii, Alaska, and Vermont, arguments are being made in the courts that a marriage license cannot be denied based on the sex of the applicants. On the other hand, some states, including Georgia, South Dakota, Texas, and Utah, have passed laws designed to thwart same-sex marriages. In 1996 the U.S. Congress passed the Defense of Marriage Act, barring the federal government from recognizing same-sex marriages and permitting states to ignore same-sex marriages performed in other states.

Even though most states do not recognize same-sex marriages, many agencies and companies are adopting "domestic partnership" policies that accept same-sex relationships. Policies range from fair housing regulations to the granting of traditional marital benefits, including insurance coverage, family leave, and bereavement leave.

Remarriage

Applicants for a marriage license who were married before must provide information regarding previous marriages, including a copy of the Decree of Divorce or a Certificate of Dissolution of Marriage or a death certificate. Clerks and other marriage licensing officials say the biggest problem that occurs for those who have been married before is that they neglect to bring the original document or a certified copy. The information the applicant needs to provide includes but may not be restricted to:

- month, day, and year of final divorce decree
- county and state where divorce was granted
- grounds for divorce
- whether former spouse or spouses are living

Similar documentation may be required for an annulment and of a widow or widower. The preciseness of the legalities makes it necessary to check and double check, since even one missing document can delay the wedding; this can be a disaster for the bride and groom who have contracted the services of countless others and then must postpone their wedding.

THE MARRIAGE LICENSE

A marriage license authorizes you to get married; a marriage certificate is the document that proves that you are married and is issued by the county office where you were married, usually within a few weeks after the ceremony. In general, a marriage license may only be used in the place it is obtained, and then only within a certain period of time (usually between 24 hours and 60 days, depending on the state); otherwise, the license expires. Some states require a three-day waiting period from the time applicants apply for a license to the time the license is issued. Those states with the strictest requirements strongly advise the bride and groom to obtain their marriage license two to three weeks before their wedding day.

HEALTH CERTIFICATES

The purpose of premarital health requirements and examinations is not to keep a person with an illness from marrying but to ensure that the future spouse knows of the condition. Even in states where no blood test or physical exam is required, failing to tell your prospective spouse that you have a venereal disease or a physical impairment (such as impotency or infertility) before you marry may make the marriage invalid.

The best advice is to find out the requirements by calling or writing the County Clerk's office or the Office of the Registrar as soon as you decide to marry. Then factor in any time restrictions into your planning along with the dates you can obtain confirmations for ceremony and reception site details.

Some states have no requirements for premarital examinations or blood tests before obtaining a marriage license. In other states, the law says you need to be examined and found free of communicable syphilis. In these states, a marriage license is denied anyone found to have communicable syphilis until he or she has undergone sufficient treatment and been ruled noninfectious. You should find out what is required in your state, since the states that do require health certificates often add further time restrictions. For example, you may obtain the certificate from a private physician or health department, but it may only be good for 60 days from the date the examination took place.

In some states, a counseling class is required before a medical certificate can be issued. In such classes or during required counseling, the physician involved must offer the woman a voluntary test for susceptibility to rubella

*Legalities
and Other
Matters*

(German measles), and the physician also discusses HIV/AIDS virus educational material with both the prospective bride and groom. Again, look into your state's requirements well in advance—classes can fill up quickly.

Some states requiring medical certificates will accept them from other states. If, however, the out-of-state certificate does not contain notes that the couple has had AIDS educational material discussed with them and that the woman was offered a voluntary test for susceptibility to rubella, the doctor who issues the certificate must write a separate letter attesting that this has occurred. Otherwise the couple must visit a doctor in the state where they will be married and have that state's form filed with the out-of-state form.

IN ANOTHER COUNTRY

Many brides and grooms dream of being married outside the United States in a romantic spot such as Tahiti or Paris or St. Thomas. But before you call that little French bakery for the perfect wedding cake or put down a deposit on a Caribbean island resort, you must first check the wedding legalities of the country in which you wish to be married. Each country has a different set of requirements. Some ask for residency requirements of a certain duration. Others require a specific number of witnesses.

You don't know where to start? There are resources available to help you. One surefire way to get answers is to telephone the country's consulate or tourist office located in the United States. The office can provide specific instructions over the phone, by mail, or by fax. In some countries, such as Mexico, the requirements vary slightly from town to town, so once you've gotten the basic information from the tourist office, you will need to call the registrar's office in the town where you want to get married. Also get all information in writing so that you have all the facts.

Wedding consultants who specialize in destination weddings and travel agents who are dedicated to helping with wedding planning can also provide information on the documentation required, plus any restrictions.

If you wish to be married in The Bahamas, for example, one member of the couple must have resided in the Islands of The Bahamas for no less than 24 hours prior to the date of the application, and both parties must be there at the time of the application. In addition, a declaration certifying United States citizenship must be sworn before a United States Consul at the American Embassy. If one member of the couple is from a country other than the U.S., a declaration certifying this fact must be sworn before a Notary Public or other person authorized to administer oaths in that country. This declaration must accompany the application for the marriage license. Regardless of country of origin, the bride and groom must produce a photo ID issued by a government office in the country where both resides. If the wedding is to be a Roman Catholic ceremony, the couple is required to complete a six-week preparation class, which they can attend in their own hometown. They must provide proof to the Church when they make arrangements for their wedding.

England also has certain regulations regarding who may marry whom. For example, a man may not marry a former wife of his father, or the daughter of a son of a former wife. Why not? That's the law. On the other hand, step-relatives and certain other relations who were formerly forbidden to marry may now do so, provided they are 21 years of age or older and did not live under the same roof before the younger person turned 18.

One more thing: If you're marrying in another country, don't forget to check on your legal and religious requirements at home as well. Check your passport, medical requirements, and the documentation you need to bring back home to ensure your marriage's validity in the United States.

FROM ANOTHER COUNTRY

Marriage by an American to a foreign national requires its own set of documents and qualifications, including certified English translation of any required documentation. You can get information on obtaining a visa for a foreign spouse from any office of the Immigration and Naturalization Service, U.S. embassies and consulates abroad, or the U.S. Department of State Visa Office.

Legalities and Other Matters

OUT-OF-STATE OFFICIANTS

If your wedding officiant is from another state, some states require that he or she have a Certificate of Authorization from the state in which the wedding will take place.

WITNESSES

Some states require that a witness, in addition to an authorized member of the clergy or public official, be present during the wedding ceremony. In some of these states, there is no minimum age for a witness, but it is suggested that he or she be deemed competent enough to testify in a court proceeding about what he or she witnessed. In other states, no witness is required other than the officiant.

WHO CAN PERFORM A MARRIAGE CEREMONY?

Nonreligious ceremonies, called civil ceremonies, may be performed by a judge, justice of the peace, or court clerk who has legal authority to perform marriages; they may also be performed by a person given temporary authority by a judge or court clerk to conduct a marriage ceremony. Contrary to popular belief, ship captains often will not perform or are not universally authorized to perform marriage ceremonies. Increasingly, however, cruise lines are working out ways for legally recognized marriages to be performed aboard ship by ship captains. A list of persons specified by law as authorized to perform a marriage ceremony is available in that each state's Domestic Relations Law and can include:

- the mayor of a city or village
- the city clerk or one of the deputy city clerks of a city with over one million inhabitants
- a marriage officer appointed by the town or village board or the city common council
- a justice or judge in most courts
- a village, town, or county justice
- a member of the clergy (priest, rabbi, or minister) who has been officially ordained and granted authority to perform marriage ceremonies from a governing church body in accordance with its rules and regulations
- a member of the clergy or minister who is not authorized by a governing church body but who has been chosen by a spiritual group to preside over their spiritual affairs
- a tribal chief (for Native American weddings)

RELIGIOUS FACTORS

Mastering government legalities is just one step toward ensuring the legality of your marriage. Some religions also have rules and regulations that must be adhered to—points that are best immediately checked with the priest, rabbi, or minister who will officiate.

In some religions, for example, "banns" must be published over a three-week period. A bann is a public statement of intent to marry that asks anyone who may object to do so. If, at the end of 21 days, no one has objected, the couple may marry. In other religions, a set number of premarital counseling sessions must be attended before the clergy person will marry the couple. In still other religions, if one or both members of the couple have been divorced, the divorce is not recognized and they may not be married in the church. There is also the matter of membership. For a wedding to take place at a Quaker meeting house, for example, at least one member of the couple should be a Quaker. Otherwise, written support for the marriage must be obtained from two adult members of the Society.

The bottom line: Even if you are a lifelong Roman Catholic, Lutheran, or Presbyterian or a convert to Judaism or the Hindu faith who has seriously studied the tenets of the religion, inquire in advance whether the church has any special requirements. If it is important to you to be married by a priest, rabbi, or minister or in a church, temple, or synagogue, you will need to know the requirements beforehand.

PREMARITAL COUNSELING

Premarital counseling, whether mandated or merely recommended, is a short-term way to work through important issues ahead of time and avoid conflict over the long haul. The purpose is to raise issues that might not have been considered, to discuss potential sensitive areas, and to give words to some of the concerns a couple may have but may not know how to express.

Most couples feel that by the time they are engaged, they know pretty much everything there is to know about each other. It is very likely, however, that they have not seriously talked through a range of issues, including their own physical and emotional needs, their respective goals and desires, and their thoughts on problem-solving and compromise. It's a good time as well to compare notes on having children, work and home priorities, coping with sickness or a crisis, money matters, and spiritual beliefs. People of different religious backgrounds often find clergy counseling extremely helpful, especially if they are planning to have children and raise them in a religious household.

This is also a good time to discuss with your future mate how family matters may best be resolved. A bride or groom might be entering into a marriage with children from a previous marriage or face parental disapproval or a divided family. They may have been on their own for a long time and aren't used to shared decision-making.

When premarital counseling is completed, it would be thoughtful of the bride and groom to write a thank-you note or a letter to their minister, priest, or rabbi to express their appreciation for the guidance they received.

NAME CHANGES

There is no law, rule, religious dictate, or mandate that says the bride must take the groom's last name. A bride may take her husband's last name, retain her own surname, or hyphenate both her own surname and her husband's surname. When Linda Graham marries Mark Richards, she may be Linda Richards, Linda Graham, or Linda Graham-Richards. Despite the range of acceptable choices, 90 percent of today's U.S. brides make the traditional choice of adopting their husband's names.

A bride who wishes to take her husband's last name may retain her given middle name or, more commonly, use her own surname as a middle name. Linda Beth Graham may become Linda Graham Richards or Linda Beth Richards.

The only law governing the name chosen by the bride (or by the groom, who has the option of changing his name as well) is that the name is used *consistently* and without intent to defraud. Any name change is effected simply by entering the new name in the appropriate space provided on the marriage license, as long as the new name consists of one of the following options:

- the surname of the bride (or the groom)
- any former surname he or she has had
- a name combining into a single surname all or a segment of the pre-marriage surname or any former surname of each spouse
- a combination name separated by a hyphen, provided that each part of such combination surname is the pre-marriage surname, or any former surname, of each of the spouses

If, at the time of the marriage, a bride (or groom) does not change her name and later changes her mind, she can file a petition for change of name with the court. The marriage license and certificate, however, cannot be changed to record the surname she decides to use after she is already married and registered with a different name.

NAME CHANGE CONSIDERATIONS

The matter of changing names is traditionally more of a consideration for the bride than it is for the groom, since it is still rare for a man to change his name upon marrying. If a woman is being married for a second time, she probably has already changed her name once. She may have kept her ex-husband's surname, or she may have reverted to her maiden name. Another marriage can

TALKING IT OVER

If premarital private counseling or group classes are not a part of your preparation for marriage, take time out to talk things over yourselves. Ask each other what you would do if you had a problem you couldn't seem to resolve together. Would you seek counseling? Enlist the advice of friends? Keep your own lines of communication open, no matter what? Talk about each other's needs. Discuss having children, career aspirations, family obligations—anything and everything that may be important to you. Don't get so caught up in interviewing musicians and choosing a photographer that you forget the most important components of your pending marriage—each other.

Legalities and Other Matters

bring about more change. If the bride has kept her married name from her first marriage, it is likely that she will take her new husband's surname—if for no other reason than to avoid confusion for all concerned. She may also do it out of consideration and love for her new husband, who will undoubtedly be pleased that she will be known by his name and not by another man's name.

Professional Versus Social

One way to deal professionally with a name change is for the bride to continue to use the name she has been using in work or professional situations. Therefore, she is known as Ms. Jane Johnson at work, while socially she is Mrs. Franklin Pierce, or Jane Johnson Pierce if she retains her maiden name as her middle name.

Children and Names

If the bride has children from a previous marriage, their last name will very likely be that of their father, while their mother may be using her maiden name or taking the name of her new husband. How this is sorted out is up to each bride and groom, but it is important to let relevant persons and organizations know who is who. You may want to type up a note stating the proper names, phone numbers, and addresses of how you are to be notified in case of any calls or correspondence. Give copies to your child's school, pediatrician and dentist, and any religious and sports groups.

NAME CHANGE: OFFICIAL NOTIFICATIONS

When a bride changes her name, she must notify a vast number of people, companies, agencies, and organizations. Use your wedding planner to list these names. Some organizations require proof of the name change and will require a copy of the marriage certificate, which is issued after the marriage. When an address change is occurring as well, it is a good idea to make both changes at the same time. Those to notify include:

- Social Security Administration
- motor vehicles department
- passport agency
- employer payroll department
- banks

- credit unions
- mortgage company
- voter registration
- financial planner (or investment firms/stockbroker)
- credit-card companies
- religious organizations
- magazine subscriptions
- school alumni organizations
- credit accounts (local stores)
- frequent travel clubs
- doctors and dentists

NAME CHANGE: ADVISING OTHERS ON NONTRADITIONAL CHOICES

Confusion often prevails when the bride decides to retain her maiden name or use some hyphenated form of both her and her husband's name. If you decide to go the nontraditional route, you will need to graciously inform those who assume you will be taking your husband's name as your own. If you need to correct someone, do so politely. Be patient: Realize that the older generation may not understand your reasoning for making a nontraditional choice. Some commonsense ways to do so include using your new name on stationery, in the return address on thank-you-note envelopes, in newspaper wedding announcements, or on "at home" cards enclosed in wedding announcements.

PRE- AND POST-NUPTIAL CONTRACTS

The matter of formalizing financial and legal matters through a prenuptial contract or premarital agreement is a sensitive one for brides and grooms, many of whom consider doing so a crass form of hedging bets on the longevity of the marriage. It is definitely an issue that needs to be discussed early in the relationship—and not something you spring on your partner-to-be right before the ceremony. Otherwise, serious doubts, hurt feelings, and even extreme anger can result.

Basically, a premarital agreement is a contract between two people that defines the rights and benefits that will exist during the marriage and after, in the event of divorce. It can expand or limit a person's right to property, life-

Legalities and Other Matters

71

insurance benefits, or support payments upon death or divorce. Usually, it
addresses the rights to property that each brings to the marriage, retirement-
plan assets, and how money accumulated before the marriage will be distributed in case of death or divorce. Without a premarital agreement, state laws
define the rights and benefits of marriage. If the couple does not want to rely
on state laws to determine their legal and fiscal fate, the premarital agreement
allows them to make their own rules.

Although anyone can have a premarital agreement, it is most often used
when the bride or the groom or both bring assets to the marriage that they
want to protect in the event of divorce or death. This is particularly true for
people marrying for the second or third time who want to make sure that certain assets are passed on to their children from a previous marriage.

What a prenuptial contract does not cover is child custody and support.
The courts will disregard the contract on this point and make a decision that is
considered in the best interest of the child. The courts will also disregard a premarital agreement that, in essence, leaves one person destitute.

A postnuptial contract is one made after a couple is married. It can
include the same categories of consideration, usually having to do with property and money, as those in a prenuptial contract. This contract is usually drawn
if the couple realizes that children from a previous marriage or other family
members would be unprotected in the case of divorce or death.

DISCLOSURE

Because one person is usually giving something up by agreeing to a prenuptial
contract, both the bride and the groom must fully disclose their finances to
each other in advance. Most states require that the premarital agreement
include separate listings that describe and show the values of each person's

assets. If the couple chooses not to do this, they are preventing one partner from knowing what he or she is losing by signing the contract—and this may constitute fraud, which makes the agreement unenforceable. For this reason, and to ensure that the agreement is written correctly and legally, it is a good idea for both the bride and the groom to seek the advice of his or her own lawyer before entering into the agreement.

THE FORM OF THE AGREEMENT

A prenuptial contract or premarital agreement must be in writing to be legally binding. It provides evidence of the terms of the agreement and demonstrates that both people understand and agree to the terms. It is generally legally binding as long as it is entered into voluntarily and without fraud and as long as it is reasonable and fair. It is not binding if a person is unfairly induced to sign the agreement or is coerced under excessive emotional pressure.

THE ART OF DIPLOMACY

It is often as difficult for those requesting a premarital contract to broach the subject as it is being asked to sign one. Again, a prenuptial contract may simply be a way of protecting assets you bring into the marriage in the (unlikely) event of divorce or death. A couple who communicates well has a head start in discussing a prenuptial contract. If you are the person requesting a premarital agreement, do so with tact, love, and honesty. Explain exactly why you are making the request and whether it affects the assets you amass as a couple (it shouldn't). Discuss the lifetime of assets you hope to build together as a couple—assets completely separate from the assets protected in the prenuptial agreement.

DOMESTIC PARTNERSHIP AFFIDAVITS

Most experts agree that before a same-gender couple enters into a domestic partnership affidavit the two should consult with an attorney. This agreement is intended to create for same-gender couples who cannot legally marry conditions equal to those of married couples of opposite genders. An affidavit can, however, contain clauses that may be unpalatable to the couple. For example, in some cities, the couple is required to live together and to "have a close personal relationship." Critics claim this is discriminatory, arguing that legal marriage does not require that a couple live together or have a close personal relationship. Signing such an agreement brings few real benefits but may include being able to participate in a partner's health insurance plan. If these situations are not a factor, organizations such as the Partners Task Force for Gay & Lesbian Couples suggest that partners desiring validation as a couple instead plan a wedding or other ceremony of commitment.

WILLS AND FINANCES

When there is no pre- or postnuptial contract, the bride and groom would be smart to put their wills and finances in order so that the disposition of their money and property is clear to each other or, should both die, to their families.

CHANGING BENEFICIARIES

Finances include such things as insurance policies and beneficiaries on retirement plan payouts. Assuming the bride and groom want to make each other the beneficiary on any existing policies they own, the couple should call an insurance broker and talk to their payroll coordinator at work to see what documentation is required to make this change.

DECISIONS ABOUT BANK ACCOUNTS

How the couple will manage their finances is purely personal, but they should discuss their thoughts. They may decide to maintain a separate accounts as well as open a new joint account, or they may pool all their finances into a joint account. If the bride is maintaining a separate account but changing her name, she needs to take care of this paperwork when she changes other legal documents. If she is changing her name and has direct electronic deposit into her account, she needs to coordinate the account change at the same time as she changes her name at work.

WEDDING INSURANCE

Weddings have taken place for centuries without wedding insurance, but no chapter on the legalities of getting married would be complete without including it as a topic of consideration for the bride and groom. In many instances, the cost of a wedding is so astronomical that the additional cost of insurance is worth every penny if it protects such a large investment.

Wedding insurance, offered exclusively by the Fireman's Fund insurance company (800–ENGAGED), may be taken out by a bride and groom to cover wedding catastrophes that are beyond anyone's control. Wedding insurance can also cover any retaking of photographs, replacement of lost or damaged wedding attire or wedding gifts, and public liability.

Wedding insurance is beneficial, for example, when a reception site suddenly cannot accommodate the party because a fire, damage, or a murder or suicide has occurred at the site, or an outbreak of a contagious disease has required a health department quarantine. Insurance will cover the cost of rebooking elsewhere.

If wedding insurance is a possibility, it is wise to consider every contingency when assessing the value and extent of the insurance you want. For example, if the reception site is suddenly not available and the wedding must be canceled because no other site is available on such short notice, other costs may be lost, such as formal-wear rental, car hire, hotel charges for the wedding party, and flower arrangements.

HOMEOWNERS' INSURANCE FOR GIFTS?

You might also check with your insurance agent about the advisability of taking out a rider on your homeowner's policy if you anticipate receiving a number of expensive gifts. If, for example, you receive place settings of sterling silver, the value is probably not covered in the insurance you presently have. It could be covered on a temporary rider until you reevaluate your future insurance needs.

Legalities and Other Matters

A WORD ABOUT CONTRACTS

While the bride and groom are busy getting their personal documents in order before the wedding, they are also likely to be contracting for myriad services, from the photographer to the reception site to airline tickets and the honeymoon hotel.

How do you make sure that ultimately you get what you pay for? In a phrase: *Get it in writing.*

If your agreement with the florist was to provide 12-inch-round floral centerpieces of roses and lilies and you arrive breathless at the reception to find jelly glasses holding daffodils, you have little recourse for a price adjustment if what you agreed to is not written clearly in a contract. If your agreement with the caterer was for brand-name liquor and you find the bartender pouring from house brand bottles, you will have trouble legally withholding full payment if that specification is not part of a contract.

It is assumed, of course, that you have done your homework carefully and checked references to ensure that you are not contracting with a disreputable or fly-by-night vendor, so you have every right to expect what you ordered. But you will have a hard time collecting if every requirement is not in writing.

THE BEST CONTRACT

"A contract of eternal bond of love,
Confirm'd by mutual joining of your hands,
Attested by the holy close of lips,
Strengthen'd by interchangement
of your rings;
And all the ceremony of this compact
Sealed in my function, by my testimony."

—William Shakespeare, "Twelfth Night"

CHAPTER 5

GUESTS AND GUEST LISTS

I t happens to almost every bride and groom: The guest list, carefully counted and coordinated within the budget, slowly but surely inflates. Don't think it can't happen to you. Indeed, as cousins you've never heard of come out of the woodwork and your mother's work friends inquire about the date, guest lists can grow at an alarming rate.

Most brides and grooms, in planning their nuptials, must work around financial considerations. The biggest factor in the cost of a wedding? The guest list. That's because the reception costs generally are the most expensive aspect of weddings today.

Guest-list grousing can turn the most compatible families into the Hatfields and the McCoys and leave brides and grooms feeling that elopement is a reasonable resolution. Insisting that all involved whittle down their lists often makes the person who is paying feel guilty and petty. The bride and groom become anxious, parents complain, and tensions rise.

TACT TO THE RESCUE

Tact and diplomacy, two of the cornerstones of etiquette, can save the day, along with a visit back to the bride's and groom's first shared vision of their wedding—*and* a budget reality check.

Number one: As the nuptial couple, don't automatically agree that cousins you've never met or Mom's office colleagues take precedence over your own friends. This is, after all, *your* wedding. Think and talk it through—calmly. You might end up inviting the cousins, but you'll be more understanding and less resentful if you agree it's the way to go.

Number two: Don't opt for the easy solution. Inviting a large number of guests to the ceremony but only a small number to the reception is no solution at all. It can be insulting to send a formal ceremony invitation to many and a reception invitation to a favored few. (The exception: inviting children to the ceremony only.) Yet, an open invitation to the ceremony issued to church or synagogue members by the priest, rabbi or minister, with your permission, carries no gift obligation for those who attend nor any obligation to the bride and groom to invite them to the reception. The reverse—inviting a small number of guests to an intimate or private ceremony and a larger number to the reception—is perfectly acceptable.

Number three: You have a choice to make. Do you want to plan your guest list and reception around a budget or make a guest list first and plan the reception around that? Either way, you will likely find that your list will require some fine-tuning.

THE GUEST LIST

A guest list consists of a magical number of family and friends that 1) suits the size of your ceremony and reception sites, 2) corresponds with the level of intimacy desired for the wedding, and 3) can be accommodated within your wedding budget (an important reality). Traditionally, each family is allotted half of the desired total guest count, a figure largely determined by the person hosting the wedding. A way of starting to decide whom to invite is to combine four lists, thus formulating the master list. Start with lists from the bride, the groom, the bride's parents, and the groom's parents. It is necessary that everyone make up their lists *realistically*. As acceptances and regrets become known, the "weights" of the lists may vary.

Some decisions that may affect your numbers: Do you plan to include children? To invite single friends to bring guests? Neither inclusion is necessary, but both necessitate "proper etiquette," meaning consideration and sensitivity.

If children are not invited, the proper way to communicate this is to write only the parents' names on the outer and inner envelopes. It is inappropriate to write "No Children" on the invitations. For the guest of a single friend, send a separate invitation to the guest, unless he or she lives at the same address.

Use all of the considerations just noted to arrive at a reasonable estimate. Then ask each half (or one-quarter) to compile a rough list of "must-have" guests, supplemented by "hopefuls" to be invited if there should be room. Remember to include in your count the officiant and his or her spouse, yourselves, both sets of parents, and your wedding party.

Cutting down an overambitious guest list is a difficult task requiring great tact, diplomacy, and even-handedness. If you know that distance will prevent certain people from attending, factor this in. To trim the guest list, try to redraw your lines equilaterally, bumping entire groupings of people—second cousins, work associates with whom you've never socialized, friends from the health club—to a "B" List. These people can be invited four weeks before the wedding if guests on the "A" List send regrets. Your list may read something like this:

- **FIRST TIER**: immediate families (parents, siblings, grandparents, the couple's own children)
- **SECOND TIER**: extended family members (aunts, uncles, cousins, nieces, nephews)
- **THIRD TIER**: family friends (parents' close friends, long-time friends and neighbors, childhood friends and their parents, if close to you)
- **FOURTH TIER**: bride and groom's friends, in progressive tiers of closeness to you (childhood friends, high school and college friends, work friends, new friends)
- **FIFTH TIER**: parents' colleagues (associates, employers, employees)

This guide should be based upon what makes sense in your case. Any planning, of course, must be adapted to your particular circumstances. If you and your intended are established professionally, perhaps marrying for a second or third time, you will probably be paying for all or most of the wedding yourselves. Perhaps your wedding will take place far from your hometown or where your parents live. Under any of these circumstances, it could make sense to switch tiers three and four, as defined above.

Your invitation guest list can be pared down in a number of ways. Following are ways to do so.

Make Across-the-Board Distinctions

To avoid hurt feelings when a guest list is limited, subdivide the levels of family across the board. For example, if numbers are limited, you could invite all aunts and uncles and forgo cousins.

Leave Out Work Associates

When space is absolutely at a premium, some couples delete work associates entirely. This can reduce the list considerably while at the same time keeping the wedding a more personal one, with only family members and close, long-time friends attending.

Forget Parental Paybacks

This is not the time for parents to insist on reciprocity for all the gifts they've given and weddings they've attended in the past, nor does your wedding need to be the occasion for them to fulfill their own social obligations.

Shower Guests Are Wedding Guests

Any guest who is invited to a shower must also be invited to the wedding, with a few exceptions—co-workers who give an office shower, for example. Keep that in mind when drawing up your guest lists for wedding showers.

DON'T FORGET THESE GUESTS

A few special guests do not fit into any of the priority tiers but should be included on the guest list. These include:

- The person who performs the ceremony, and his or her spouse (necessary)
- The parents of ring bearers and flower girls (necessary)
- The parents of the bridesmaids (not necessary, but a nice gesture when feasible, especially when the bride knows them well)
- Counselors, advisors, or mentors to the bride or groom who are not close friends but who have been an important part of their lives (not absolutely necessary but often meaningful)

One of the most common problems is that of restricting the number of children attending the reception. In large families, with dozens of cousins, nieces, and nephews, the costs of inviting them all may be prohibitive. Yet, some relatives feel so strongly that their children be included that they will consider refusing the invitation altogether if the children are left out.

No easy answer exists. You can, however, discourage the youngsters' attendance one of two ways. You can enclose a note to those friends and relatives who may be the most understanding about your situation, explaining that costs and space prevent your asking all children under a certain age. You may also talk to close friends and relatives, explaining the problem and asking them to help by spreading the word. You can also offer to hire a baby-sitter during the hours of the wedding celebration to watch the children of out-of-town guests, either at a relative's home or at the hotel where the guests are staying.

Once you've established an age limit, however, you must make no exceptions. Outside of your own children or your own brothers and sisters, you must refrain from inviting one child under your age limit—or the hurt feelings incurred will far outweigh the money saved.

If you are planning to invite more than just a few children to your wedding celebrations, finding ways to keep them occupied can be great fun. You could have your floral designer create a piñata filled with inexpensive toys. Or you could set up a designated children's table with coloring books and favors. If children are seated with parents, you could still provide each with a coloring book and a small box of crayons. Make sure, too, that your menu includes some kid-friendly foods. Another consideration is to hire a baby-sitter or two to help out. Some reception sites even provide a separate room where children can color, watch a video, or just gather. In that case, the kids should be supervised, and baby-sitters are a must.

OUCH!

Instead of throwing rice or rose petals, blowing bubbles, or gently tossing birdseed at the newlyweds, guests in Rumania used to throw sweets and nuts at the couple as their wish for prosperity. This tradition is generally a thing of the past, for obvious reasons (including the sheer weight of flying objects!).

Guests and Guest Lists

ORGANIZING A GUEST LIST

A beautifully organized and orchestrated wedding, most brides will tell you, is the happy result of lists—and lots of them. One of your most important lists is your guest list. After you have made the final decisions on whom to invite, you will need to coordinate your many sources of lists: your personal address book, your computer address files, handwritten names and addresses from the groom's mother and stepfather, and a typed list from the bride's stepmother and father—not to mention the groom's lists and those of the other parents (your mother and the groom's father). Then there are the loose scraps of paper cluttering up an old address book. After the bride and groom review everyone's lists they can incorporate them into their own.

Make one alphabetical master list from the various lists, then incorporate it into your wedding planner or computer spreadsheet. You will refer to this list endlessly as the weeks go by—to address invitations, figure out who needs maps and directions, check off acceptances and regrets, and record gifts received and thank-you notes written. You will also use this list to count heads. The master guest list is the foundation of your wedding plans, and as such should be carefully maintained. It should include each guest's full name, address, telephone number, and relationship to the bride or groom. You should have spaces to indicate whether a guest has sent an R.S.V.P., a description of any gift received, and the date a thank-you note was sent.

DESTINATION GUESTS

If you are planning a destination wedding to a site where guests will have to travel a good distance, the sooner you can share your plans with them, the better. While costs are considerable for any travel, they can be astronomical if the venue is an exotic island or out-of-the-way hamlet. The sooner your guests can start making their travel arrangements, the less it will cost them. A long lead time also allows them to arrange for time off from work and perhaps even plan a family vacation around the wedding. This does not mean you should send out invitations a year in advance. A telephone call or note is all your guests need to begin planning; the written invitation can follow.

STANDBY GUEST LIST

Ask everyone involved in choosing the guest list for the names and addresses of "wait list" guests; then you and your partner can prioritize them. Plan for enough time for responses from the master-list guests to be received—no less than four weeks—to invite guests who are on the "B," or standby, list. Making this choice early in your planning process makes sending the second group of invitations out quickly much easier. Create a list separate from the master guest list, and once guests from the standby group accepts, incorporate the name into the master list in your planner.

Some couples are hesitant to have standby lists, but these lists do provide a practical solution for controlling the numbers—and budget. If you and your intended (and parents) apply discretion, making sure that guests do not even know that you have "A" and "B" lists, feelings won't be hurt, and guests won't feel slighted if those later invitations are mailed promptly, four weeks before the wedding.

WEDDING ANNOUNCEMENT LIST

If you plan to have wedding announcements mailed after the wedding, put together a list of the names and addresses of people who will be receiving announcements so that you can order the announcements well in advance. This way, you can address and stamp them beforehand, and arrange for a friend or relative to mail them, preferably the day or next few days after the wedding.

HELP! WHAT DO I DO ABOUT. . .

1. . . . INCLUDING PARTNERS? Partners of invited guests must be included in a wedding invitation, whether they are married, engaged, or living together and whether anyone in the wedding party knows them. It is nice—but certainly not required, and often not realistic—to suggest that single guests who aren't attached to a significant other bring a date.

   A single invitation addressed to both members of a couple who live together is sent to their shared address, while invitations to an engaged or long-standing couple who don't live together are sent separately to each address. Envelopes addressed to a single friend may include "and Guest," indicating that he or she may bring an escort or friend. If it is possible to obtain the name of the guest, the name would be included on the invitation to the friend. Or a second invitation may even be sent directly to the date at his or her home address instead.

Occasionally, a single guest will become engaged or reunite with a separated spouse after the invitations have been mailed. In that case, it is perfectly correct for the bride or groom to extend a verbal invitation to the guest's friend or spouse.

2. . . . GUESTS WHO ASK TO BRING A GUEST? The answer is straightforward: It is impolite of a guest to ask if he can bring a date—but it is not impolite of you to refuse. If you discover, however, that the two are engaged or living together, it is polite to invite your friend's partner, whether verbally or by invitation.

3. . . . INVITATIONS TO OUT-OF-TOWN GUESTS WHO CAN'T POSSIBLY ATTEND? Many people prefer not to send invitations to those friends and acquaintances whom they think cannot possibly attend the celebrations. They feel that doing so makes it look as if they are merely inviting those friends to send a gift. In most cases, those friends should receive a wedding announcement instead, which carries no obligation whatsoever.

There is the flip side to this dilemma. Some good friends who live far away might actually be hurt if you do not send invitations, even if your intent was to spare them from feeling obliged to send a gift for a wedding so far away. These friends, upon hearing news of your engagement, may actually have been planning to travel to your wedding. In general, invite truly good friends—even if they live far away.

OUT-OF-TOWN GUESTS

The bride and groom are certainly not obligated to plan entertainment for out-of-town guests who are not part of the wedding party. But it is a nice touch to offer activities, gatherings, and other forms of hospitality to those who have come from far away to celebrate your nuptials.

EVENTS FOR OUT-OF-TOWNERS

At the time of your engagement, you will probably be approached by friends and relatives offering to help out or to host a gathering or meal for out-of-town guests. In some cases, the costs and preparations are shared by a group of your friends and family. You will need to provide the hosts of these parties with a list of names and addresses so that they can send invitations, if necessary, and plan their party accordingly. You can get a good idea of the number of out-of-town guests by referring to your master guest list (in the space to check whether a guest is from out of town). If out-of-town guests are staying in private homes, their hosts should be invited to the events and parties as well. Thus, be sure to provide the party hosts with the names and addresses of those who are providing accommodations. Don't forget to send thank-you gifts or flowers to the party hosts, along with your words of appreciation. These parties may occur:

- **DURING THE REHEARSAL DINNER.** Friends and relatives may offer to host a cocktail party, barbecue, or other gathering for guests while the wedding party is attending the rehearsal and rehearsal dinner. Note: Many rehearsal dinner hosts invite certain out-of-town guests to the event—a perfectly appropriate choice if space and budget allow.
- **ON THE DAY OF AN EVENING WEDDING.** Other friends might host a brunch or luncheon for guests on the day of a wedding that's held in the late afternoon or evening.
- **AT A POST-WEDDING BRUNCH.** Out-of-town guests at an evening wedding generally stay the night. For them, a breakfast or brunch makes for a nice send-off.
- **OPTIONAL ACTIVITES.** If there is free time in the wedding-celebrations schedule, you may want to provide your out-of-town guests with a list of local activities, sports centers, museums, and other attractions, along with addresses and phone numbers.

Guests and
Guest Lists

Here's where you can get creative: Your town may have a singular attraction that may be a must-see for any person new to the area. You might even provide tickets or passes. Don't make an activity mandatory, however—simply provide enticing options. You might ask a friend to gather local information for you to give to out-of-town guests.

LODGING FOR OUT-OF-TOWNERS

Out-of-town guests are expected to pay for their own lodging; the exception is if they are members of the bridal party. Bridal-party members are expected to pay for any extra hotel charges (such as movie rentals, room service, health-club fees) when they check out. An extra-courteous touch: Leave a note of welcome at the desk for each guest with a list of other guests who are staying there.

Following are some ideas for helping your out-of-town guests find places to stay.

- It is a courtesy—but certainly not obligatory—for the bride and groom to take responsibility for finding or recommending lodging for out-of-town guests. But if yours is a large wedding with a good number of out-of-town guests expected, it's a smart idea to pre-reserve a block of rooms in a hotel; some hotels are able to discount room rates if a minimum number is booked in a block. Be sure to have guests make their reservations as early as possible.

- Some friends may offer to put up out-of-town guests at their homes. If the guests do forgo a hotel room, it is up to you to make the best match so that all involved are comfortable with the arrangement.

Either you or the hosts can send the out-of-town guests the names, address, and telephone number of their host and hostess and directions to their home, and let the guests know what to expect (whether their hosts have a pet, a swimming pool, children, and the like). Make sure the hosts are clear on the guests' arrival and departure dates and times. Remember to give a thank-you gift to those who are providing lodging.

GUESTS' RESPONSIBILITIES

R.S.V.P

The most important obligation a guest has upon receiving a wedding invitation is to respond immediately, particularly if he or she can't attend. This allows the bride and groom to promptly send out another invitation in his or her place, if desired. At the very least, the hosts will have realistic numbers of guests to relay to the caterer and others—as long as guests abide by the R.S.V.P.

Gifts

Guests invited to the ceremony and reception have an obligation to send a gift, whether they are attending or not. There *are* a few exceptions. Those who receive an announcement after the wedding has taken place have no obligation to send a gift, although it is always nice to acknowledge the receipt of the announcement by sending a card or note expressing best wishes to the couple.

A request for a contribution to a charity in lieu of gifts, particularly in the case of an older couple or a remarriage, should be respected and adhered to by guests.

Attending

Just as it is impolite of a guest to ask if he or she may bring a guest, it's doubly so to simply show up at the celebration with a surprise guest. Unfortunately, reports abound that it does happen: Some guests arrive with dates, children, extras in general—unannounced. The courteous thing for the hosts to do is graciously grin and bear it, when possible.

Best Behavior, Please

Just as there are guidelines to help the bride and groom and their families organize the most wonderful wedding possible, there are guidelines for guests who sometimes, in their enthusiasm, pose thorny problems. Guests have the responsibility to behave with decorum, and this responsibility extends to immediate family members as well. No matter how many sets of parents each of you have, and no matter what level of rancor may have been reached in their relationships with one another, a wedding is not the place to wage war. Best behavior is the code, so guests should practice civility during any and all proceedings in which they are participating:

1. *During the ceremony*
   - Guests should respect the sanctity of the occasion and not talk during the wedding ceremony or interrupt the service by taking pictures with a flash camera. This is also not the time to mingle or greet friends and acquaintances.
   - Guests should participate in as much of the ceremony as their own religion and that of the ceremony permits. If a mass or communion is offered and they choose not to participate, they should remain quietly in their seats. Otherwise, they should stand when others stand and sit when others sit. They are not required to kneel if this is offensive to them or recite prayers that are contrary to their own beliefs.

2. *During the reception*
   - Some behavior may seem harmless and trivial in casual circumstances, but within the context of a special occasion it can appear ill-mannered and unruly. The custom in some regions of the country for guests to clink their forks or spoons against their glasses indicating that the bride and groom should kiss should be kept to a minimum. It is annoying to those who are trying to speak; it is annoying to the bride and groom who are trying to greet guests or simply enjoy the food; it is annoying, period.
   - Neither should guests grab the microphone to croon a few favorite numbers or tell stories or jokes, no matter how impressive their singing voices or how humorous they think they are. The bride and groom have taken great care to orchestrate a few hours of entertainment that do not include an amateur hour. Only if a bride and groom request that a guest sing a number should he accept—but he should keep the performance short and sweet.
   - Don't monopolize the bride and groom in the receiving line. Guests in the receiving line should introduce themselves to the first person in the line, then keep their comments to the bare minimum: "What a lovely wedding!" "I'm so happy for you." They should then move quickly on. The same brevity of comment is appreciated during the reception, since the bride and groom have so many people with whom to speak.

- A bride and groom held captive by a garrulous guest can gently extricate themselves by saying, "We have so much to catch up on. Let's make a pledge that when we get back from the honeymoon we get together and talk for hours! I'm so glad you're here. . . thank you for coming. . . ."

3. *After the reception*
- It is quite inappropriate for guests to grab the centerpiece upon departing, scoop up matchbooks, or request that any uneaten portion of their meal be put in a doggie bag to take home. The centerpieces should be left in place unless the bride and groom have actually encouraged guests to take them; asking for leftover food is not in keeping with the elegance or dignity of the event. Guests also should not assume that flowers, if not given away, will be thrown out. The bride and groom may have made arrangements to have flowers delivered to shut-ins, to hospitals or nursing homes, or to guests unable to attend the festivities because of health or family issues. The flowers, in other words, belong to the bride and groom to dispose of as they wish.

SEATING SAVVY: GUESTS ONLY

The bride and groom and their families have taken great care in planning seating for their guests, both at the ceremony and at the reception. It is important for the guests to respect these plans.

At the Ceremony
When guests arrive at the ceremony, they should tell the usher whether they are to be seated on the bride's side or the groom's side. If there are a disproportionate number of guests on one side or the other, the usher might ask a late-arriving guest if he or she would mind sitting on the other side. It is courteous of the

---

PICTURE THIS

Ask guests to bring a copy of a picture of themselves with you and/or the groom, or with your parents, siblings, or other family members. Put a friend in charge of pinning the photos to a poster board that's on display at the reception. It will be great fun for guests to look at during the reception, and a wonderful beginning to your first photo album as a married couple afterward.

guest to comply with this request, since it truly makes no difference—and it is only a tradition, not a hard and fast rule, that there are "sides" to take in the first place.

If guests have been sent a pew card or a "within the ribbon" card, they present this card to the usher who seats them accordingly. A pew card has a number on it: the lower the number, the closer to the front the guest is seated. A guest holding a "within the ribbon" card is seated anywhere in a number of pews that have been reserved, as indicated by ribbons across the entrance to the pew. The usher escorts the guests to that section and removes the ribbons so the guests may enter.

Unlike at a regular church or synagogue service when guests move in to make room for later arrivals, guests at a wedding who have arrived early enough to have an aisle seat do not need to lose their preferred seat to those who come after. Instead, they rise or step into the aisle to let the new arrivals move in to the center of the pew, then reseat themselves.

> ## MORE MEMORIES
>
> Instead of a memory book to be filled in at the reception, send a small memory card with your invitations, along with the request that each guest write on it a memory either of you or of you as a couple and return it with their response. Paste these memories into a book and put this book near your guest book for guests to look through at the reception.

At the Reception

Guests should never alter place cards or switch tables at a wedding reception. Instead, it is their responsibility to be as cordial as they can be wherever the bride and groom have designated they sit. Don't stand on ceremony and wait to be introduced to tablemates and others either. Introduce yourself and add a little explanation: "I'm Lorrin's aunt from Hawaii" or "Jen and I were roommates in college."

It is kind but not required for men at a table to ask single women to dance at some point during the reception, and for anyone at the table to offer to assist an older or infirm guest with a buffet meal.

CHAPTER 6

INVITATIONS AND OTHER PRINTED ITEMS

Because it reflects the degree of formality of the celebration, your invitation is the first indication to your guests of the style and tone of your wedding. It is also a keepsake for the bride and groom to cherish forever, and as such, your choices should be based on personal preferences. The couple who enjoys a long engagement has the luxury of having more time to mull over choices available to them before making a final selection.

Even with a long engagement, choosing, printing, and mailing invitations must be planned well enough in advance to allow time for the invitations to be mailed and guests to respond. The rule of thumb is to allow at least six to eight weeks for printing formal invitations and their related enclosures. Try to plot out the time so that you will be addressing your invitations no later than two months before the wedding and mailing them out six to eight weeks before the wedding date.

Of course, customs have loosened as busy couples find themselves pressed for time. For the bride and groom who decide suddenly to marry, tradition is often thrown to the wind. A couple may telephone, fax, or overnight-mail their requests for the honor of the presence of their family and close friends.

INVITATION STYLES

These days, the range of invitations is infinite, but the general categories can be broken down into third-person formal invitations, semiformal invitations, or in the case of a small, intimate wedding, handwritten notes on beautiful stationery.

Shop around before making a final decision. You can get catalogs from the many wedding stationery companies that advertise in the pages of bridal magazines. Local stationers and printers also have a wealth of sample books and catalogs on hand.

When writing the name of the recipient on a formal engraved or printed invitation, it is imperative that the inner and outer envelopes are double and triple checked with the invitation before mailing, ensuring that all names are the same. If the envelopes are being addressed separately, take a few minutes to put them in alphabetically ordered stacks before assembling them so that, for example, the top outer envelope is "Mr. and Mrs. Robert Adams" and the top inner envelope is "Mr. and Mrs. Adams." You wouldn't want the Adams, with their correctly addressed outer envelope, to find "Mr. and Mrs. Norwood" written on their inner one.

The elements to consider when choosing invitations are paper shades, paper weight, typeface, size, and wording. Visit several vendors and check costs for these and for coordinating inserts and envelopes as well. Then compare prices and the length of time required for printing. While some stationers require several weeks for an order to be placed and returned to them, printers who do the work themselves can often guarantee a faster turnaround time. If the delivery time is considerable, ask if you can receive your envelopes early so that you can get a jump on the often time-consuming task of addressing them.

Don't forget to keep samples of what you order so that you can coordinate the design scheme of other printed accessories—whether inserts, place cards, or personalized napkins—with that of the invitation.

FORMAL INVITATIONS

The correct shades for the most formal and traditional wedding invitation are ivory, soft cream, and white. The heaviest-weight paper in these shades may cost a bit more, but its appearance and feel are substantial and bespeak formality. You may want your paper flat or prefer a raised plate mark or margin. It is correct to use either a large double sheet, which is folded a second time, or a smaller single sheet.

After choosing paper shade and weight, you should select a typeface. For formal invitations, shaded and antique Roman faces are traditional choices. Remember: Simple styles are in better taste than ornate and flowery styles—and are easier to read as well. No other ornament should be added to a formal invitation, with the exception of a coat of arms (if the bride's father's family has one). A coat of arms or a crest may be used without color at the top center of the invitation.

ALTERNATIVES TO TRADITIONAL INVITATIONS

Printed invitations that do not follow the traditional, third-person wording style can be quite beautiful. If the wedding is to be a simple and nontraditional celebration, the invitations may be printed on paper with a design or border (often in a color carrying out the color scheme of the wedding), while being engraved or thermographed in as formal a style as traditional ones.

PRINTING CHOICES

Formal and semiformal invitations may be printed in several ways. Whatever you use is a matter of personal preference and budget, of course, but in general the more formal the wedding, the more formal the printing style.

ENGRAVING

Engraved invitations are the most traditional printing style for formal invitations, if only because the engraving method has been around the longest time. Engraving results in raised print that is pressed through so that it can be felt on the back of the paper. It is also the most expensive form of printing.

THERMOGRAPHY

Thermography results in raised print that is shinier than engraved print and does not press through the back of the paper. Thermography is less expensive than engraving.

LITHOGRAPHY

Lithography imprints lettering with ink but results in neither raised nor pressed-through lettering. It is less costly than either engraving or thermography.

> ## YOU'RE THE EXPERT
>
> You can often save on costs when you decide to use a local print shop for your invitations and enclosures. Most print shops do not do engraving but can manage other printing processes, including desktop and laser printing programs. Remember, though, that the printer's expertise is printing, not necessarily layout, design, and invitation etiquette. If you go this route, do your homework so that you can be prepared to make the big decisions yourself.

Invitations and Other Printed Items

LASER

Invitations can be produced on a laser printer, either at a professional print shop or at home. The result is similar to that produced by lithography. Blank invitation forms are available at better stationers. A word of caution: Great care must be taken to ensure that the forms are fed through the desktop printer straight and evenly. You should also choose a typeface that is formal, crisp, and easy to read, duplicating other professionally produced print. Laser printing is the most inexpensive form of printing, and when it is used for a formal wedding it can also *look* inexpensive. Make sure to print out a few practice invitations to get the look you want before it's too late to have invitations professionally printed.

HANDWRITTEN

A personal invitation may be handwritten on lovely stationery when it is an invitation to a very small wedding or when the bride and groom want to personalize their invitations, no matter how formal the ceremony may be.

The most formal invitations have the name of the recipient written by hand on an otherwise printed card. You may want to employ the services of a calligrapher for this form of invitation, unless you or someone close to you has beautiful penmanship. It is also possible to use a desktop laser printer to "write" in the name of the recipient, but to ensure a handwritten result it is imperative that a type font that duplicates a calligraphic style is used. Make sure, too, that the invitation (which, because of printer limitations, must be a single sheet, not a fold-over style) can be fed evenly through the printer.

DOCTOR AND MRS. REID W. COLEMAN

REQUEST THE HONOUR OF THE PRESENCE OF

Mr. and Mrs. Christopher Wicke

AT THE MARRIAGE OF THEIR DAUGHTER

LAURA JEANNE

TO

MR. PATRICK DESMOND WHELAN

SATURDAY, THE EIGHTH OF MAY

AT HALF AFTER ELEVEN O'CLOCK

ST. JOHN'S CHURCH

REHOBOTH, MASSACHUSETTS

INVITATION WORDING

TRADITIONAL WORDING

For the bride and groom who cherish long-standing traditions, conventional wording and spelling will govern their invitation choices. Some specific rules for *formal* wedding invitations are as follows:

1.   The invitation to a wedding ceremony in a house of worship reads "Mr. and Mrs. Henry Stuart Evans request the *honour* [using the traditional "u" spelling] of your presence. . . ." "*Favour,*" as in "the favour of a reply," also uses the traditional spelling.

2.   The invitation to a reception reads: "Mr. and Mrs. Henry Stuart Evans request the pleasure of your company. . . ."

3.   When a Roman Catholic Mass is part of the wedding ceremony, invitations *may* include "and your participation in the offering of the Nuptial Mass" beneath the groom's name.

4.   No punctuation is used except after abbreviations, such as "Mr." or "Mrs.," or when phrases requiring separation occur in the same line, as in the date.

5.   Numbers in the date and time are spelled out, as in "the twenty-seventh of August," but long numbers in the street address may be written in numerals: "1490 Kenwood Parkway."

6.   Half-hours are written as "half after four o'clock"—not "half past four" or "four-thirty."

7.   Although "Mr." is abbreviated and "Junior" may be, the title "Doctor" is more properly written in full.

8.   If the invitation includes the handwritten name of the recipient, the full name must be written out. The use of an initial—"Mr. and Mrs. Scott E. Jenkins" —is not correct.

9.   The invitation to the wedding ceremony alone does not include an R.S.V.P.

10.   On the reception invitation, the terms "R.S.V.P.," "R.s.v.p.," "RSVP," and "The favour of a reply is requested" are equally correct. If the address to which the reply is to be sent is different from the one appearing on the invitation itself, you may use "Kindly send reply to," followed by the correct address.

11.   Traditionally, the date of the wedding on a formal invitation does not include the year, but today it is considered correct to include it, spelled out: "Nineteen hundred and ninety-nine." (The year has traditionally been a part of wedding announcements.)

Invitations and Other Printed Items

Traditional Formal Invitation

The most common traditional wording used today for a formal wedding given by the bride's parents reads:

Mr. and Mrs. Henry Stuart Evans
request the honour of your presence
at the marriage of their daughter
Katherine Leigh
to
Mr. Brian Charles Jamison
Saturday, the twelfth of June
nineteen hundred and ninety-nine
at half after four o'clock
Village Lutheran Church
Briarcliff Manor

The traditional wedding invitation is issued by the bride's parents. Note that although the bride's name is not preceded by "Miss," the groom's is preceded by "Mr."

Less Formal Wording

When less formality is desired, alternatives to traditional third-person wording can be used. These invitations may be engraved or printed by a stationer in just as formal a style as traditional invitations:

SHOP THE MUSEUMS

If your wedding is not so formal that it requires traditional invitations, look in museum gift shops for beautiful fold-over cards that replicate antique lace patterns on cut-out paper. If they're too delicate to go through a print process, you could print the invitation on pastel paper and cut it to fit within the fold.

TRAVEL INFORMATION FOR GUESTS

If you have the time and the inclination, gather as much travel and lodging information as you can for your out-of-town invited guests. This information can be sent after you receive a response or can be included with the invitation—perhaps laser-printed on a card or a single sheet of small stationery. Helpful information to include: the names of airlines that fly into nearby airports; hotels, motels, inns, and bed-and-breakfast lodging; ground transportation services; and car rental rates. If events are planned for out-of-town guests, this information should be sent as soon as a response is received, along with travel information; that way your guests can best plan their arrival and departure times. Along with the travel information, the schedule of events can be printed right from your own desktop computer and coordinated in color and paper, if possible, with the other printed pieces.

Our joy will be more complete
if you will share in the marriage of our daughter
Carole Renée
to
Mr. Dominick Masullo
on Saturday, the fifth of June
at half after four o'clock
7 Old Elm Avenue
Salem, Massachusetts
We invite you to worship with us,
witness their vows, and join us
for a reception following the ceremony
If you are unable to attend, we ask your
presence in thought and prayer
Mr. and Mrs. Earl Rinde
[or Lorraine and Earl Rinde]

R.S.V.P.

When the invitation is to come from both sets of parents, it might be worded:

Sharon and Elliot Karp
and
Hialry and Kenneth Cohen
would be honoured
to have you share in the joy
of the marriage of their children
Leah Rachel
and
Jonathan
This celebration of love will be held on
Sunday, the ninth of September
at five o'clock
Temple Shalom
Englewood, New Jersey
A reception will follow the ceremony
at the Palisades Lodge
Palisades Parkway

Kindly send reply to
Mr. and Mrs. Elliot Karp
[address]

Less formally, the bride and groom may design and print or hand-write their own invitations on a simple card:

Anne Bell McKune and Michael Smithson
invite you to celebrate their marriage
on
Saturday, June the 5th
2001
at four o'clock
2 Fox Run
Danville, Kentucky

R.S.V.P.

Personal invitations to very small weddings are often issued in the form of a personal note. It is a most flattering gesture and typically would read:

Dear Aunt Ruth,

Sean and I are to be married at Christ's Church on June tenth at four o'clock. We hope you and Uncle Don will come to the church and afterward to the reception at Greentree Country Club.

With much love from us both,
Laura Jeanne

Other personal forms of invitation for weddings that make no pretense of being traditional may be as original as the couple or the bride's parents wish, as long as the invitations are dignified and sincerely reflect the sentiments of the bride and groom and their families. Among the loveliest and most meaningful is the following example, written as a letter from the bride's parents.

Our daughter, Lisa, will be married to Frank Adams O'Gorman, on Saturday, the fifth of February, two thousand, at half after seven o'clock in the evening. Their vows will be spoken at St. John's Lutheran Church, Mamaroneck, New York.

We invite you to worship with us, witness their vows, and be our guest at the reception and buffet that follow at the Beach and Tennis Club, New Rochelle.

If you are unable to attend, we ask your presence in thought and prayer.

Helen and Davis Wilson

WORDING FOR SPECIAL CASES

The wording in an invitation may undergo slight changes for different circumstances. For example, if a formal invitation is to the ceremony only, the traditional wording should not include an R.S.V.P. When a reception follows, a separate reception invitation or response card is inserted in the mailing envelope with the invitation to the ceremony. Circumstances dictate what kind of invitation is mailed, whether one to the ceremony only, one to both the reception and the ceremony, or one to the reception only.

To the Ceremony and Reception

When all the guests invited to the wedding are also invited to the reception, the invitation to both may be combined:

Mr. and Mrs. Kenneth McGuigan
request the honour of your presence
at the marriage of their daughter
Joanne Marie
to
Mr. Stephen Dempsey
Saturday, the ninth of April
two thousand
at half after five o'clock
Church of the Resurrection, Evanston
and afterward at the reception
Lake Michigan Shore Club

The favour of a reply is requested
Twenty-three Soundview Avenue
River Forest, Illinois 60601

To the Reception Only

When the wedding ceremony is private and a large reception follows, the invitation to the ceremony is extended orally or by personal note, and the wording of the reception invitation is:

Mr. and Mrs. Douglas Charles Campbell
request the pleasure of your company
at the wedding reception for their daughter
Deirdre Mary
and
Mr. Jeffrey Keller
Saturday, the twenty-fourth of June
two thousand and one
at seven o'clock
Horseshoe Harbour Yacht Club
Larchmont, New York

R.S.V.P.

Reception Cards

A reception card, which is an invitation to the reception, is often sent when the ceremony and reception are held at different locations. The reception card is enclosed with the wedding invitation.

The reception card is also used when the guest list for the ceremony is larger than that for the reception. Here, the reception cards would only be enclosed with the wedding invitations for those being invited to the wedding *and* reception. The most commonly used form is:

Reception
immediately following the ceremony
Knolls Country Club
Lake Forest
The favour of a reply is requested

226 Lakeside Drive, Lake Forest, Illinois 61300

Invitations to a Belated Reception

When a reception is not held at the time of the wedding, the couple or their parents may have one later, possibly when the newlyweds return from their honeymoon. Although the party is held to celebrate the wedding, the wording must be slightly changed:

Mr. and Mrs. Wayne Matteis
request the pleasure of your company
at a reception
in honor of
Mr. and Mrs. Scott Nelson
[etc.]

At Someone's Home

Even though the wedding and reception are to be held at a friend's house, the invitations should be written in the name of the bride's parents or sponsors or in the name of the bride and groom:

Linda Lanier-Samuels and Gregory Samuels
request the honour of your presence
at the marriage of her daughter
Anne Van Arsdale
to
Mr. Bryan Keith Oettl
Saturday, the twelfth of October
at half after three o'clock
at the residence of Mr. and Mrs. Robert Cozza
Thirty-three Fall Creek Drive
Kansas City, Missouri

R.S.V.P.

SAMPLE INVITATIONS

A growing number of wedding invitations issued today do not follow the traditional, formal style illustrated in the previous sections but instead reflect the often complicated makeup of modern families. A bride may have two divorced and remarried sets of parents giving her away. A groom may have the blessing of one divorced parent but not the other. Even birth mothers of adopted children may be involved. For brides and grooms in these situations, there is no need to panic. Etiquette accommodates most any circumstance with elegance. These sample invitations are just a few that cover a variety of complex situations gracefully:

When the Bride Has One Living Parent
When either the bride's mother or father is deceased, the invitation is issued only in the name of the living parent:

Mr. [Mrs.] Daniel Watson Driskill
requests the honor of your presence
at the marriage of his [her] daughter
Susan Patricia
to
Mr. Drew Randolph Donney
[etc.]

There are circumstances, however, when the bride very much wants to include the name of the deceased parent. This is acceptable, as long as the invitation does not appear to be issued by the deceased. In other words, don't word the invitation so that it reads "... the late William Tierney requests the honor of ...":

Diane June Tierney
daughter of Mary Ann Tierney and the late William Tierney
and
James Thomas Duffy
son of Mr. and Mrs. Lawrence David Duffy
request the honour of your presence
at their marriage
Saturday, the fifth of October
[etc.]

When the Bride's Mother Is Divorced
A divorcée giving her daughter's wedding by herself sends out her daughter's invitations using her own first and last names:

Mrs. Ann Syverson
requests the honour of your presence
at the marriage of her daughter
[etc.]

When Divorced Parents Give the Wedding Together
In the event that relations between the bride's divorced parents (one or both of whom have remarried) are so friendly that they share the wedding expenses and act as co-hosts, both sets of names should appear on the invitation. The bride's mother's name appears first:

Mr. and Mrs. Shelby Goldring
and
Mr. Michael Levy
request the honour of your presence
at the marriage of their daughter
Rachel Lynn Levy
[etc.]

If, however, the bride's parents are not sharing expenses, yet the bride wishes both parents' names to appear, a different situation exists. If the bride's mother is not contributing to the cost of the wedding, the bride's father's name appears first on the invitation, and he and his wife (if he has remarried) host the reception. The bride's mother is then only included as an honored guest at the reception.

When the Bride Has a Stepfather

When the bride's mother has been widowed or is divorced and remarried and she and her husband are hosting the wedding, the invitations are worded:

> *Mr. and Mrs. Kevin Michael O'Callaghan*
> *request the honour of your presence*
> *at the marriage of her daughter [or Mrs. O'Callaghan's daughter]*
> *Kelly Elizabeth Quimby*
> *to*
> *[etc.]*

If the bride's own father has no part in her life and her stepfather has brought her up, legally adopted or not, the invitation reads:

> *Mr. and Mrs. Kevin Michael O'Callaghan*
> *request the honour of your presence*
> *at the marriage of their daughter*
> *Kelly Elizabeth Quimby*
> *to*
> *[etc.]*

When the Bride Is an Orphan

"Miss," "Ms.," or "Mrs." are rarely used before the bride's name. The following case is an exception:

Mr. and Mrs. Paul John Carey
request the honour of your presence
at the marriage of
their niece
Miss Rosemary Wendorf
to
Mr. Karl Andrew Rauch
[etc.]

When the Bride and Groom Issue Their Own Invitations
A bride and groom who send out their own invitations would also use a title
("Miss," "Mrs."):

The honour of your presence
is requested
at the marriage of
Miss Andrea Kraft
to
Mr. Robert White
[etc.]

[OR]

Miss Andrea Kraft
and
Mr. Robert White
request the honour of your presence
at their marriage
[etc.]

[OR] less formally,

Beth Holland and Christopher Saladino
invite you to attend
their marriage
on
Saturday, the twenty-ninth of October
two thousand
at half after three o'clock
The Hopewell School
Richmond, Virginia
A reception on the grounds will follow the ceremony

R.S.V.P.
Ms. Beth Holland
87 Grace Street
Richmond, Virginia 23223

Mature couples or couples who have been living together may prefer to send out wedding invitations in their own names and not use social titles:

Mary Ann Schmidt
and
George James MacLellan
invite you to share with them
the joy of their marriage
Saturday, the tenth of July
nineteen hundred and ninety-nine
at half after four o'clock
First Congregational Church
Baton Rouge, Louisiana

R.S.V.P.

When Other Relatives Issue Invitations
If the bride has siblings or other relatives who are giving the wedding, then the invitations should be sent in their names:

Mr. Robert Mazzone
requests the honour of your presence
at the marriage of his sister
Elizabeth Ann
[etc.]

When a bride and groom's grown children are giving their wedding, the invitation may be issued in their names, with the bride's children listed before the groom's. When several children are involved, their names are given in the order of their age, from the oldest to the youngest in each family. When the bride's son and the daughter and son of the groom are giving the wedding together, the invitation should read:

Mr. and Mrs. Brendan Shine
Miss Christine Shine
Mr. and Mrs. William Barrett, junior
request the honour of your presence
at the marriage of their parents
Madolyn Whitefield Shine
and
William Wyndham Barrett
Sunday, the tenth of September
two thousand
at half after three o'clock
Belle Haven Club
Greenwich, Connecticut

R.S.V.P.

When the Bride Is a Young Widow or Divorcée
Invitations to a young widow's second wedding may be sent by her parents using the same wording as that of the invitations to her first marriage. But if she continues to use her married name, it should be included:

Doctor and Mrs. Daniel Thomas McCann
request the honour of your presence
at the marriage of their daughter
Margaret O'Neill
[etc.]

A divorcée's second wedding invitation may read the same way. The bride's name would be the one she is using—either her first name, maiden name, and ex-husband's last name or, if she has dropped her ex-husband's name, her own middle and maiden name.

A more mature woman whose parents are deceased or a divorcée who has been independent since her divorce would, along with her groom, generally send out her own invitations.

A widow or divorcée's invitation would read:

The honour of your presence
is requested
at the marriage of
Mrs. Susan Green Millman
and
Mr. Elliot Franklin Aiken
[etc.]

If the bride prefers, she may drop the title and have her name simply read "Susan Green Millman."

When the Bridegroom's Family Gives the Wedding
When the bride's family lives far away and she is alone, the groom's parents may give the wedding and issue the invitations. This is also true if the bride's family disapproves of the wedding and refuses to take part in it.

Mr. and Mrs. Wendell William Orr
request the honour of your presence
at the marriage of
Miss Latoya Kenisha Anderson
to
their son
Joshua Allen Orr
[etc.]

If any announcements of the marriage are sent out to friends and colleagues who weren't invited to the wedding day celebrations, they should be sent by the bride's family, if possible. Otherwise, the groom's family should send them, including the names of the bride's parents on the announcements.

Including the Groom's Family in the Invitation

Increasingly, there are occasions when the groom's family shares in or pays the major part of the wedding expenses. In such a case, it is only fair that their names appear on the invitations. The bride's parents' names would be first, and the wording would be:

Mr. and Mrs. David Zimmermann
and
Captain and Mrs. John Gonzalez
request the honour of your presence
at the marriage of
Cynthia Ann Zimmermann
and
John Howard Gonzalez, junior
[etc.]

When both the bride and groom's parents have been divorced and have remarried, but all are participating in giving the wedding and hosting the reception, it is not unusual for all their names to appear on the invitation. In this instance, the bride's mother and her husband would appear first, the bride's father and his wife second, the groom's mother and her husband third, and the groom's father and his wife fourth:

Mr. and Mrs. Michael Hannigan
Mr. and Mrs. Lawrence Anvik
Doctor and Mrs. Russell Healy
Mr. and Mrs. Jeffrey Jacobs
request the honour of your presence
at the marriage of
Lindsay Catherine Anvik
to
Andrew Lloyd Jacobs
[etc.]

A form followed in some foreign countries provides for a double invitation with the bride's family's invitation on the left and the groom's family's invitation on the right:

Mr. and Mrs. Arturo Mendel	*Mr. and Mrs. Roberto Perez*
request the honour of your presence	*request the honour of your presence*
at the marriage of their daughter	*at the marriage of their son*
Angelina Ruth	*Eduardo Robert*
to	*to*
Mr. Eduardo Perez	*Miss Angelina Mendel*
[etc.]	*[etc.]*

When the Bride Has a Professional Name

If the bride is well known by a professional name and has many business friends to whom she wishes to send invitations or announcements, she may include on the invitations her professional name in parentheses engraved or printed below her real name:

Margaret Marie
(Meg Drake)
to
Mr. Carl Louis Valentine
[etc.]

Military Titles

When the groom is a member of the armed services or is on active duty in the reserve forces, he uses his military title.

Officers whose rank is captain or higher in the Army or lieutenant, senior grade, or higher in the Navy should have the title appear on the same line as the name:

Colonel Graham O'Gorman
United States Army

Those with lower ranks should have their name and title engraved in this form:

John McMahon
Ensign, United States Navy

In the case of reserve officers on active duty, the second line would read "Army of the United States" or "United States Naval Reserve."

First and second lieutenants in the Army both use "Lieutenant" without the numeral.

A noncommissioned officer or enlisted man may, if he wishes, include his rank and his branch of the service below his name.

Henry Delucia
Corporal, Signal Corps, United States Army

[OR]

Marc Josephson
Seaman Apprentice, United States Naval Reserve

High-ranking officers of the regular armed forces should continue to use their titles, followed by their branch of service, even after retirement, with "retired" following the branch of service:

General George Harmon
United States Army, retired

When the father of the bride is a member of the armed forces, either on active duty, a high-ranking retired officer, or one who retired after many years of service, he uses his title in the regular way:

Colonel and Mrs. James Booth
request the honour of your presence
[etc.]

When the bride is on active duty, both her rank and the branch of military is included in the invitation. The name of the bride appears on one line with her rank and the branch of the military on a separate line:

marriage of their daughter
Joanne
Lieutenant, United States Navy

Other Titles

Medical doctors, dentists, veterinarians, clergymen, judges, and all others customarily called by their titles should have those titles included on their own wedding invitations and on the invitations to their daughters' or sons' weddings.

Holders of academic degrees do not use "doctor" unless they are always referred to in that way.

Women use their titles only when the invitations are issued by themselves and their grooms:

The honour of your presence
is requested
at the marriage of
Doctor Laurie Neu
and
Mr. Norbert Rudell
[etc.]

Otherwise, she is "their daughter, Laurie."

The bride's mother uses the title "Doctor" on her daughter's invitation if she feels strongly about it: "Doctor Lynn Josephson and Mr. Marc Josephson request. . . ." Otherwise, the invitation would read, "Mr. and Mrs. Marc Josephson request. . . ."

Same Gender Unions
A formal invitation to a gay or lesbian commitment ceremony may be issued by the couple themselves or by one or both sets of parents:

> *The honour of your presence*
> *is requested*
> *at the marriage of*
> *Susan Beth Gibson*
> *and*
> *Georgia Lee O'Dell*
> *[etc.]*

[OR]

> *Mr. and Mrs. Franklin Johnson*
> *Mr. and Mrs. Jason Benson*
> *request the honour of your presence*
> *at the marriage of their sons*
> *Victor Kenneth Johnson*
> *and*
> *Marc William Benson*
> *[etc.]*

A gay or lesbian couple formally joining together may decide to use a different phrase than "marriage" on their invitation, depending on their feelings and the type of ceremony in which they are participating. Choices include commitment ceremony, affirmation ceremony, celebration of commitment, rite of blessing, relationship covenant, and union ceremony.

Double Weddings

Double weddings almost always involve the marriage of two sisters, and the form, with the elder sister's name first, is:

Mr. and Mrs. Roderick Thorn
request the honour of your presence
at the marriage of their daughters
Jessica Ann
to
Mr. Bradley Peterson
and
Amanda Lynn
to
Mr. Richard Suarino
Saturday, the twenty-second of October
at four o'clock
Good Shepherd Church

In the event that two close friends decide to have a double wedding, the invitation reads:

Mr. and Mrs. Richard McMillan
and
Mrs. Karen Clark
request the honour of your presence
at the marriage of their daughters
Kerry Ann McMillan
to
Mr. Stephen Bonner
and
Amanda Louise Clark
to
Mr. Kenneth Kienzle
[etc.]

WEDDING ANNOUNCEMENTS

Printed or handwritten wedding announcements sent through the mail can serve a useful purpose. These are generally sent to those friends and family who were left off the guest list, because the celebration was too small to accommodate them, or to acquaintances or business associates who, while not particularly close to the family, might still wish to hear news of the marriage. Sharing the happy news after the wedding in the form of printed or handwritten announcements is never obligatory, but it is a nice idea.

Announcements carry no obligation for the recipient to present a gift to the bride and groom, so many families send them rather than invitations to friends who are not expected to attend or to send a present. They are never sent to anyone who has received an invitation to the ceremony or reception.

Ideally, announcements are mailed the day after the wedding but may be mailed up to several months later.

Announcements were traditionally sent in the name of the bride's parents, with wording as follows (still perfectly correct):

Mr. and Mrs. James Welch
have the honour of
announcing the marriage of their daughter
Amy Sue

to

Mr. Jonathan Scott Jamison
Saturday, the twelfth of June
one thousand nine hundred and ninety-nine
Mansfield, Pennsylvania

Several other variations are equally correct. You may use "have the honour to announce" or merely "announce." The year is always included. The most formal wording is "one thousand nine hundred and ninety-nine," but "nineteen hundred and ninety-nine" is more commonly used.

Today, however, when the attitude toward marriage is that it is a "joining" rather than a "giving" of a woman to a man, there is no reason that announcements should not go out in both families' names. Although this privilege has always been accorded the bride's family, the parents of the groom are also presumably proud and happy to share the announcement. The wording is as follows:

Mr. and Mrs. James Welch
and
Mr. and Mrs. Dewey Jamison
announce the marriage of
Amy Sue Welch
and
Jonathan Scott Jamison
on
[etc.]

The variations in circumstances, names, and titles follow the rules under wedding invitations (page 95). In general, the wording used for the wedding invitation is the basis for the wording of the wedding announcement.

ENVELOPES

ONE OR TWO?

When formal, third-person invitations are written, they are traditionally inserted into two envelopes, an inner envelope and an outer envelope. The outer envelope is the one that is addressed and stamped, while the inner envelope bears only the names of the people to whom the mailing envelope is addressed. For example, a married couple's inner envelope is addressed to "Mr. and Mrs. Anderson" with neither first names nor address.

This convention serves a useful purpose—it permits the bride and groom to be very specific as to whom is invited. If, for example, a close friend is invited and the bride and groom want her to bring a guest (whose name they don't know), the outer envelope is addressed to the friend, and the inner envelope reads "Miss Smith and Guest." Not only would it be awkward to address the outer envelope this way, but there is no other way, short of a personal note or telephone call, to let Miss Smith know that a guest is welcome. An inner envelope that reads only "Miss Smith" clearly indicates that Miss Smith is not supposed to bring anyone else.

Of course, this kind of communication may be unnecessary for the type of guest list you have, and you may want to dispense with the custom of the inner envelope altogether; it is correct to do so.

If you do plan to use inner envelopes, you may write the names of intimate relatives and lifelong friends in informal and familial terms. For example, it is perfectly fine to write "Aunt Deirdre and Uncle Tom" or "Grandmother."

ADDRESSING ENVELOPES

Wedding invitations are always addressed to both members of a married couple, even though the bride may know only one or knows that only one will attend. Invitations to an unmarried couple who reside at the same address should be addressed to "Ms. Nancy Fellows and Mr. Scott Dunn," with each name appearing on a separate line.

Just as abbreviations are not used in the wording of the invitation, so are they not used in addressing the envelopes. A person's middle name may or may not be used. If it is, it must be written out in full, as should "Street" and "Avenue." The name of the state is traditionally not abbreviated, but because the post office prefers the use of two-letter state abbreviations and no comma between the city and the state, it is fine to do so.

Children over 13 years of age should, if possible, receive separate invitations. Young brothers and sisters may be sent a joint invitation addressed to "The Misses Smith" or "The Messrs. Jones" on the outer envelope, with "Andy, Doug, and Brian" written on the inner envelope to make perfectly clear that all are invited. If there are both boys and girls, the outer envelope address may read:

The Messrs. Jones
The Misses Jones

If children are not receiving a separate invitation, their names may be written on a line below their parents' names on the inner envelope and do not have to be listed on the outer envelope at all. If no inner envelope is used, however, their names *must* be written on the outer envelope or their parents will not know that they are included in the invitation.

When possible, it is wise to be specific and list names. Occasionally, however, it is difficult to know all of the names and relationships within a family. If, for example, relationships are so complicated or children so numerous that it seems simpler to address the envelope "Mr. and Mrs. Vito Sessa and Family" you may do so—but *only* in the following circumstances:

1. When it is clear that you are inviting just the people living under that roof, not the aunt and uncle next door.
2. When the children are young (adult children who reside in the house should receive their own invitation).
3. When every person living under the same roof is intended to be included in the invitation.

The U.S. Postal Service requests that all first-class mail bear a return address. This information also lets invited guests know where to send replies and gifts if an R.S.V.P. address does not appear on the invitation. The postal service prefers that the return address be printed or handwritten on the upper left-hand corner of the envelope. It is nonetheless acceptable to clearly emboss the return address by stamping it on the envelope's flap (although the embossing is sometimes difficult to read).

INSERTIONS

In addition to the invitation, several enclosures may be placed in the inner envelope (or the outer envelope if you omit an inner one).

Admission Cards

Admission cards are only necessary when a wedding is held in a popular cathedral or church that attracts sightseers. To ensure privacy in these circumstances, each guest is asked to present his card at the entrance. It is generally engraved or printed in the same style as the invitation and reads:

Please present this card
at
St. Patrick's Cathedral
Saturday, the twelfth of June

Pew Cards

Small cards with "Pew Number _____" engraved on them may be enclosed with the invitations going to those family members and close friends who are to be seated in reserved pews. Recipients simply take the pew cards to the ceremony and show them to ushers, who escort them to their seats.

Similar cards are sometimes engraved "Within the Ribbon." This indicates that reserved pews or seats with white ribbons across the ends have been set aside for special guests. When ushers escort recipients of these cards to their seats, the ribbon is lifted and then replaced after the guests are seated. Guests receiving pew cards can sit anywhere within these seats.

Pew cards are sometimes sent separately after acceptances or regrets are received, when the bride knows how many reserved pews are needed.

At-Home Cards

If the bride and groom wish to let friends know what their new address will be, they may insert an at-home card with the invitation or wedding announcement. These cards traditionally read:

> *At home [or Will be at home]*
> *after July second*
> *3842 Grand Avenue*
> *Houston, Texas 77001*
> *(898) 555–4321*

The problem with the preceding example is that many people receiving these cards often put them away, intending to enter them in an address book or file at some point in the future. When they come across the card weeks, even months, later, they may find they can't recall just who will be "at home at 3842 Grand Avenue after July second." Therefore, even though you are not married at the time the invitation is sent, it is perfectly all right to have an at-home card printed with the couple's names:

> *Mr. and Mrs. Bruce Moore*
> *will be at home*
> *[etc.]*

An at-home card also gives the woman who plans to keep her own name the opportunity to let friends know. In this case, the at-home card would read:

Katherine Bowlin and Bryan Hailey
will be at home
[etc.]

Reception Cards

When a separate reception card is used, it is placed in front of the invitation to the wedding ceremony. (See suggested wording for reception cards earlier in the chapter, "Reception Card.")

Response Cards

It used to be that the only correct response to a formal invitation was an equally formal reply, handwritten by the invited guest. Such replies are still correct, but because fewer and fewer people will take the time to pen a formal reply, in the last decade or so response cards have replaced the handwritten reply in popularity. The response card is inserted with the invitation and is engraved or printed on card stock in the same style as the invitation, in the following form:

M_____
accepts _____
regrets _____
The favour of your reply is requested by July 26

The "M" precedes the space where the guest writes his or her title and name, as in "Miss Phyllis Reynolds" or "Mr. and Mrs. Joseph DeRuvo."

A printed, stamped envelope is included so that all the guest has to do is write in his, her, or their names—"Mr. and Mrs. Stephen Nelmes"—check by "accepts" or "regrets," place the card in the envelope, and mail it. When one guest is able to accept and the other is not, it is necessary to make this clear on the response card.

To avoid confusion, a response card should *not* include the phrase "number of persons," which could lead the recipients to think that other family members may be included, even though their names didn't appear on the inner or outer envelopes—a misunderstanding that could result in a wedding overflowing with guests. The absence of other family members' names means they are not invited.

When one invitation is received by a couple whose children are included, every name must be written in on the response card.

If one invitation is sent to a friend with "and guest" written on the envelope, the friend should write in the name of the guest so that his or her name can be written on a place card. If the friend is not bringing a guest, then only the friend's name should be written on the response card.

Handwritten Formal Reply

When a formal invitation does not include a response card insert, a guest may certainly send a formal handwritten reply. The formal reply should be written in blue or black ink on plain or bordered letter paper or note paper. The lines should be evenly and symmetrically spaced on one page. The formal reply, which follows exactly the form of the invitation, should read if accepting:

> *Mr. and Mrs. Mark Ross*
> *accept with pleasure*
> *Mr. and Mrs. McCullough's*
> *kind invitation for*
> *Saturday, the twenty-second of May*

[OR]

> *Mr. and Mrs. Mark Ross*
> *accept with pleasure*
> *the kind invitation of*
> *Mr. and Mrs. Frank McCullough*
> *to the marriage of their daughter*
> *Kristin Lynn*
> *to*
> *Mr. Brent Brown*
> *Saturday, the twenty-second of May*

Regrets are sent in the same manner:

Mr. and Mrs. Charles Coletti
regret that they are unable to accept
Mr. and Mrs. Aliberto's
kind invitation for
Sunday, the fourteenth of March

When one invited guest is able to attend and the other is not, the form reads:

Mrs. Lawrence Hires
accepts with pleasure
Mr. and Mrs. Benson's
kind invitation for
Saturday, the fifth of February
but regrets that
Mr. Hires
will be unable to attend

Tissues

The delicate tissues that are sometimes included in a wedding invitation are optional today. Their prior usage had a real function: to keep the oils from the ink on engraved invitations from smudging as it slowly dried. Improved printing and engraving techniques have made tissues unnecessary for decades, but their use continues as a bow to tradition. While the tradition is fine, it is perfectly correct to exclude the tissues if a couple chooses to do so.

Maps

You can insert maps and directions to the wedding sites in a number of ways. You may enclose them with the invitation or you may mail them after you have received an affirmative response to your invitation. Sometimes maps are provided by the ceremony or reception sites. If they are not, you will have to order them or design them yourself. Be sure your directions are clear and accurate, and that they are written in as concise and abbreviated a manner as possible to avoid adding extra bulk to the invitation.

Rain Card

When a ceremony or reception is planned for outdoors, you must have an indoor emergency plan of action in the event of inclement weather. A rain card is a small card that gives the alternate location for either. It might read, "In case of rain, the ceremony and reception will take place at 33 Elm Street, Traverse City."

STUFFING THE ENVELOPES

When two envelopes are used, the invitation (folded edge first for a folded invitation, left edge for a single card) and all enclosures are put in the inner envelope, facing the back. The inner envelope is then placed, unsealed, in the outer envelope, with the flap away from the person inserting it.

When there are insertions, they are placed in front of the invitation, so they face the flap (and the person inserting them). In the case of a folded invitation, they are placed in the same direction but within the fold.

A CHANGE IN PLANS

WHEN THE WEDDING IS CANCELED AFTER INVITATIONS ARE MAILED

If the decision to cancel the wedding is a last-minute one, guests must be notified by telephone. If there is time, printed cards may be sent out:

> *Mr. and Mrs. Oliver Grant*
> *announce that the marriage of*
> *their daughter*
> *Debra*
> *to*
> *Mr. Christopher Bronner*
> *will not take place*

WHEN THE WEDDING DATE IS CHANGED

When it is necessary to change the date of the wedding and the new date is decided upon after the invitations have been printed but before they are mailed, it is not necessary for the bride to order new invitations. If there is time, she may enclose a printed card saying, "The date of the wedding has been changed from March sixth to April twelfth." If there is not time for the card to be printed, she may neatly cross out the old date on the invitation and write in the new one by hand.

If the invitations have already been mailed, she may mail a card or a personal note or, if the guest list is small, telephone the information.

When the wedding is postponed, not canceled, and there is time to have an announcement printed, it would read:

> *Mr. and Mrs. Roy Westgate*
> *regret that*
> *the invitations to*
> *their daughter's wedding*
> *on Saturday, December fourth*
> *must be recalled*

[OR]

Mr. and Mrs. Scott Pierce
announce that
the marriage of their daughter
Janet Ann
to
Mr. Peter Norton
has been postponed

If the new date is known, it is added: "has been postponed to February third." If there is no time to have a card printed, the information must be communicated by telephone, fax, e-mail, or handwritten note.

INVITATION DO'S

Order Extras

Even the most carefully held pen can experience a slip-up, so it is the wise bride who orders at least a dozen extra invitations and envelopes. At the very least, order extra envelopes. It is far less costly to print extras that you may not need than to go back to the printer to order more. Remember to order an extra for yourselves, to include as a keepsake in your album or planner.

HAVE YOUR TICKETS READY. . .

It should go without saying that you are inviting guests, not a paying audience, to your wedding. Don't even consider charging a fee or suggesting a ticket price. An appalling invitation? The one that includes a suggested guest price and states "includes dinner, dancing, and gift."

Where to R.S.V.P.

Do think about where you want responses sent, given that gifts are usually sent to the return address on the envelope or to the address printed by the "R.S.V.P." If the bride lives in New York City but her wedding will be held where her parents live in Chicago, it is far handier to have gifts sent to her New York City home than to her mother, who will have to pack them up and ship them to New York. Then there is the question of who is keeping track of responses. If it is the bride, then by all means her address should be used. If it is her mother, then the question of which is easier to ship back and forth—responses or gifts—is the determining factor.

Allow Plenty of Time

This is both an invitation "Do" and "Don't." Don't run out of time. Do allow plenty of time to carefully address, assemble, and mail your invitations, especially if you are using a calligrapher to do the writing. If other obligations leave you pressed for time, ask to have envelopes sent to you well in advance of the invitations so that you can start addressing early.

Get Organized

Develop a system of organization that makes the process of addressing and mailing your invitations pleasurable, not painful. Prepare in advance by writing in your wedding planner the names and addresses of everyone on your guest list; some brides find a computer database or file cards helpful. Otherwise, you'll spend all your time looking up addresses in the phone book and other sources.

Use proven time-management systems and, if possible, handle each piece only once. Arrange each element that goes into an invitation in a stack, in the order it will be picked up, assembled, and inserted.

As replies are received, make helpful notes to yourself, such as "friend of Andy's parents" or "Susie's date," so that you'll know who's who when finalizing your table arrangements and greeting guests in the receiving line.

Check Postage

It would be extremely annoying to mail all your invitations only to have them returned because of insufficient postage. Before you buy stamps and use them, take an assembled invitation to the post office and have it weighed. It's likely

---

MAKING MEMORIES

It was the custom in the 19th century for brides and grooms to give each of their guests a beautiful wedding program detailing the ceremony. Today, a program can be embellished with art, poetry, or fine calligraphy, or it can simply list the order of the service in a fold-over bulletin. The bulletins can often be ordered from the diocese, synod, or home center of the church or synagogue; or, they can be printed on a desktop publishing system.

that the inserts, or even an unusually shaped envelope, will require extra postage. Remember that maps and other directional inserts sent to out-of-town guests will create a heavier invitation than those to local guests and may require a postage adjustment. In that case, be sure to assemble two sets and have both weighed—and pay close attention when affixing postage so that the appropriate stamps go on the right envelopes.

Spell Check

Ask for the business cards of the contacts at your ceremony and reception sites before you order your invitations. You'll want to get the titles and spelling of the sites absolutely correct. Guests directed to "St. John's Church" could easily miss the wedding ceremony at "The Evangelical Lutheran Church of St. John."

Miss "X"

It is much warmer and more welcoming to use the correct names of those who will be guests of your friends on invitations and place cards. Whether you also send these guests their own invitation or include their name on your friend's invitation is up to you, but the guest feels personally invited when his or her name is actually written on the envelope. This also enables you to write a place card using his or her name instead of writing "and guest" on your friend's place card or making a card that reads "Miss Johnston's Guest."

> ## ORGANIZING PLACE CARDS
>
> There are many ways to look at your reception seating plan, whether by preparing lists on a database, using your wedding planner, or by handwriting lists. One way to envision who will be where is to write your place cards as responses are received and place them in stacks, by table. Review each stack to make sure that you haven't, by accident, seated together people who are antagonistic toward each other. Actually "seeing" names on place cards helps you imagine the makeup of a table even better than a printed list.

Titles

It is most flattering when invitations are addressed correctly. This means using correct titles, as well as spelling names right. Some professional titles that are also used socially and that would be used when addressing an invitation include *The Honorable* (judge, governor, mayor, United States Senator, member of Congress, cabinet members, ambassadors) and *The Reverend, The Most Reverend* or *The Right Reverend*. When in doubt, ask before addressing.

Invitations and Other Printed Items

INVITATION DONT'S

Certain information should not be included on or placed inside a wedding invitation:

Registry or Gift Information

Although a wedding invitation demands a gift in return, it is in extremely poor taste to insert a "helpful" list of places the bride and groom are registered or a checklist of the things they want or don't want. This information should be shared with parents and attendants who can be resources for guests who want to know.

"No Gifts"

Often a second-time bride or groom or an older couple feels that they have everything they need and prefer that their guests do not give them a gift. Regardless, the joy and happiness a wedding represents include the giving of gifts to celebrate that happiness, and the printing of "No Gifts, Please" on the invitation is not acceptable. Again, family members and attendants can share this information with guests or can provide the name of a favorite charity to which guests may contribute in lieu of giving a nuptial gift.

"No Children"

Never print "no children" or "adults only" on an invitation. The way an invitation is addressed, whether on the outer or inner envelope, indicates exactly who is—and by omission, who is not—invited to the wedding.

Bulletin Board Invitations

It is not a good idea to post an invitation on a bulletin board at work. It implies that anyone reading it is welcome to attend, and each person may feel he or she is also welcome to bring a spouse, a date, or children—which would surely skew the count for the reception. Instead, it is better for each person to receive his or her own invitation at home, not at work, particularly if some colleagues are invited and others are not.

Dictating Dress

It is incorrect to put "black tie" or "white tie" on the invitation to the ceremony. If it seems essential to include this directive, it can be added only to the invitation to the reception and is placed in the lower right-hand corner. Avoid writing "black tie invited" or "black tie preferred."

Labels

Do not use labels to address wedding invitation envelopes, even when inviting hundreds of guests. Instead, plan ahead and take the time to handwrite every envelope (or hire a calligrapher to do so) so that it is in keeping with the personal tone of the wedding.

Entrée Choice

It is best not to put entrée choices on the response card or the envelope. If you are offering menu choices, work out the arrangements with the club, restaurant, or caterer to provide French service—where each wait-staff member carries a tray with both or all entrées already plated and offers each guest his choice—or have the wait staff ask each guest his preference at the table before serving. The wait staff could also offer a little of each entrée to each guest.

Alcohol Information

It is unnecessary to put "alcohol-free" or "wine and beer only" on the invitation. Surely this information will not enter into the decision whether to attend: You are inviting them to a wedding, not a cocktail party.

> ### NOT A NICE TRY
>
> There are those parents who go right ahead and write their children's names on the response card, even though the kids clearly weren't asked to attend. Some do this intentionally, believing they can bully the bride into having them; others truly believe it is understood that the children are included. Whoever is hosting the wedding may call immediately and explain in kind terms that the children are not being invited. If this results in an angry "then I'm not coming either," so be it. The breach of etiquette is theirs, not yours.

Don't Underestimate Your Time

Count on the printing of your invitations and their related inserts to take six to eight weeks. Keep in mind that for a large, formal wedding, invitations should be mailed six to eight weeks in advance. Remember that it can take an extraordinarily long time to address, assemble, and mail invitations, so don't underestimate your time. Instead, allow several extra weeks in your schedule to prepare your invitations for mailing.

OTHER INVITATION BULLIES

To friends who ask for invitations or whether they can bring a guest, you need only say, "I'm so sorry, I wish you could be there (or that your friend could join you), but we are having a fairly small wedding only for family and our immediate circle of friends." Never over-explain or go into detail about how you could have chosen a bigger, more ho-hum reception venue over the charming smaller site—it sounds as if you decided that location was more important than guests. Oops! No wordy, profuse apologies are necessary: You're doing the best you can!

Don't Mix Typefaces

Once you have selected a typeface for your invitation, use the same one for all related printed insertions and other printed material. The typeface you choose is part of your overall theme, and even though you may love both a shaded Roman and a flowery script, a well designed invitation avoids mixing them.

Don't Offend Your "B" List

When a bride and groom draw up a longer list of guests than they can accommodate, they must pare it down. They can do so in a number of ways: They can include first cousins, for example, but not second; they can invite only the friends from work with whom they've socialized before. The second cousins and other work pals should not be forgotten, however, and can be invited if several guests on the "A" List send regrets. A word of caution: Do not invite your "second tier" of guests less than three weeks before the wedding. Inviting people at the last minute makes it obvious that they are on your "B" List—a notion that may make them feel more unwelcome than if you had not invited them at all.

PROGRAMS

Programs can be good additions to your ceremony and are especially helpful to guests of other religions who may not be familiar with your service. This is particularly true when the wedding is a mix of religions and cultures, and not all guests necessarily understand the liturgy or ritual. Programs are not Broadway playbills, however, and are not the forum for profiling the bride, the groom, their attendants, or their families. Therefore, avoid any biographical write-ups. Under no circumstances should programs be advertisements for wedding service providers, such as florists or consultants. They may, however, include the names of soloists (particularly if they are contributing their talents as a gift to the couple), the officiant(s), and the attendants, altar assistants, organist, and readers.

Program elements that are appropriate and helpful can include:

- processional
- service music
- translations
- the order of the service
- explanation of symbolic meaning of service components
- text for group prayers or readings
- poem or thought of thanks and love

DISTRIBUTING PROGRAMS

Ushers can hand programs to guests as they seat them, or children can hand them out as guests arrive. Programs can also be placed on pews or chairs or in baskets by the door. Flower girls can offer them to arriving guests if they are at the ceremony site earlier than the rest of the bridal party.

PLACE CARDS

Although the use and placement of place cards is reviewed in Chapter 12, "Planning the Reception," they are mentioned here because they are a stationery item that is often ordered with the other paper and printed items.

Place cards should be written or done in calligraphy in one hand. Because they will be placed together on one table, they should have a uniform look. Place cards may be decorated, have a gold or colored border, or be simple white or colored fold-over card stock. Place-card forms are available at better stationers. Place cards created and printed by computer (using an 8½" x 11" sheet to run through a laser printer) are acceptable as long as 1) the typeface chosen looks handwritten and 2) the individual cards are separated carefully so that no rough edges are left, indicating that they came from a tear-off form.

PRINTED ACCESSORIES

Some couples like to have personalized cocktail napkins, matchbooks, or other memorabilia at their receptions. If this is your choice, it is a good idea to see whether they can be printed by the printer who is handling your invitations, announcements, and other inserts. Sometimes you can get a better price when ordering everything from one source.

PERSONAL STATIONERY

Don't forget stationery for your thank-you notes. Fold-over note cards are perfect for this purpose and can be printed with your monogram or name on the front. Remember: The groom can also write thank-you notes. You might want to order "his" and "hers" stationery to use before you are married and, at the same time, stationery with your married name, monogram, or initials to use after you are married. A monogram of only the initial of your last name or "Mr. and Mrs." stationery can be used by both of you.

NEWSPAPER WEDDING NOTICE

Most newspapers request wedding information at least three weeks before the big day. The wedding announcement generally appears the day following the ceremony. Since newspapers often receive more wedding announcements than they can print, the sooner yours is sent and the clearer and more concise the information, the better your chance of having it published.

Each paper generally uses as much of the information as it wishes and rewrites it to match the paper's style. It is a good idea to call the paper ahead of time and request a form, but in general, you should provide the following:

- The bride's full name, age, and town of residence
- The bride's parents' names and town of residence
- Bride's parents' occupations
- Bride's maternal and paternal grandparents
- Bride's school, college, and degree, if any
- Bride's occupation
- Groom's age, full name, and town of residence
- Grooms parents' names and town of residence
- Groom's parents' occupations
- Groom's maternal and paternal grandparents
- Groom's school, college, and degree, if any
- Groom's occupation
- Date of wedding

- Location of wedding and reception
- Names of bride's attendants and relationship to bride or groom, if any
- Names of groom's attendants and relationship to bride or groom, if any
- Description of bridal gown and bouquet (optional)
- Description of attendants' gown (optional)
- Name of minister, priest, or rabbi
- Name of soloist, if any
- Where couple will honeymoon
- Where couple will reside (town) after wedding

A newspaper announcement is also a way for a bride who intends to keep her own name to make it known. When the announcement is for a second marriage, it isn't necessary to include the previous marital status of both bride and groom, although some couples choose to do so.

If a photograph of the bride is to be included, the photo needs to be taken in time to be provided with the announcement information. If a photograph of the bride and groom together is to be included, the announcement is usually printed a week or two after the wedding so that a portrait can be taken on the day of the wedding.

> ## MYSTERY GUESTS
>
> It's bound to happen—a guest who forgets to write his name on the line provided on the response card. A solution? In addressing your invitations, put tiny numbers on either the card or the response envelope and write corresponding numbers for every name on your guest list.

CHAPTER 7

GIFTS, GIFT REGISTRIES, AND THANK-YOU NOTES

The showering of gifts on the newly betrothed is a tradition that only seems to get more deeply ingrained with time. And no wonder: Wedding gift-giving is big business. The idea behind wedding gifts, however, is a special one. It is a tangible representation of love and support, a generous offering to help young marrieds get a head start in their lives together.

Customs regarding gifts vary by culture and ethnic groups; in some cultures a wedding gift is given as a shower gift, for example, or money is presented. In other cultures the groom's family gives lavish gifts of jewelry to the bride at her engagement party, draping necklaces around her neck and bracelets on her wrists. The gift suggestions in this chapter, however, are based on traditional American customs. Use them as a base from which to begin. If you are uncertain of custom when invited to the wedding of friends of a different cultural or ethnic background, simply inquire of other guests-to-be or of any acquaintances who belong to that culture or ethnic group.

MAKING A WISH LIST

The bride and groom should take an active role in determining the types of gifts they will be receiving. This is the time for couples to seriously consider their needs, whether basic appliances or fancy silver, thereby simplifying the gift-giving process for guests and allowing the bride and groom to get the things they want and need.

For you and your intended, a wish list is in order. First off, go on a shopping expedition. Take a good look at home furnishings, hardware, sports equipment, and little luxuries. A hardware store is just as promising a gift source as a fine crystal and china shop. In fact, many brides and grooms prefer nontraditional gift choices over traditional: registering with travel agents, for example, opening mortgage accounts for a future house, or having family and close friends make a contribution toward a trip.

When the two of you go on shopping expeditions, look in different kinds of stores for ideas; it's perfectly all right to register at several. If your lifestyle is casual, you may not be interested in formal crystal, china, and silver—all traditional wedding gifts. Still, there is nothing wrong with planning for the day when you will appreciate a formal setting, and registering for patterns is a time-honored bridal tradition.

Your shopping forays will help you select which gift registries to choose. Once you've decided that you prefer everyday pottery to formal china, or an electric sander over crystal wine glasses, prioritize your list. Then start filling out bridal registration forms.

THE MODERN-DAY TROUSSEAU

Times have changed from the days when a couple couldn't get married without a dowry, a trousseau, and sufficient household goods to completely furnish a home. Today it is often a combination of shower and wedding gifts that creates the "trousseau" that begins the marriage. While a bride and groom who have been living at home with parents or sharing an apartment with friends might bring an odd assemblage of furnishings into the marriage, it is unlikely that they have enough between them to fill a household's worth of furniture, appliances, and dishes. In this case, a wish list would include more basic household needs.

USING A BRIDAL REGISTRY

Gift registries are showing up in the most unusual places these days. While the tradition of registering at department and gift stores for china, silver, and crystal continues to be as popular as ever, more and more couples are also selecting other types of gifts—particularly in second- and third-time couplings, where multiple sets of china and crystal have already been amassed. In response, creative retailers are offering registries for nontraditional wedding gifts. A national chain hardware store started the trend, opening a gift registry in 1991 in an effort to draw women customers to the stores. The idea took off, with many prenuptial couples choosing practical items such as lawnmowers, kitchen fixtures, even camping equipment, in addition to—or instead of—expensive china or glassware.

Today, couples can register at garden and home centers, national chains, specialty stores, and recreational-sports stores. They're choosing items such as shrubbery and patio furniture, kayaks and binoculars, and exercise equipment. Registering in national chain stores works especially nicely for out-of-town guests, who can order easily from the companies' 800-numbers and have the gifts delivered by mail. Online couples can register for gifts on one of the growing number of retail chains' websites—allowing friends to place an order while simply sitting at their computer.

Registering at stores means completing a list of things you would like to have, in the quantity you would like to have them. It's a good idea to register for items in a variety of price ranges, since guests have a wide range of finances. The store provides the form, which includes your name, wedding date, and the address to which gifts are to be sent. A store well-versed in registering gifts can do more: Salespeople will help you choose patterns; figure the correct number of items ordered on your list in relation to your guest list; and give you a printout updating the latest purchases. A store registry generally keeps all pertinent information on file for up to several months after the wedding date.

How do you get the word out that you've registered at a particular store? The old-fashioned way: word of mouth. Tradition still holds that the practice of including lists of gift registries on wedding invitations is considered tacky and unacceptable; a simple phone call to you or a close friend or relative will provide guests with all the information they need. Another way to get the word out: Once you have registered, give your mothers and your maid of honor a list of the stores, mail-order catalogs, Internet addresses, and other places that you are registered to share with guests when they ask for gift ideas.

Do not register for the same things at different stores. A national store or catalog service will remove items that have been bought for you from your list so that you don't get duplicates of those items, or they will mark that they are no longer available. One store does not coordinate with another, however, so if

GLOBAL REGISTRY

If family and friends are so far-flung that accessing your registries is difficult, explore the Internet as an option. There are numerous national chain stores and merchants that offer online registries and shopping services. Try the Wedding Registries Directory Home Page (www.wedreg.com), which lists stores, catalogs, and manufacturers that offer computerized registries across the United States.

you register for eight woven place mats at store A, don't also register for them at store B. Otherwise, you're likely to end up with more place mats than you'll ever need.

It is a good idea to register as soon as you can, with your registries completed by the time invitations go out.

GIFTS FOR THOSE WHO ARE MARRYING AGAIN

Although family members usually give a gift to a bride being married for the second time, friends who gave gifts the first time around need not do so. If it is the first marriage for the groom, it is fine for his family and friends to give the couple gifts. If you are being married again and prefer that guests forgo gifts, it is considered incorrect to include that information on the invitation; the word that gifts are not expected should be spread by family and close friends.

ENGAGEMENT AND SHOWER GIFTS

ENGAGEMENT GIFTS

Traditionally, engagement presents are given only by close relatives and intimate friends upon the announcement of your engagement and are almost always intended especially for the bride. When the engagement party is a small dinner, cocktail party, or luncheon and a guest wants to give a gift, he or she takes it to the party. If *everyone* brings a gift, the bride-to-be may open them as part of the festivities. When the party is a large reception or cocktail party, gifts are not generally taken; if they are, they should not be opened during the party, to avoid embarrassing those guests who (correctly) did not bring any.

The bride-to-be may decide to give her fiancé a small engagement present, such as a pair of cuff links, a watch, or a key chain. These items may be engraved with the date of the engagement.

WEDDING-SHOWER GIFTS

Unless culture and custom dictate that shower gifts should be the equivalent of wedding presents, gifts given to the bride or engaged couple at a shower should not be elaborate. Traditionally, shower gifts were handmade for the occasion, and such gifts are still treasured. If the shower has a theme, gifts should be

*Gifts, Gift
Registries,
and
Thank-You
Notes*

137

IN JAPAN, GIFTS FOR GUESTS

Japanese brides and grooms sometimes give their wedding guests "kohaku manjyu," round steamed buns with sweet bean paste in the middle. A pair of buns, one red, one white, are made and given to guests in a special box. Other gifts for guests? A pair of chopsticks imprinted with the date and perhaps the names of the bride and groom, tied with a ribbon; a collection of origami cranes; or a bag of candied almonds. The reasoning behind this reverse gift-giving? It is believed that guests bring so much luck with them that the bride and groom should thank them in return.

appropriate to the shower. At a bath or kitchen shower, for example, guests comply by bringing towels or small appliances. Sometimes, guests contribute to a joint gift for the bride or the couple.

Shower gifts are to be presented to the bride, or the bride and groom, at the shower. If an invited guest can't attend, it is not obligatory that she send a gift. (Often, close friends or relatives wish to, however, which is fine.) If a non-attending invitee does send a gift, she should send it directly to the shower hostess—not from the store directly to the bride. The gift should be accompanied by a card to let the guest of honor know the name of the donor. Shower gifts are opened at the party, and each donor is thanked personally then and there. The bride may write thank-you notes later if she wishes: It is much appreciated if she does, but it is not absolutely mandatory—unless the donor was not there or did not receive thanks from the bride in person.

Sometimes the invitation asks each guest to bring a gift for a Wishing Well, in addition to the shower gift. The Wishing Well gift is a small, inexpensive item, such as a measuring spoon or cup, an herb or spice, or a bar of scented soap. These presents may be wrapped or not, accompanied by a card or not, and put into a small model or replica of a well. Under no circumstances should these be large items, since the shower guest has invested in a shower gift and most likely a wedding gift, too.

GIFTS FOR SECOND-MARRIAGE SHOWERS

It is perfectly acceptable to have a shower for a second marriage or for an older couple who have been independent for a number of years. For couples who may already have all of the basic necessities, food showers, garden showers, and ticket (to some entertainment) showers may be more appropriate than traditional kitchen or linen showers. In general, the guest list is made up of new friends of the bride or couple or very close friends and relatives. It is better to not invite friends who attended a shower for the first marriage.

WEDDING GIFTS

It used to be considered obligatory for anyone invited to a wedding to send a gift, whether they attended the wedding or not. This is still true when the recipients are friends whom you see from time to time or who live nearby. In the days when that held sway, people did not move around as much as they do today, and invitations were sent only to those within a reasonable distance. Because invitations still carry a gift-in-return obligation, it is more proper to send a wedding announcement, which carries no gift obligation, to mere acquaintances or distant friends you haven't seen in years. If you do send an invitation to people who are not close to you and they do not attend the festivities, you should not expect a gift in return.

Any formula wherein a wedding gift should cost at least as much as the bride and groom are spending on entertaining each person at the reception is a *myth*. Such extravagance is impractical, uncalled-for, and ostentatious—and

---

FOR THE COUPLE WHO HAS EVERYTHING

When you've been married before and have little need for traditional gifts, think beyond the usual. Consider registering at the following:

- a local nursery for a plant, tree, or shrub for your garden or terrace
- a liquor store for a selection of wines or champagne
- a caterer for a special meal after the wedding
- a gallery for a contribution to an "artwork" account
- a ticket agent, for ballet, opera, or theater tickets

If a couple is shy about registering, friends might want to surprise them with any of the above, or something else.

Gifts, Gift Registries, and Thank-You Notes

therefore in poor taste. Fortunately, guests are learning that they have no such obligation. It is not the cost of the gift but the thought, the sentiment, and the practicality that count. The cost of a gift is based on the guest's affection for and relationship with the bride, the groom, or their families. No one should be made to feel that he must spend more than can be afforded. That doesn't mean, however, that guests have the green light to be stingy in purchasing a gift. Each guest should simply give what he or she can afford, along with love and best wishes.

GIFT DELIVERY

Wedding gifts are generally delivered to the bride's home or the home of her parents before the wedding, and are addressed to the bride in her name. Gifts may be sent out as soon as a guest receives an invitation, mailed by the donor or sent directly from the store where they were purchased. Sometimes gifts are delivered in person. When gifts are sent after the wedding, they are sent to the couple at their new address, if known, or to their parents' home. When a couple is living together before their wedding, gifts are either sent to them at their home address or to the bride's parents if they are hosting the wedding. The circumstances are the guide.

In some localities and among certain ethnic groups it is customary for guests to bring a gift to the wedding reception rather than deliver it ahead of time. Gift packages should be put on a table set up for them. The newlyweds are not expected to open these gifts during the reception, but they should delegate the tasks of making sure they're safe at the reception and of packing them up and transporting them from the reception to a safe place. In other cases, checks are handed to either the bride or the groom in the receiving line or sometime before the end of the reception.

CREATE YOUR OWN REGISTRY

If you crave something from a store that doesn't have a bridal registry, ask whether the store will set one up for you. Before finalizing the arrangements, make sure the store gives you positive answers to these questions:

- Will you keep a log that lists what has already been purchased to let other guests know?
- Will you accept telephone orders from those who don't live nearby?
- Will you insure gifts that you send to us?

KEEPING A RECORD

As soon as the invitations are mailed, develop a system for keeping track of gifts as they arrive. You can use your wedding planner, a computer database system, or a handwritten log—whatever is easiest for you. Record the article, the date it was received, the name and address of the donor, and the store the gift came from, if necessary. Include a column to indicate the date you sent a thank-you note. If you are numbering gifts for display or insurance purposes, add a column for that. Your system might look something like this:

NO.	DATE REC'D	GIFT	SENT BY/ ADDRESS	WHERE BOUGHT	THANK-YOU SENT
1	6/21	SILVER PLATTER	MR./MRS. ALLAN ANDERSON 2 HILL ST., PEEKSKILL, NY 10960	TIFFANY	6/22
2	6/22	8 LINEN PLACE MATS	AUNT RUTH 24 MILLSTONE LANE, SOUTHAMPTON, NY 11968	HILLBERTS, SOUTHAMPTON	6/24

DISPLAYING GIFTS

If you simply want to show your gifts, or if your reception will be held at your home, you may choose to display them in a room easily accessible to others. If you want only close friends and relatives to see your gifts, place them in a back room.

Gifts are rarely displayed at the club, hotel, or hall where the reception is held. Instead, relatives and friends are invited to the home in the days before the wedding to see the gifts.

Often, tables are set up and may be covered in plain white cloths or sheets. Sheets can hang down to the floor so that the boxes for presents can be concealed underneath.

You won't want to step on any toes in displaying the gifts guests have given to you. Take care in placing the gifts so that comparisons aren't made. A piece of silver plate should not be stuck next to costlier pieces of sterling, for example.

Gifts, Gift Registries, and Thank-You Notes

There is no rule about whether the cards sent with the gifts should be displayed. Showing them saves answering the question, "Who sent that?" over and over again, but some couples feel that it is a private matter, while others believe it is fine to let others know who sent what.

When wedding gifts are numerous and valuable, it's wise to hire a security guard to watch the house while everyone is at the wedding and reception. Also, be sure to check with your insurance company about additional coverage or a rider on your policy to cover the value of the gifts. Your itemized list of gifts received serves as a record.

Displaying Checks

Ordinarily it is in bad taste to display gifts of money. But to be fair to a generous relative or friend who sent a wedding check, it is quite proper to display it—albeit with the amount concealed. If you have more than one, simply lay the checks out on a flat surface, one above the other, so that the signatures alone are disclosed. The amount of the one at the top should be covered with a strip of paper. Then place a sheet of glass over the whole thing to prevent snoopy guests from taking a peek.

You may also write on plain white gift enclosure cards "Check from Mr. and Mrs. Harold Brown" and display just the cards.

EXCHANGING GIFTS

You may exchange duplicate presents without telling anyone you have done so. If friends who have given a gift realize that you have more than one, they should encourage you to exchange theirs for something else. If a gift is not a duplicate but rather is something you neither like nor need, you may exchange it as well, unless doing so risks hurting a close friend. If the gift is from someone you rarely see, simply write a thank-you note for the gift they sent, even if you've exchanged it for something else. You should not, however, exchange the presents chosen for you by your own families unless you are specifically told to do so. Nor should you discard a gift that was especially made for you.

When you write a thank-you note for a duplicate gift that you have exchanged, simply thank the giver for the present she sent, with enthusiasm. You don't have to tell her that you exchanged her gift for something else.

BROKEN GIFTS

If a gift that was sent directly from the donor arrives broken, immediately check the wrapping to see if it was insured. If so, notify the person who sent it at once so that he can collect the insurance and replace it. If it is not insured, you may not want to mention that it arrived broken; otherwise the person who gave it may feel obligated to replace it. When a broken gift arrives directly from a store, simply take it back without mentioning a thing to the donor. Any reputable store will replace merchandise that arrives damaged.

RETURNING GIFTS

The only time that gifts are returned are when marriages are either canceled or immediately annulled.

When wedding plans are canceled, gifts that have already been received must be returned. If the wedding is postponed indefinitely but the couple does intend to marry, the gifts that have arrived are carefully put away until the ceremony takes place. If, after a period of six weeks to two months, it becomes doubtful that the wedding will take place at all, the couple must send the gifts back to donors to return.

GREAT GIFT FOR THE BRIDE

The maid of honor is not expected to take a gift to each shower and party she is invited to, but she can bring a small token. A great gift idea: a little emergency kit for the day of the wedding. In it she could place an extra pair of panty hose, a mirror, hair spray, hairpins, a small comb, a nail file and nail polish, all sizes of safety pins, a small sewing kit, white masking tape, a package of tissues, bottled water, breath mints, scissors, super-adhesive glue, or packages of hand wipes.

GIFTS TO AND FROM THE ATTENDANTS

It is customary for the bride and groom to give each of their attendants gifts as a thank-you for their participation in the wedding. It is also customary for the bride and groom's attendants to give a gift in return.

FROM GROOM TO USHERS

The groom's gifts for his ushers are either put at their places at a bachelor dinner, presented at the rehearsal dinner, or given just before leaving the rehearsal when no dinner is planned. Any kind of small, personal item—a nice pen, a leather wallet, or cuff links—is suitable and may be engraved or mono-grammed. The groom's gift to his best man may be the same gift he gives to the ushers or a more elaborate one.

FROM BRIDE TO BRIDESMAIDS

The bride's gifts to her bridesmaids may be given at a bridesmaids' luncheon shortly before the wedding, at the rehearsal dinner, or just after the rehearsal when no dinner is planned. A piece of jewelry that can be worn to the wedding, such as earrings or a necklace, is a perfect gift. The bride's gift to her maid or matron of honor may be the same gift she gives to her bridesmaids or a more elaborate one. If you plan to give an engraved gift, such as a silver picture frame, have the wedding date and your initials engraved to commemorate the occasion.

ATTENDANTS' GIFTS TO BRIDE OR GROOM OR BOTH

It is often customary for bridal attendants to give a joint gift to the bride, for the groomsmen to give a joint gift to the groom, or for both sets of attendants to give a large gift to the couple. This is in addition to any shower and other gifts they may wish to give along the way. These gifts can be personal or house-hold items.

Because they bear considerable costs to be a part of the wedding party, it is not always necessary for the attendants to give an individual wedding gift to the couple. The traditional custom of attendants giving individual gifts to the couple is becoming optional. If the joint gift is an extravagant one and an atten-dant is already stretched beyond his or her means, the bridesmaid or usher need not feel another gift is a mandate. He or she should feel comfortable deciding what is appropriate: a small, meaningful token, a traditional gift, or none at all.

GIFTS FOR EACH OTHER

Often the groom will give his bride a present apart from the wedding and engagement rings. The bride may also wish to give her groom a wedding pre-sent separate from the wedding ring. It might be jewelry engraved with the date of the wedding or a beautiful book. The couple could also buy themselves gifts for their new life together—matching mountain bikes, for example, or a hammock for the backyard.

GIFTS FOR PARENTS

Although it is not necessary to give your parents a gift, it's a nice way to thank them for everything they have done. One touching gesture is for the bride and groom to each present a rose, along with a kiss on the cheek, to their parents just after the bride's father or escort is seated. Have the roses placed near the spot you will stand after the processional.

GIFTS FOR YOUR CHILDREN

If either of you has been married before and has young children, give them an extra-special gift to make them feel a big part of your wedding festivities. Be sure to buy them something they've been asking for, especially if the nuptials have left them feeling anxious and uncertain. One lovely gesture is to present children with a family medallion during the ceremony.

GIFTS AND THANKS TO HOSTS

When friends, neighbors, or relatives offer to take in out-of-town guests or host a party or shower during the wedding festivities, you should of course thank them. It is also a nice idea to give them a thank-you gift. It needn't be elaborate—an arrangement of flowers delivered before or after the wedding or event is a suitable token of your appreciation. You could also buy them tickets to an upcoming concert if they like music, or take them out to lunch or dinner if time permits.

Your card with flowers or a small gift can read simply "with thanks and love" or "what a wonderful shower" or "thank you so much for giving shelter and respite to Frank and Judy." Later, you can send a heartfelt thank-you note that mentions their kindness at length. Some sample notes are shown at the end of this chapter.

WEDDING FAVORS

Gifts from the bride and groom to their wedding guests, referred to as wedding favors, are only necessary when part of a cultural tradition. European brides and grooms, for example, have long given their guests favors, as have some brides and grooms in the American South.

Favors are a special gesture from the newlyweds to guests for being a part of the occasion. Traditional favors include a piece of groom's cake boxed and wrapped or a miniature box of chocolates. Favors can also be tiny pots of flowers, miniature bottles of champagne or wine, or keepsakes made by the bride.

Unfortunately, the concept of presenting favors to wedding guests has become big business, and many brides and grooms are pressured to feel that they must offer them. It cannot be said too often that, while favors are a lovely thought, unless they are part of your tradition they are completely unnecessary and yet another drain on your budget.

THANK-YOU NOTES

Whatever the gift, whether a place setting or a gift of time or talent, it must be acknowledged. Thanks takes many forms, but all share one common guideline—that they be prompt. This is particularly true when gifts have been sent in the mail or delivered by a store; it lets the sender know his gift has arrived safely.

A separate, handwritten thank-you note must be sent for each wedding present you receive. If humanly possible, you should write each note of thanks on the day the present arrives; otherwise, the list will soon get ahead of you, and the first weeks of your marriage will be spent writing thank-you notes. A note of thanks should also be sent to those who send congratulatory telegrams on the day of the wedding. There is no excuse for not having all thank-you notes written within three months of the wedding—at the most—especially now that it is expected that the groom shares in this task.

Every thank-you note, no matter how short, should include a reference to the present itself. You certainly don't have to lie about your feelings for the gift, but you must express your appreciation for the thought and effort. You must never let on in your thank-you note that you dislike a gift; describe it instead as "unique," "a conversation piece," or even "interesting." Display it when you know the donor is coming for a visit; otherwise, put it away and hope that its absence will go unnoticed.

PREPRINTED THANK-YOU CARDS

It is difficult to overemphasize the rudeness of a couple who sends a printed or even an engraved card of thanks with no personal message added. If you prefer a card that says "thank you" or has a poem or message on it, choose one that is simple and dignified, then add your *own* note, mentioning the gift by name and why you are so happy to have received it. Since you *must do this* in any case, it seems silly to go to the expense of buying cards that probably cost more than a box of plain note paper.

Some brides and grooms order preprinted thank-you cards from the photographer, who inserts their portrait in little corners designed for this purpose. The recipient of the note then receives not only a personal thank-you, but a souvenir photo as well. Unfortunately, the wait for these kinds of cards can be up to two or more months—much too long a time between the giving of a gift and the thank-you. You can get around this problem by having a portrait taken a month or so before the wedding—whether during the photograph sittings for newspaper shots or formal portrait shots—so that the cards and photographs can be ready and waiting for you when you return from your honeymoon. Also, you can get the photographer to supply you with blank cards before the photograph is ready. You'll be able to write your notes as gifts arrive, adding the photographs (and dates on the notes) a little later.

STATIONERY

No special stationery is required for writing thank-you notes. You can use paper printed or engraved with your maiden-name initials, your married initials, or a monogram of your last name. If you've taken your husband's name and you are using initials, however, you should wait until after your wedding to send initialized notes. Use plain paper or notes printed with your maiden name until your new name is "official."

The paper can be bordered, white or colored, ecru or ivory. In fact, plain, fold-over notes are just fine. There is no excuse, therefore, to delay writing your notes simply because personalized note cards have not arrived from the printer.

WHAT'S IN A NOTE?

Notes are written by one person, so they should be signed by one person. If the bride writes, she should mention the groom's thanks in the note, and vice versa.

Dear Mr. and Mrs. McKune,

How did you ever find those perfect candlesticks? They are wonderful, and John and I want to thank you a thousand times! We have just rented a great apartment with a fireplace, and your candlesticks will be just right on the mantel.

Thank you so much!
With love from both of us,
Christine

Dear Aunt Ruth,

Catherine and I truly love the quilt you made for us. It is perfect on the bed, and we're so excited about it that we take friends right into the bedroom to see it, practically before they get their coats off. The colors are perfect and the quilt is beautiful, but the best part is feeling the love you put into making it for us. Come visit us soon. We miss you already and still treasure the time we could spend with you right before the wedding.

Love,
Richard

When gifts of money are given, it is fine for you to state the amount in your thank-you note, just as you would mention the specific item if the gift was a place setting of china or a kitchen accessory. The thank-you note should also, if possible, indicate how you intend to spend the money.

Dear Aunt Kate and Uncle Reid,

Wow! You have no idea how wonderful it was to open your card and find that generous check for $100.00. We used it to help buy the Ernest Garthwaite painting we've been saving for to hang in the living room, and when we look at it, we'll think of you. Thank you, too, for rearranging your schedules so that you could be with us at the wedding. Laura and I didn't think we could get married without you there to share the day with us, and we know what trouble you went through to be there. It meant the world to us.

Laura sends her love with mine,
Jeremy

Dear Mr. and Mrs. Brown,

You know how much Ted and I love camping, and we want you to know that your $75 check has gone right into our tent fund. We can't thank you enough for such a generous gift, and who knows? You might wake up some morning and look out your kitchen window to find us camped out right in your backyard on our way to the mountains.

Thank you again!

Love,

Cindy

No Thanks Given?

When the donor of a gift to the bride and groom receives no thank-you note after three months have gone by, he should feel no hesitation in calling or writing to ask whether the present ever arrived. The question may serve to clarify the situation for both parties. Wording is important; the donor should sound concerned rather than critical. If the newlyweds have not received the gift, the donor can then trace it, or replace it. If, on the other hand, the couple has not sent thanks because of thoughtlessness, they deserve the embarrassment a call or letter will cause.

Thanks for Acts of Kindness

There will probably be many people who help out with any variety of elements at your wedding, from attendants to a neighbor who stamped your envelopes. These acts of kindness are often the best gifts of all and should be acknowledged with a note of thanks.

Dear Mrs. Hausler,

I'm sure the invitations to the wedding would not have been mailed on time if you hadn't come to the rescue and helped. I really appreciated it and loved spending time with you and hearing about your and Mr. Hausler's wedding. It was one of my favorite wedding moments. Thank you so much.

Love,

Helen

Dear Nancy,

Well, we're back from Lake Tahoe, and I can't wait to tell you all about it. In the meantime, I wanted to say thank you. I honestly couldn't have made it without you. I know you will just say "that's what friends are for," but your support, not to mention everything you took care of and did, was bigger than that. Once we were in the plane and on the way, what I thought about most was how lucky I am, and have been for fifteen years, to have you for a friend. Thank you for helping me organize the list and address envelopes, for finding such wonderful "old, new, borrowed, and blue," for dashing out for pink lipstick at the zero hour, for holding my hand, for being so nice to Aunt Ginny, for making the list for the photographer, for staying up with me 'til 2 o'clock baking cookies when I couldn't sleep, for dragging my train around, for keeping me calm, and for just being there. I'll never forget.

Love,

Lisa

Dear Mrs. McCaffery,

I never saw you, but I knew you were there. There's no other way everything would have been ready so perfectly for the wedding. Thank you so much for taking care of letting the florist in, for the new candles on the altar, and for making sure the acolytes were doing their job. The

HOW TIMES HAVE CHANGED

In 1922, Emily Post wrote, "If the bridegroom-elect has plenty of means, she [the bride] may not only accept flowers but anything he chooses to select, except wearing apparel or a motor car or a house and furniture—anything that can be classified as 'maintenance.' It is perfectly suitable for her to drive his car, or ride his horse, and she may elect furniture for their house, which he may buy or have built. But, if she would keep her self-respect, the car must not become hers nor must she live in the house or use its furniture until she is given his name. . . it would be starting life on a false basis, and putting herself in a category with women of another class, to be clothed by any man, whether he is soon to be her husband or not."

church has always been lucky to have you quietly taking care of so many details, but I was the lucky one last month. Steve and I look forward to seeing you soon, and thank you again.

With affection,

Joanne McGuigan

Dear Mr. and Mrs. Werner,

    My bridesmaids had so much fun staying at your house that they could hardly tear themselves away to get ready for the wedding! I don't know how to begin to tell you how much it meant to all of us that you took them in, and then took such good care of them, too. I know Mom has told you how grateful we were, but I wanted to add my thanks to hers and Dad's for your, as always, incredible generosity.

    Rob and I can't wait to see you and will ask Mom to let you know the next time we're visiting to see if we can find some time to get together. In the meantime, please accept our thanks for everything you did, from practically running your own inn to shuttling everybody back and forth to being two of our favorite guests at the wedding.

Love,

Cassie

MONOGRAMMING AND ENGRAVING

If the bride and groom want to have linens monogrammed or silver engraved, they should include on their registry information the initials they want to have used.

Marking Linen

Katherine Leigh Adams, who will marry Brian Charles Jamison, may have linens initialed with her married initials, KJ or KJA, or her future husband's last initial, J. Often the single initial embellished with a scroll or pretty design is more effective than three initials, and the cost may be less. The bride who is keeping her own name may have her last initial and that of her husband divided by a dot or design:

A ~ J

Towels are marked at the center of one end so that the monogram shows when they are folded lengthwise in thirds and hung over a rack.

Long rectangular tablecloths are marked at the center of each long side, midway between the table edge and the center of the cloth.

Small square cloths are marked in one corner midway between the center and the corner so that the monogram shows on the table.

Dinner napkins are marked diagonally in one corner or centered on a rectangular fold.

Sheets are monogrammed so that when the top is folded down, the letters can be read by a person standing at the foot of the bed. Pillowcases are marked approximately two inches above the hem.

Marking Silver

If silver flatware is monogrammed, a triangle of block letters—last name initial below and the first name initials of the bride and groom above—works well on modern patterns. When Polly Marshall marries Charles Harrison, the configuration would be

P C
H

If a single initial is used, it is the last name initial of the groom.

Monograms on flat silver have always been placed so that the top of the letter is toward the end of the handle. In other words, when the piece is on the table, the monogram is upside down as seen by the diner at that place. If you prefer, you can have initials engraved the other way so that they can be read more easily.

CHAPTER 8

ATTENDANTS

I t is believed that the custom of selecting attendants to witness the matrimonial ceremony has its roots in early England, when it was customary for a
bride to walk to her wedding surrounded by friends who were dressed exactly
as she was. This way, evil spirits jealous of her happiness could not tell who was
who and thus could not put a curse on the bride.

While the custom remains, attendants are no longer chosen to help ward
off evil spirits. Whether bridesmaids or ushers, they are chosen as witnesses to a
couple's matrimonial union in a gesture of love, friendship, and support.

Most couples these days choose to have attendants in their wedding. The
nuptial celebration is one of shared happiness and joy, and including friends and
loved ones in this happy milestone is one of society's most cherished customs.

There are no set rules decreeing the size and shape of your wedding party,
no magic number of attendants allowed, no standard ratio of ushers to bridesmaids or men to women. You may have two maids of honor or two best men.
You can have male attendants for the bride and female ushers if you wish. You
can even choose to have no attendants at all—although you will need witnesses.

While rules don't dictate the selection of attendants, there are practicalities to consider. The size and formality of your wedding will likely be the main
determiners of the size of your wedding party. If you plan a small, intimate
gathering, you won't want attendants outnumbering the guests. If the ceremony
site itself is small, you may have room for only one or two attendants. If you're
pulling out all the stops and planning a large, extravagant celebration, you may
want to match it with an equally large wedding party.

What, then, is the number of attendants in the average wedding party?
The average formal or semiformal wedding party includes four to six bridesmaids and at least that many ushers. The number of ushers is usually determined by the "one usher for fifty guests" guideline—a good gauge for seating
guests expediently.

Another practical factor: your budget. The more attendants you have, the more of a burden it puts on your expenses. The bride and groom are responsible for all bouquets, boutonnieres, and wedding-party gifts. They are expected to pay for their attendants' accommodations. The more attendants you have, the larger your reception guest list will be, because you are responsible for feeding and entertaining not only your attendants but your attendants' partners as well.

One other determinant may be religious restrictions. Some religions have strict rules regarding official witnesses. Your honor attendants, at least, may be required to be members of your faith or even to attend pre-ceremony instruction classes before they can participate. Check with your officiant before asking anyone to be in your wedding.

CHOOSING YOUR ATTENDANTS

Attendants are invited to be in a wedding soon after the engagement is announced and the couple has some idea of the celebration type and size. Bridesmaids and ushers are traditionally chosen from among the bride and groom's families and close friends. But when you have a limited number of possible attendants and a large contingent of close friends and family, don't be overly concerned. There are other honors you can bestow, including reading a passage at the ceremony, serving as guest-book attendant, or working with the photographer to organize candid pictures and formal portraits.

In choosing your attendants, consider first the people to whom you are closest. Then consider those friends and family members you can count on, who share a willingness to help. At the same time, keep in mind that the people you choose are bridal attendants, not a hired work force. While they can *help* you have a wedding day free from worry, be sure to respect their own commitments and delegate duties only to those who have offered to help.

Another important consideration: the financial obligations attendants will be incurring on your behalf, from travel expenses to clothing bills to possible participation in parties and showers. If attendants are coming from far away, they are expected to pay their own travel costs. For those friends and family who would find it a serious financial strain to serve as attendants, you might thoughtfully ask them instead to participate in a different, less expensive way. This is especially true if you are being married for the second time or having a large second wedding. Friends who served you at your first wedding may be reluctant or unable to spare the costs required to serve as attendants again.

If cost is a concern for a good friend you can't imagine being married without, you can certainly offer to pay his or her bills. No one but you and your friend has to know of this special financial arrangement.

DIFFICULT CHOICES

Sometimes choosing attendants is easy. When, however, the number of close relatives and good friends is large, it can become difficult. The possibility of inadvertently hurting someone's feelings always exists. There can also be hurt feelings when the bride chooses one of two best friends to be her maid of honor and asks the other to be a bridesmaid, or the groom chooses one brother over the other to be his best man.

Fortunately, times and etiquette's guidelines have changed. When a decision is impossible to make, an acceptable solution is for the bride to have two maids or matrons of honor or the groom two best men. While only one attendant for the bride and one for the groom need serve as official witnesses when papers are signed, the other duties can be shared. More important, hurt feelings are spared.

It is in the spirit of family unity to ask the bride's brothers to be ushers or the groom's sisters to be bridesmaids, but it is not mandatory—and sometimes only possible when the wedding party is large.

It is a good idea to be direct in explaining to relatives or friends why you

SURROUNDED BY HER ATTENDANTS

Long ago, Greek women generally married when they were 15, surrounded by a flock of older, married women who had been happy and fertile in their own marriages. It was believed that their wisdom and good fortune would rub off on the bride and, by osmosis, steer the inexperienced girl into a happy and fertile marriage of her own. By virtue of their number, it was also believed that they protected her from evil forces. Traditionally, young girls walked before this group, tossing grains and herbs in the bride's path as tribute to the gods who could ensure the bride's fertility.

have chosen others to be in your wedding party. Choosing siblings or even parents over friends needs no explanation, whereas a choice between friends might. Be forthcoming, but convey anything you say in a kind and loving manner. You can explain that you literally flipped a coin (or even do so in their presence) or that you have known the person you chose longer than the other friend.

Another change in etiquette is that the bride and groom's attendants no longer need to be evenly paired. This is always a relief to any bride and groom who have been struggling to equalize their numbers to create matched sets. You can have more bridesmaids than ushers in your wedding party, or vice versa—a sign of how times have changed, since it was until recently unacceptable to have more bridesmaids than ushers. As more than one wedding planner has said, this is not the passenger list for Noah's Ark.

WHEN TO ASK

Generally, you should ask anyone you want to be in your wedding soon after the engagement is announced. You'll probably want to have some basic plans in order, mainly the wedding date and location. Your invitation may be issued in person, by telephone, or by letter. Before your friends and relatives agree or decline, let them in on the plans so far: the dates and times of the ceremony, reception, and rehearsal; your overall ideas for the degree of formality; and any known pre-wedding events that would involve them.

If you are planning a destination wedding, whether to Disney World or a Caribbean island, it is especially important that you make this clear in your initial invitation. You could say, for example, "We're getting married in Bermuda! If you can get yourself there, we'll pick up the tab of your accommodations, as we've rented several villas where everyone will stay. We hope you can come on Wednesday and stay until Sunday, so you can have a little vacation at the same time." While the bride and groom are responsible for paying for the wedding

Emily Post's Weddings

party accommodations, the other costs fall to the attendants themselves, the reason they will need to know what basic costs to anticipate before deciding to participate.

In any event, you and your partner should not press for an immediate answer but should give those you invite a few days to review their calendars and bank accounts. If the answer is no, graciously hasten to say that you are disappointed but understand, and you hope that they will be able to attend the wedding anyway.

APPEARANCE IS NOT EVERYTHING

It goes without saying that friends' looks are not the criteria for their selection for the wedding party. A good friend's large size should play no part in your decision to ask her to be an attendant. You are not producing a magazine layout; you are getting married in the loving company of relatives and friends. The same is true if a friend is pregnant, disabled, short, tall, or not a physical match with the rest of the wedding party. Whatever you do, don't make it an issue. Welcome your friends to your celebration warmly; they will respond by being comfortable, confident, and happy to be sharing your special day.

If you have friends or relatives who decline because they aren't comfortable in the role of attendant, be sensitive and understanding. As long as you make it clear that their conditions don't matter one way or the other to you, you must respect their decision to decline. If you know that accepting will make them feel miserable, don't press the issue.

A LITTLE LUXURY

Treat attendants (and moms and little sisters, too!) to a little luxury a few days before the wedding. Hire a facialist or licensed esthetician to give everyone a herbal facial and a manicure and pedicure. Or make appointments for all to get massages. Or you might have a hairdresser on hand to help pin up hair, tuck in flowers, and add finishing touches the morning of the wedding. Turn part of the house into a "women only" retreat for some fun, relaxing time together. If the wedding is to occur later in the day, a light lunch of tea sandwiches and fruit is the perfect accompaniment.

WHEN AN ATTENDANT BACKS OUT

It used to be that the only reason an attendant could back out of a wedding commitment was because of ill health or a death in the family. Today, the press of careers is as urgent for women as it is for men, and a critical business trip or other work-related issue can force either an usher or a bridesmaid to back out altogether. If this happens early in your planning and before you have announced the names of all your attendants, you may easily ask someone else. It is generally incorrect, however, to ask someone else to fill in at the last minute, although there are exceptions, such as asking a close friend who would be honored to help out.

SHARING THE DETAILS

Once you have affirmative answers from all your attendants, you should keep them informed of your ongoing plans. Details can be shared by telephone, letter, or e-mail. Keeping your attendants informed helps everyone stay organized and more familiar with the rest of the wedding party—an especially nice touch if they've never met. The information could include:

- list of names, addresses, and phone numbers of the wedding party
- dates and times of parties and showers to which they will be invited (they are not obligated to come, but it is nice for them to know when the events are occurring)
- rehearsal time and place
- rehearsal dinner arrangements
- where they will stay
- what their wardrobe needs might be—from wedding attire to clothes for other activities (such as shorts for a picnic)
- reminders to bridesmaids and ushers to break in their shoes
- any plans for breakfast, lunch, or tea before the wedding
- where they will dress
- the time and place for any pre-wedding photos
- transportation arrangements to the ceremony and reception

DUTIES AND RESPONSIBILITIES

The traditional roles for attendants are no longer strictly followed. It has been customary, for example, for the maid or matron of honor to help the bride dress and change outfits and coordinate bridesmaids' activities, but this is no longer considered mandatory. Moreover, a married woman, or "matron," may be chosen instead of a maid of honor, and on rare occasions both a maid and a matron of honor may attend the bride. Traditionally in this case, the "maid" takes precedence, holding the bouquet and serving as a witness.

Whether a bridesmaid or a groomsman, an attendant has certain responsibilities, which are usually determined by the bride and groom. Some of these responsibilities are derived from tradition; others are based on practicalities. Following are descriptions of the traditional and modern duties of wedding party attendants.

HONOR ATTENDANTS: DUTIES AND RESPONSIBILITIES

An "honor attendant" is another, more modern term for the matron or maid of honor and the best man. Honor attendants have two primary roles in the wedding. The first responsibility is to be a best friend—to be wholly supportive of their respective charges on the day of the wedding, from the moment they wake up to the time the newlyweds leave for their honeymoon. The second responsibility is to make sure bridesmaids and ushers are where they should be and that they are organized and ready to do their own jobs.

Today, if the bride chooses a male friend to be her honor attendant, she would obviously alter some of the following duties, such as help with changing clothes. There would nonetheless still be plenty of ways for him to assist her. Adaptations and personal touches agreed on by the bride and attendant are fine. One bride's male honor attendant chose to hand the bride's bouquet to her grandmother seated in the front pew. The grandmother was thrilled to hold the bouquet during the ceremony, and it was a task the male attendant felt comfortable doing.

Similarly, the best man traditionally serves as the groom's right hand, helping the groom dress. A female "best" or honor attendant for the groom, would obviously not perform these duties.

THE BRIDE'S MAID OR MATRON OF HONOR: DUTIES AND RESPONSIBILITIES

Honor attendants may fulfill any or all of the following:

- Helps the bride select bridesmaids' attire.
- Helps address invitations and place cards.
- Attends as many prenuptial events as possible.
- Organizes bridesmaids' gift to the bride; usually gives individual gift to the couple.
- Makes sure that the bridesmaids, flower girl, and ring bearer are on time for fittings, the rehearsal, the ceremony, and photo sessions.
- Holds the groom's wedding ring.
- Helps the bride dress and get ready for the ceremony.
- Arranges the bride's veil and train before the processional and recessional.
- Makes sure the bride's gown is "picture perfect" throughout the day.
- Holds the bride's bouquet during the ceremony.
- Witnesses the signing of the marriage certificate.
- Stands on the receiving line.
- Keeps the bride on schedule.
- Helps the bride change into her going-away clothes.
- Takes care of the bride's gown and accessories after the reception.
- Pays for own wedding attire and transportation to wedding city (not lodging).

THE GROOM'S BEST MAN: DUTIES AND RESPONSIBILITIES

The best man may fulfill any or all of the following:

- Organizes a pre-wedding party for the groom.
- Coordinates the groomsmen's gift to the groom; usually gives individual gift to the couple.
- Gets the groom dressed and to the ceremony on time.

FIERCE BEST MAN

In ancient times, a best man was more often chosen for his ferocity than for his other impressive characteristics. As a warrior friend of the groom, it was thought he would be best able to shield the bride from abductors.

- Makes sure the groom's wedding-related expenses are prepared (clergy fee, for example).
- Makes sure the groom has the marriage license with him.
- Gives payment to ceremony officiant.
- Takes care of and holds the bride's wedding ring.
- Makes sure all ushers are properly attired and in place on time.
- Helps welcome guests.
- Offers first toast to bride and groom at reception.
- Dances with the bride, maid of honor, mothers, and single female guests.
- Witnesses the signing of the marriage certificate.
- Drives the bride and groom to reception if no driver hired.
- Helps the groom get ready for the honeymoon.
- Gathers up and takes care of the groom's wedding clothes after he changes.
- Has a car ready for the bride and groom to leave the reception, or perhaps drives them to their next destination.
- Coordinates return of rented apparel.
- Pays for own wedding attire and transportation to the wedding city (not lodging).

BRIDESMAIDS: DUTIES AND RESPONSIBILITIES

Assuming that the maid of honor is able to take care of her responsibilities, the main charges to the bridesmaids are to help the maid of honor in any way they can and to take care of their own dress and accessory fittings. They may help with a shower for the bride (although this is entirely optional), and may look after the flower girl and ring bearer before and during the ceremony.

Bridesmaids' duties may include:

- Take responsibility for dress fittings.
- Assist the maid or matron of honor in any way they can.
- Attend as many prenuptial events as possible.
- Possibly co-host a party or shower (not mandatory).
- Assist bride with errands.

BUSY BRIDESMAIDS

When appropriate, add some favorite traditions from other countries to the list of bridesmaids duties. Czech bridesmaids pin a sprig of rosemary on each guest as a symbol of constancy, while Polish bridesmaids unbraid the bride's hair before the wedding—a symbolic gesture representing her abandoning her "maidenly" single status on the way to becoming a married woman.

- Contribute to bridesmaids' gift to the bride; usually give an individual gift to the couple.
- Arrive at dressing site promptly.
- Possibly participate in receiving line.
- Dance with ushers and single male guests.
- Help gather guests for the first dance, cake-cutting, and bouquet toss.
- Look after elderly relatives or friends.
- Pay for their dresses and transportation to the wedding city (not lodging).

USHERS: DUTIES AND RESPONSIBILITIES

Ushers serve as the official greeters of all guests at the ceremony and as such should be in place at least one hour before the ceremony begins. Very often a head usher is appointed to oversee the ushers, which relieves the best man of both attending to the groom and keeping watch over the ushers.

The head usher should receive any lists of guests who are to be seated in a specific pew and should be aware of the importance and sequence of seating special guests, including the mothers and grandmothers of the bride and groom. He also makes sure that programs, if used, are handed to guests when they are seated.

The head usher is also the recipient of a list of people who are given special flowers or corsages on arrival if the flowers have not been delivered to the recipients beforehand. The people who receive these special tokens of affection or thanks may include relatives (mothers or grandmothers, for example) or friends who have helped out in some way or who have been given an honor role.

Finally, the head usher should check that all ushers are dressed properly and wearing their boutonnieres on the left side, stem down. He also makes sure that the ushers know how to usher: how to greet guests, how to offer an arm to a single woman guest, and how to precede a couple to their seats.

When the seating in the church is imbalanced—when one side, whether the bride's or the groom's, has more people than the other—the head usher is to instruct the ushers to ask guests whether they would mind sitting on the other side.

The head usher should also help gather the wedding party for photographs either before or after the ceremony and ensure that transportation arrangements have been made for all members of the wedding party to and from the ceremony.

In general, ushers have the following duties:

- Participate in a party for the groom.
- Contribute to the groomsmen's gift to the groom; usually give an individual gift to the couple.
- Review any special seating situations with the head usher before the ceremony begins.
- Greet guests as they arrive.
- Seat the eldest woman first if a group of guests arrives simultaneously.
- Ask guests whether they are to be seated on the bride's side (left, from the back) or the groom's side (right, from the back).
- Offer his right arm to female guests (with the guest's escort walking behind) or ask a couple to follow behind as he leads the way to their seat.
- Walk to the left side of a male guest.
- Hand guests a program when they are seated.
- Put the aisle runner in place after guests are seated, before the processional begins.
- Know the order for seating: special guests, grandmothers of the bride and groom, groom's mother, and bride's mother last.
- Remove pew ribbons, one row at a time, after the ceremony.
- Close windows and check pews for articles left behind or discarded programs after the ceremony.
- Be prepared to direct guests to the reception site (perhaps having extra maps available).
- Dance with bridesmaids and other guests at the reception.
- Look after elderly relatives or friends.
- Participate in garter ceremony, if there is one, and encourage other single men to participate, too.
- Coordinate return of rented apparel with head usher or best man.
- Pay for their own wedding attire and transportation to the wedding city (not lodging).

JUNIOR BRIDESMAIDS: DUTIES AND RESPONSIBILITIES

Junior bridesmaids are girls between 8 and 14, who are too old to be flower girls and too young to be bridesmaids. Their single duty is to walk in the procession, as instructed. They are not expected to give showers, although they may be invited to attend, nor do they stand in the receiving line unless asked.

They are expected to attend the rehearsal and may be included at the rehearsal dinner, depending on their ages. Having junior bridesmaids in your wedding is entirely optional.

FLOWER GIRL: DUTIES AND RESPONSIBILITIES

The flower girl is often a young relative of the bride, who is between three and seven years old. She walks directly before the ring bearer in the procession and directly behind him in the recessional. Although she attends the rehearsal, she does not usually go to the rehearsal dinner, nor does she stand in the receiving line. Her dress and accessories should be paid for by her family. The bride may ask one of the bridesmaids to look after the flower girl, taking charge of checking her appearance, making sure she is present for formal pictures, helping her manage her meal, and escorting her to the ladies room.

The flower girl may scatter petals from a basket she holds, although this is often too overwhelming for a young child to manage in front of a large group of people. It is usually easier for her to carry either a small basket of flowers or a tiny nosegay of flowers similar to those carried by the bridesmaids. As with junior bridesmaids, having a flower girl in your wedding is optional.

RING BEARER: DUTIES AND RESPONSIBILITIES

A small boy between three and seven years old is chosen for this duty, which is entirely optional. The traditional dress is short pants with an Eton jacket, preferably white but occasionally navy; sometimes ring bearers wear blazers. Small editions of the ushers' costumes are not worn except by some groups in other countries, where identical dress is the tradition. The ring bearer immediately precedes the bride in the processional.

The ring bearer carries the rings, or a facsimile of the rings, on a white velvet or satin cushion. If the rings are actually the ones that are to be used, they should be fastened to the cushion with a very thin thread or placed over a firmly fixed hat pin. The best man takes the rings from the cushion at the proper moment.

TRAIN BEARERS AND PAGES:
DUTIES AND RESPONSIBILITIES

Train bearers and pages may be included in the wedding party, although they usually participate only in very elaborate, formal weddings. The presence of too many very young children in the wedding party may detract from the solemnity of the ceremony. Unless the bride's gown is so elaborate that the maid of honor can't manage it or unless the pageantry of the processional and recessional calls for the addition of train bearers and pages, the flower girl and ring bearer suffice as the youngest participants.

OTHER HONOR ROLES

In some parts of the country, particularly in the South, it is often the custom to have relatives and friends who have a special relationship with the couple help out at the ceremony or reception. Those who fill these "honor roles" are identified by matching corsages in wedding colors and can be found pouring coffee or tea, serving cake at a house wedding, greeting guests, distributing rose petals, birdseed, or bubble-blowers, or handing out ceremony programs. They also may serve as liturgical assistants, such as readers, lectors, soloists, cantors, deacons, and altar assistants.

Eliciting the help of these special relatives and friends bestows honor on them and gives them a way to participate without having to invest in the cost of wedding party attire. They should be included in wedding photographs with the bride and groom, and their names should be listed in a newspaper announcement along with those of the wedding party.

CHAPTER 9

WEDDING EVENTS AND PARTIES

A wedding party or pre-wedding event can be as fun, joyous, and celebratory as the wedding itself. It wasn't always so: In some cultures, pre-wedding get-togethers were anything but happy. Arranged marriages, a matter of course in many countries, seldom led to joyous celebrations. In the Middle East, women would gather and sing mournful songs until the day of the wedding, regretting and lamenting the loss of the bride and the life she was about to enter.

Today things are different, and free choice indicates a happy choice, permitting joy to surround everything having to do with a wedding. While no events other than the wedding itself are necessary for the marriage to be celebrated, those that occur should be festive occasions that heighten the excitement of the impending big day.

WEDDING SHOWERS

A wedding shower is a gathering of friends in honor of a forthcoming marriage. It is a celebration distinguished by the "showering" of gifts on the guest of honor, the bride, or increasingly, both the bride and groom. A shower may take the form of a morning coffee, a luncheon, a tea, a cocktail party, or a buffet dinner, and may be held on any day of the week that is convenient for the guest of honor, the hostess, and the majority of guests.

Ideally, wedding showers should be held from two weeks to two months prior to the wedding. A shower that takes place too close to the wedding date may be more of an inconvenience than a party for the bride, who is likely to be inundated with chores in the last busy days. A shower held too early may occur before the bride knows what she needs and before her wedding plans are firm. There are, however, many varying circumstances, particularly due to complicated logistics, school calendars, and work schedules. Exceptions to the timing guideline may well be necessary!

WHO HOSTS THE SHOWER

Contrary to some misconceptions, bridesmaids are *not required* to host a shower, although they certainly may do so. One of an attendant's duties is to "host or co-host a shower"—*if* she chooses to do so. Friends of the bride and groom, friends of parents, and members of the wedding party who are not immediate family may host a shower, as may an office staff or other colleagues. Traditionally, the bride or groom's immediate family members do not host a shower; doing so can appear self-serving—and be seen as a request for gifts. This guideline can be broken under extraordinary circumstances. For example, when a bride-to-be comes from a far distance to visit her future family prior to the wedding, the groom's sisters or mother may correctly give her a shower. Etiquette is meant to make life easier, not impose unnecessary or impractical rules. When the circumstances warrant it, as they do in this case, the rules of etiquette are bent—and a bride far from home is given a warm welcome.

THE GUEST LIST

A shower guest list is generally made up of close friends, attendants, and family members. Normally, anyone invited to a shower should be invited to the wedding. One exception would be when coworkers wish to throw an office shower for the bride, even though all are not being invited to the main event. The shower in this case is their way of wishing the couple well.

Since the hostess is the person paying the bills and providing the space, it is she who decides on the number of guests. If the shower is not a surprise, it is sometimes wise to elicit input from the bride about the guest list.

Attendants and mothers are generally included on lists for wedding showers but are not required to bring gifts to each party. They can, if they wish,

PRACTICE BOUQUETS

The bride and her attendants need something to carry during the wedding rehearsal so that they can learn how to hold their arms and manage their bouquets. The solution? Practice bouquets made at showers. A bridesmaid or other friend pokes holes in paper plates and affixes the bows and ribbons from the bride's gifts to the top, tying them underneath. Voilà! Something to carry.

Wedding Events and Parties

THE FIRST SHOWER

The first wedding shower was said to have taken place in 18th-century Netherlands, when a bride's father did not care for her choice of a husband, a poor miller. Accordingly, he refused to give her a dowry, thereby eliminating her chance of marrying her beloved. The groom was not to be deterred, however, and he shared his plight with the townspeople. Because he had always been generous to hungry families in the community, giving them flour at no charge, they joined forces and shared their wares and riches with the couple, showering the bride with enough of a dowry to make the marriage possible. The father was so impressed by the neighbors' "shower" that he consented to the marriage.

bring small, joint, inexpensive but thoughtful presents. Other guests should not be invited to multiple showers, since being invited to many parties puts a serious strain on their budgets. In fact, showers for the bride and/or couple ideally are limited to two, with different guests being invited to each.

If the bride has been married before, she may be given a shower, but it's better to cut back on inviting friends and relatives who were invited to a shower for her first wedding; of these she should invite only those who would feel slighted not to be included. If the bride is marrying for the first time but her groom has been married before, she certainly may have a shower.

One final word about guest lists: A huge shower that includes almost everyone invited to the wedding is in poor taste. The idea of an intimate party is lost, and the party becomes no more than a demand for more gifts. As such, it is little more than an imposition on those invited.

THEME SHOWERS

A shower needs no theme other than to celebrate the upcoming marriage of a couple. Sometimes, however, a hostess narrows or custom-designs the focus of a shower (often after discussions with the bride regarding the wedding couple's needs) to a certain theme. Guests are expected to bring gifts related to that theme, and the hostess may even provide theme-related food and decorations. The ideas for themes that might be applied are limitless. Some choices are as follows:

- **KITCHEN AND BATHROOM SHOWER.** Towels, utensils, soaps, everyday glasses, trivets, tablecloths.
- **SPA SHOWER.** Massage certificates, aromatherapy oils, grooming articles, robes.
- **HONEYMOON SHOWER.** Travel clock, travel kit, travel book.
- **LEISURE TIME SHOWER.** Movie tickets, board games, videos and CDs, cocktail glasses and napkins.
- **GOURMET COOK SHOWER.** Gourmet foods, gourmet utensils, books.
- **THE GREAT OUTDOORS SHOWER.** Badminton net, flower seeds and gardening tools, picnic basket, Japanese lanterns.
- **HAPPY HOLIDAYS SHOWER.** Decorations for every holiday of the year.
- **ROUND-THE-CLOCK-SHOWER.** Each guest brings a present appropriate for a different hour of the day. For example, if the hour is four in the afternoon, a guest might bring a teapot and a gourmet tea.
- **RECIPE SHOWER.** Guests are given recipe cards and asked to make up a menu including their favorite recipes. These cards are collected as they arrive and are put into a recipe box provided by the hostess. At some recipe showers, guests may even prepare one of their recipes.
- **LABOR OF LOVE SHOWER.** Promises, not gifts, are brought to this shower, where friends pledge to paint, wallpaper, garden, or donate their talents in any number of ways.

ABSENTEE SHOWERS

A proxy shower is one given for a bride who cannot attend or who lives far away. Although a proxy shower is an acceptable way of celebrating, it can pose problems for the hostess who is responsible for sending the gifts to the bride. The hostess asks guests to bring their gifts unwrapped so that everyone can see them, after which she provides a variety of wrapping paper and ribbons for the guests to wrap their gifts. She then packs the gifts into large cartons and mails them to the bride. At most proxy showers, a telephone call is made to the bride or the couple so that they can thank their friends.

SHOWER INVITATIONS

Invitations to wedding showers are often written on commercial fill-in shower cards, which are available in a great variety of styles. They may also be short personal notes or informal cards. In some cases, invitations are telephoned or issued in person, as might occur when a hostess asks her coworkers to a shower for one of their colleagues.

The name of the guest of honor and the theme and related gift (if there is a theme) should be noted on every invitation. In the event of a kitchen or bathroom shower, the couple's color preferences should be noted. In the case of a lingerie shower, the bride's sizes should be included. The invitation must not, however, include a registry list; guests who need to know where the couple is registered should call the hostess and ask.

OPENING GIFTS

Showers are the one event where gifts are always expected; in fact, by definition guests "shower" the bride with gifts. In general, shower gifts should be inexpensive. Guests can, however, pool their resources and go in on one large, expensive gift for the couple instead of several smaller ones.

The opening of gifts is the high point of all showers. After refreshments are served, the guests gather around while the bride (or the bride and groom together if it is a joint shower) opens the packages one by one and thanks each giver.

One of the bridesmaids sits beside the bride and makes a list of the gifts and who gave them, making sure the gift cards are kept with their respective gifts. Very often, gifts are passed around the room so that everyone can see them.

THANKING GUESTS AND HOSTS

In general, the bride is not required to send thank-you notes for shower gifts—as long as the giver is present at the shower and is thanked directly, in person. If time permits, however, it's a very nice touch to follow up a verbal thank-you with a written one. In some communities it is customary for the bride to send thank-you notes regardless of whether she personally thanked the giver. The bride must always send a thank-you to those she was unable to thank at the party and those who have sent a gift but were not able to attend the shower. When the shower is a surprise, the bride can send an arrangement of flowers to her hostess with a personal note of thanks, preferably on the day after the shower. At the same time, she should phone the hostess to say thank-you.

When the shower is not a surprise, the bride should give the hostess a thank-you gift, as a way of showing her appreciation. She can give her a personal gift or send flowers beforehand so that they can be used by the hostess as a shower decoration. After the shower, the bride follows up with both a thank-you call and a note.

BRIDESMAIDS' LUNCHEON

In many communities, the bridesmaids host a "farewell" luncheon or tea for the bride, either in addition to a shower or instead of a shower. This luncheon usually takes place close to the wedding, particularly if bridesmaids live in a different community and will be arriving only in time for the wedding celebrations.

In other communities, the bride and her mother host a luncheon or tea for the bridesmaids as a respite in the midst of a busy time—and as a thank-you to the attendants for their presence and support.

A bridesmaids' luncheon is little different from any other lunch party. The table may be more elaborately decorated, and the linens are often white or the bride's chosen wedding colors. The bridesmaids' luncheon is an opportune time for the bride to give her bridesmaids their individual gifts, thanking them for being a part of her wedding.

For the bride and attendants who work during the day, a more convenient get-together may be after work, at a small cocktail party or intimate dinner. Another venue could be a day spa, where they all could share a pre-wedding pampering.

BACHELOR PARTY

The bachelor party of legend is a sodden good-bye to old bachelor days, an event where the groom and his ushers share an evening of abandonment a night or two before the wedding that usually includes a great deal of drinking. The reality these days is that bachelor parties and dinners are much more low-key affairs and aren't even held as often as they used to be, in part because ushers and friends may be scattered far and wide. Work can also prevent a wedding party from gathering for a bachelors' night out.

Traditionally, the bachelor party included the breaking of glasses, a custom that originated during toasts to the bride's health. The stem of the wine glass was broken so that it "might never serve a less honorable purpose." This highly impractical custom has been retired for decades, its only remnant being a toast toward the end of the dinner, when the bridegroom rises, holds his glass aloft, and says, "To my bride!" The other men rise and drink the toast standing, and thus ends the party.

If a dinner is held, it is usually hosted by the ushers and held in the private dining room of a restaurant or in a club. Aside from toasting the bride and reminiscing, the bridegroom's farewell dinner is like any other dinner among friends, although it might include the groom's father, brothers, and the bride's brothers. Instead of a dinner party, the groom and his buddies might spend the day on a boat, at the beach, on the golf course, playing baseball or football, or enjoying a picnic.

A bachelor party is certainly not off-limits for a second-time groom. His status as a bachelor alone fits the bill.

BACHELORETTE PARTY

As a recent invention designed in the spirit of equality, the bachelorette party is given by a bride's female friends. It differs from the bridesmaids' luncheon by usually being held at night including toasts and a dinner. The guest list also includes other friends in addition to the attendants.

APPRECIATION PARTY

Instead of trying to schedule a series of luncheons and bachelor and bachelorette parties, a couple might host an appreciation party instead. Invited are attendants and anyone else who has given generously of their time and ideas to help make the wedding wonderful. The appreciation party is often a casual affair—a barbecue or picnic, perhaps—especially if the rehearsal dinner is to be formal. It is usually held just before the wedding, when everyone has gathered, and is another prime opportunity for the bride and groom to give their attendants gifts of appreciation. An appreciation party can also be held after the couple returns from their honeymoon, if their attendants and special friends live close enough to attend.

PRE-WEDDING LUNCHEON

For a late-afternoon wedding, a small luncheon for the bridal party may be given by friends or neighbors. This takes the burden off the busy mother of the bride to host yet another entertainment on her daughter's wedding day. It may be as elaborate as the host and hostess wish, but a simple and relaxed lunch may be just the ticket to put an excited and nervous bridal party at ease.

The bride and groom aren't required to attend; it depends on their schedule. If they don't attend, it should never be because of that musty old superstition that the bridegroom should not see his bride before the ceremony on the day of the wedding. The superstition stems from the days when marriages were arranged and the groom might never have seen the bride. Because there was the chance that he might take one look at her and bolt, it was safer for them to meet for the first time at the altar!

PARTIES FOR OUT-OF-TOWN GUESTS

A lovely gift from relatives or friends is a party for out-of-town guests and early-arriving wedding attendants. This relieves the bride's parents of extra meals and housework before the wedding and gives guests a chance to spend time together in an informal atmosphere. Invitations should be sent well in advance so that guests can plan their travel itinerary accordingly. Often the party is put on by multiple hosts, who share the expenses and work in order to have a bigger, more elaborate fete.

These parties can be held at home or in a club or restaurant. In warm weather they may take the form of a barbecue or a swimming party. In the winter, a sleigh ride or a skating party could be organized, followed by a cozy fireside buffet. Included may be the attendants, the couple's families, their close friends, and friends of their parents.

THE REHEARSAL

The only people required to attend the rehearsal are the bride and groom, the attendants, and the bride's parents. Since the groom's parents have no active part in the ceremony, they needn't be present. If they are invited by the bride to attend, they should accept graciously but recognize their roles as observers only; unless asked, they should not express their opinions regarding the proceedings. Also present will be the officiant and the organist or musician playing the processional and recessional, along with soloists and readers. The wedding consultant, if you have one, should also be on hand to help instruct the ushers, line the wedding party up correctly, and help with the spacing and pace of each person as they practice walking up the aisle. If there are young children participating in the ceremony, their presence is required only if the rehearsal is not held too late at night. If they attend, they are generally accompanied by their parents.

A tradition in years past held that it was bad luck for the bride to take part in the rehearsal, so her part was taken by a stand-in. The modern bride is no longer that superstitious and recognizes the need to rehearse and feel comfortable in following the ceremony.

Although the traditional marriage service is a familiar one to most, it is easy to forget the sheer volume of details that go into its planning. Add to that the excitement and nervousness all involved may be feeling on the big day. It is essential, therefore, that the wedding-party participants pay close attention to the officiating clergy during the rehearsal. It is even more important to pay attention when a service is unfamiliar or nontraditional.

WHEN TO HOLD THE REHEARSAL

The rehearsal is scheduled with the officiant at a time when all attendants will be present. For a Saturday wedding, it is usually held on Friday afternoon or early evening. The closer to the wedding the rehearsal takes place, the better the chances that everyone will remember what to do and all will go smoothly.

WHAT TO WEAR

People taking part in the rehearsal or attending as observers should remember that they are in a house of worship and dress accordingly. This means no shorts or jeans and, in some houses of worship, no bare arms or legs. When the wedding is taking place at a secular location, clothing might be more informal, unless the rehearsal is to be followed immediately by a dinner requiring dressier attire.

If the bride's gown has a long train, she will need a simulated train for the rehearsal. She can do so by pinning a sheet or a length of fabric to her outfit so that she can practice walking with it. This also gives her maid of honor an opportunity to practice keeping the train in place during the ceremony and the recessional.

DURING THE REHEARSAL

The actual service is not read at the rehearsal. The officiant simply tells the couple the order in which the words of the service come and what their responses will be. The couple do not repeat the responses or vows. The officiant might ask the bride and groom to recite one verse, however, so they can find the right tone and volume.

An aisle runner, if there is one, is discussed with the ushers. The timing and signals of placing the runner is determined and discussed so that the officiant knows when the bride's mother has been seated, that the bride has arrived, and when the service should begin.

The organist is also present at the rehearsal and plays the processional so that pace and spacing can be practiced, and any soloists or readers accompanied.

The order of the procession is established, and the attendants walk up the aisle two or three times until all goes smoothly.

Everyone is placed at the chancel to make sure that all fit comfortably and that the lineup looks symmetrical. The maid of honor learns when to take the bride's bouquet and how to monitor whether the bride's gown or train needs rearranging without fussing or attracting attention to herself.

The best man and the maid of honor learn when to give the rings to the officiant and how to remove the rings if they are affixed to a pillow carried by the ring bearer.

The officiant should know in advance whether the bride will be wearing a face veil. He can then explain when it should be turned back, and a decision is made on who will do so.

The ushers are instructed by the officiant or the wedding consultant on their roles in escorting guests. They will be shown how to offer an arm and how to remove pew ribbons, noting which pews have been set aside for special seating. They will also learn how to escort guests into the ceremony site and how to help them exit in an orderly fashion at the ceremony's end. Because the ushers are the first people guests see, they should be confident about what they are doing and look as though they have done it for years.

The manner in which attendants will leave the chancel—whether in pairs or singly—is arranged at the rehearsal. All should practice the recessional at least once, just to ensure that they will know how to exit. (The pace of the recessional will be set by the bride and groom on the day of the wedding, and the attendant will follow at a natural walk.)

REHEARSAL DINNER

The rehearsal dinner generally takes place the night before the wedding, regardless of when the rehearsal is held. It has become custom but not obligatory for the groom's family to host the rehearsal party. If they do so, they may elicit the help of the bride or her mother in selecting a location—especially if they are from another town and unfamiliar with what is available. In this case, preliminary plans are made by telephone or confirmation letter, and the final arrangements are made when they arrive for the wedding celebrations.

If the groom's family does not or cannot give the rehearsal dinner, it may be arranged by the bride's family. It may take the form of a beach party, a picnic, a simple buffet, or a formal dinner. The only guide is that the rehearsal party should not be more formal than the wedding reception will be, particularly if the party is given by the groom's parents.

REHEARSAL PARTY GUEST LIST

Those invited to attend a rehearsal party should include the members of the wedding party (except for the flower girl and the ring bearer), the officiant, parents and grandparents of the bride and groom, and siblings of the bride and groom if they are not in the wedding party. If the bride and/or groom have stepparents, they are invited with their spouses if they have remarried but should not be seated next to their former spouses. The wedding party's husbands, wives, fiancées, fiancés, and live-in companions should be invited, but dates are not included. The children of the bride and groom from a previous marriage also attend, unless they are too young. After that, it is optional that any number of people may attend, including out-of-town guests, close friends, aunts and uncles, and godparents. Junior bridesmaids and junior ushers may attend if the hour is not late, as may the flower girl and ring bearer (if supervised).

INVITATIONS

Invitations are generally written on informals or fill-in cards or may simply be handwritten or telephoned. If you are inviting a good number of out-of-town guests, the written invitation is the best way to go; it serves as a tangible reminder of the time, date, and address of the party.

DURING THE DINNER

The rehearsal dinner is the perfect occasion for the presentation of the couple's gifts to the bridesmaids and ushers, if they haven't already given them. It is also a good time for the attendants to present their gifts to the bride and groom, usually by the maid of honor and the best man and often accompanied by a short speech or toast.

Toasts should be made during dinner, not after; otherwise, the night can drag on interminably. The host—often the groom's father—should make the first toast, welcoming the guests and expressing his feelings about the forthcoming marriage. He is generally followed with a return toast by the bride's father and then by toasts from ushers, bridesmaids, and anyone else who wishes to say something.

The attendants' toasts, while sentimental to some extent, are often filled with anecdotes, jokes, and poems regaling guests with tales from the bride and groom's past. Sometimes the bride and groom stand and speak about each other, and they generally end by proposing a toast first to their respective parents and then to all their friends and relatives in attendance.

THE AFTERGLOW

When out-of-town guests are staying overnight on the day of the wedding, the bride's family might invite them home for a late snack or even for dinner after an afternoon reception. This is not at all necessary or expected. In fact, the last thing the parents of the bride may want to do is entertain, but often the afterglow of all the events leading up to that moment carries them on to another gathering with friends.

The post-wedding entertainment, which can be provided by a close friend or relative, can be as simple as takeout pizza offered to guests who have changed into comfortable clothes or as elaborate as a next-day brunch.

The fun of the gathering is in hearing post-wedding stories and impressions. Often the parents are so busy and swept up in the emotion of the occasion that they miss some of the details.

The invitations to such gatherings are often spontaneous, with the host and hostess encouraging people to stop by before they go home or back to their hotels.

If the reception ends late and guests prefer to turn in for the evening, the after-wedding party can take the form of a breakfast or brunch the next day. In this case, the gathering is probably planned, and it is generally the bride's parents or a friend who offers to host the occasion. Notes or informal invitations are sent to guests ahead of time so that they can plan their departure time around the party.

A BELATED RECEPTION: THE WEDDING PARTY

Couples whose wedding is small and private may decide to throw themselves a party in the weeks following the ceremony to share their happiness with friends. It can be as formal or as informal as they like and can even have a wedding cake to be cut and served to guests. No gifts are expected—only the good wishes of those present.

HOSTED BY THE BRIDE'S FAMILY

When a couple is married privately or away from home and returns shortly thereafter, the bride's family may want to give them the reception they weren't able to have. It may include all the components of any wedding reception. If the bride wore a wedding gown for the ceremony, she may wear it again at the reception, if she so chooses. Invitations would read:

Mr. and Mrs. William DeRosa
request the pleasure of your company
at a reception
in honor of
Mr. and Mrs. John Nelson

THE GROOM'S PARENTS' CELEBRATION

If the bride and groom were married in her hometown and the friends of the groom and his family live too far away to attend, his mother and father might give a reception for them the first time they come to visit after the honeymoon. They may even host a reception if the couple visits them a short time before the wedding takes place.

Invitations to such a reception are generally fill-in cards or informals, with "In honor of Priscilla and James" or "to meet Priscilla Holmes" written at the top. They should be mailed two to four weeks before the party.

This party does not parallel the couple's wedding reception. There is no wedding cake, and the couple and any attendants who live near enough to be there do not wear their wedding clothes. When the party is held after the wedding, however, and the groom's mother would like guests to see the wedding gown—and the bride would like to wear it—she may certainly receive in it and then change after everyone has arrived.

The party is usually in the form of a tea or cocktail buffet. The host and hostess stand at the door with the newlyweds and introduce them to everyone who has not met them. The bride's parents are invited as well, but they should not feel that they must attend.

Chapter 10

PLANNING THE CEREMONY

THE DETAILS OF YOUR CEREMONY

Start firming up the plans for your wedding ceremony by making an appointment to see your chosen officiant. You will need to confirm the responsibilities and details of your ceremony, as well as discuss any issues or concerns you may have. You will also want to discuss the ways you might like to personalize the ceremony.

Among the details you will want to confirm:

- Date, time, and length of ceremony
- Site of ceremony: church, side chapel, synagogue, wedding facility, home, other
- Number of guests the site will comfortably hold

If your chosen officiant is a priest, rabbi, or minister, before doing *anything,* you will need to let him or her know if yours is an interfaith marriage or if neither of you are practicing members of that particular faith. You will need to discuss whether you plan to marry in a house of worship or at a secular site. Each religion has different standards, rules, and restrictions. Clergy often have restrictions on whom they can marry and where they can marry them. (Catholic priests, for example, can only marry couples in a Catholic church.)

Many religions also require that couples wishing to marry provide certain documents according to church or synagogue law. A Baptismal certificate, First

---

WHY DO WE "TIE THE KNOT?"

A Chinese legend says that the gods tied an invisible red string around the ankles of a man and a woman destined to be husband and wife. With every year that passes, the string, which can never be untied, becomes shorter until the couple is finally united in marriage.

MARY-ELIZABETH TONDREAU

and

PATRICK JAMES O'NEILL

request the honor of your presence

at their wedding on

Saturday, May 8th, 1993

at three o'clock

St. Paul's Chapel

Columbia University

New York, NY

PLEASE ENTER THROUGH
THE MAIN GATE AT
116TH STREET &
BROADWAY

Ms. Katharine Wilhe...
8

Miss Sharada Strasmore
9

Ms. Emily Wilheim
1

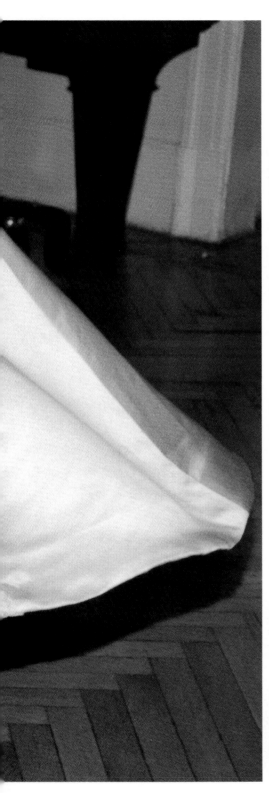

Communion certificate, and Confirmation certificate, for example, are often required in Catholic churches. If you plan to marry in a parish separate from the one to which you belong, you may need to provide a letter of permission to marry from your priest.

QUESTIONS TO ASK AT THE CEREMONY SITE

Be prepared for your meeting with the officiant and/or ceremony site manager. Make a list of all of your concerns and questions, which may include:

- What kinds of restrictions does the ceremony site have?
- Are there restrictions concerning dress? Bare shoulders or arms? Head coverings? You will need to know this before you select the bridal and attendants' gowns.
- What latitude do you have in writing some or all of your ceremony yourselves?
- Is photography and videography allowed? If so, when and how may photographs and/or videotape be taken? Before, during and/or after the ceremony?
- When should you make an appointment with the organist or music director to select music?
- Can you have instrumental or vocal soloists?
- What kinds of floral arrangements/decorations are permitted?
- How do you arrange access for a florist to decorate? What is the site policy on the disposition of flowers after the ceremony?
- Are any other weddings scheduled the same day as yours?
- Is there a room for dressing prior to the service?
- Is there a way to assure that space is left vacant for the cars that will carry the bride and her attendants to the front of the building?
- Is it permitted to throw rose petals or birdseed outside the building?
- Is an aisle carpet or runner provided?
- For a Christian ceremony: Will communion be part of the ceremony?
- For a Jewish ceremony: Who will provide the *chuppah* and may it be decorated with flowers?
- What fees are required for the use of the facility? For the organist, the cantor, and additional musicians? For the sexton? For the priest, minister, or rabbi?
- May a receiving line be formed at the ceremony site?

Planning the Ceremony

181

If you haven't already done so, be sure to make a reservation for the wedding rehearsal at this meeting. You should do so as soon as possible—a site schedule that is heavily booked on your wedding day is likely to be equally tight on the day before, the traditional time to hold the rehearsal. Ask if there are restrictions or rules for the rehearsal, such as clothing regulations or guidelines on who may attend. Find out how long the rehearsal will run so that the rehearsal dinner can be planned (if you're having one). Make sure to include a few extra minutes in the schedule in case the rehearsal runs overtime.

If you and your partner plan to participate in premarital counseling from the officiant (and some religions require that you do so), this is also the time to set the dates for appointments.

The answers your officiant provides about the wedding ceremony will probably inform your other decisions. For example, if the taking of photographs or videotaping is only allowed during certain times in the ceremony, you can discuss this with the photographer and decide how you will work around it.

PERSONALIZING YOUR CEREMONY

Often couples like to include personal readings, musical interludes, or self-penned vows in the wedding ceremony. It's a lovely idea, but keep in mind that any additions will lengthen the total time of the ceremony and affect the timing of your reception.

Vows and Readings

If you want to write your own vows or select additional readings, ask the officiant whether this is permissible. If so, ask for a copy of the liturgy for the wedding ceremony and ask the officiant to mark those places where you may add a reading. Find out whether the readings must be scriptural or can include secular pieces; your officiant may even be able to provide a list of reading choices. Finally, find out whether the officiant needs to review your selections.

Music

Some houses of worship stipulate that any musician performing in a wedding ceremony must be engaged through the music department of the church or synagogue. Ask the officiant whether the prelude, processional, ceremony, and recessional music must be all sacred music, or if the church allows secular, classical, or popular selections. You can discuss specific choices with the music director or organist once you know the choices that are available to you. Discuss, too, whether you want hymns sung at your ceremony, and if and where in the ceremony additional music can be inserted, such as a solo by a flutist, trumpeter, guitar player, or vocalist.

Some houses of worship even have modernized sound recording equipment and can provide audiocassettes as mementos.

Additional Clergy

If you want a co-officiant at your wedding—a relative, perhaps, or a retired minister to whom you are particularly close—ask your officiant if this is permissible. If so, provide his or her name, telephone number, and address, and send the reciprocal information to the visiting clergy. That way, they can communicate directly, if they wish, and plan the order of officiating. If the visiting clergy is from another faith, your officiant may be unable or unwilling to include him. If he agrees to the arrangement, however, discuss with him ways the service may be structured.

Flowers

Ask whether there are any restrictions governing flowers and decorations. Some houses of worship will not let you remove flowers used in holy ceremonies. Ask if there is any problem with your removing the flowers after the ceremony, whether to use as reception decorations, to deliver to shut-ins, area hospitals, or nursing homes, or to give to friends.

Discuss the types of arrangements that are permitted at the site. Find out the name of the person the florist should contact so that he can arrange access to the site on the day of the wedding.

INTERFAITH MARRIAGES

If yours is an interfaith marriage, you will need to make sure that performing your ceremony is acceptable to the officiant and that the ceremony site allows interfaith marriages to be performed. If not, you will either have to select a different site for your ceremony or find a different officiant.

It is important for you and your intended to meet with officiants from both faiths, especially if you plan to have children and want to teach them the ways of both your faiths.

OTHER WEDDINGS

Ask your officiant to let you know if any other ceremonies are booked the same day. If there are other weddings scheduled the same day, you will need to know the times of these weddings in relation to yours. Having another wedding in close proximity to yours could affect the time you have to work on decorations, the arrival of your ushers, and the use of dressing rooms.

TRAFFIC OFFICER

From previous experience, the clergy person will know what kind of traffic congestion occurs when weddings take place and whether the services of a traffic officer are advisable. In some towns, they are required. If you are advised to have a traffic officer, call the local police department to make arrangements to hire an off-duty police officer or security guard.

The traffic officer or the officiant will also need to clear the area in front of the building to permit cars bringing the wedding party to the ceremony to park.

ROSE PETALS?

If you have your heart set on being showered with rose petals or some other celebratory symbol, be sure to ask your officiant if this processional option is allowed. Most churches don't permit the festive tossing of anything at the bride and groom as they leave the ceremony for the reception, because cleanup is too costly. Also, if you have your heart set on having rose petals scattered before you during the processional, keep in mind that petals are notoriously slippery. Instead of rose petals, some couples provide their guests with tiny bottles of bubbles, used for blowing toward them during the recessional. One warning if you do consider celebrating with bubbles: If they float onto your gown, they could cause staining. Other options: colored streamers or confetti. In any case, you should offer to pay extra for cleanup.

Do remember also that many couples decide to forgo scattering anything, for practical reasons. Rice is rarely used anymore, even though as a symbol of fertility it is deeply rooted in tradition. Rice can be damaging to birds and other wildlife, who cannot digest uncooked grains of rice. It is also almost impossible to rake, scoop, or pick up from grass and flower beds.

AISLE CARPET

Do you want a white carpet rolled up the aisle before the bridal attendants' and bride's procession? Some houses of worship have them available as a service or for a small fee. If not, most florists or limousine services can provide them. The "white carpet" is actually just a pressed-fiber strip, although sometimes canvas runners are still used. (Ask your officiant's advice. Some feel that aisle carpets are a terrible trip hazard.) Confirm when and how it is rolled out and how many ushers are required to place it successfully. It is a good idea, if possible, for the ushers to rehearse this maneuver.

RECEIVING LINE

Many brides and grooms prefer to receive at the ceremony instead of the reception site. Whether to have a receiving line directly after the ceremony can be discussed with your officiant. Your rabbi, priest, or minister will know best if the space and layout of the building lends itself to having a receiving line.

FEES

There is no time like your first meeting with your officiant to discuss fees. Ask what amounts are customary and when payments should be made for both his own duties and any ceremony costs. Pencil the figure and date into your planner.

AT-HOME CEREMONY TIPS

- Borrow or rent chairs from a church, school, social club, or rental company for seating your guests.
- Hang a wedding banner from the flagpole and decorate the banister with white satin ribbons.
- Recruit children to usher and take guests' coats.
- Hire off-duty police or responsible teens as parking valets.
- Refrain from watering the lawn the day of your ceremony so that you don't have muddy footprints in the house.

A few other items that should be confirmed at your first meeting with the officiant include:

- Whether there will be other service participants such as altar boys or acolytes, and whether it is the officiant's duty to arrange for them to be there. Find out whether they should be paid and, if so, how much, and whether they will attend the rehearsal.
- If you are using the services of a wedding consultant or coordinator, you should tell the minister, priest, or rabbi. If possible, arrange for them to meet or speak to discuss ceremony and rehearsal plans.
- Whether you will have premarital counseling sessions and ways to prepare for the counseling.
- Advice on guest parking so that you can include the information with the map and directions inserts in the invitations.
- The names you want your officiant to use in the ceremony. Also mention whether you will be taking the groom's last name.

ARRANGEMENTS FOR A CEREMONY AT ANOTHER SITE

Even if you plan to marry at a site separate from the officiant's church or synagogue, many of the preceding questions for the officiant still apply. In addition, you will need to know:

- Are there any restrictions on the kind of ceremony you can have if it is not conducted in a house of worship? If so, what? If not, is there perhaps more room to deviate from the standard wedding service?
- What are the travel needs of the officiant? Would he prefer to arrive at the ceremony in a hired car? Can you reimburse him for time, gas, and mileage if he chooses to drive?
- Will you need to provide an altar? A kneeling bench or cushions? An altar cloth? Candles? Any other liturgical items? If the answer is yes to any of these questions, ask for the names of resources who provide them. Ask whether makeshift arrangements will do, such as a table that can be used as an altar or a table runner that doubles as an altar cloth. If the ceremony site is a frequent wedding location, you may find that these items are already available.

A CIVIL CEREMONY

In general, you will need to make few arrangements for a civil ceremony to be held at the office of a justice of the peace or at town hall. The ceremony itself is simple and brief. The only things you'll need to do are fulfill the legal requirements and, often, provide two witnesses.

If a civil ceremony is to be conducted at another site, such as the bride's home, a garden, or a rented facility, the same arrangements need to be made as those for a religious ceremony outside of a house of worship—the exception being the need for liturgical items that aren't required for a civil ceremony.

If the bride and groom wish to personalize the order of a civil ceremony, they should arrange to meet with the justice of the peace or whoever will officiate to discuss the length of the service, any requirements, and a list of elements they may add to the service.

CLERGY FROM OUT-OF-TOWN

If you are having a clergy person from out of town officiate at your wedding, and you want to marry in a church or synagogue that he or she is not affiliated with, talk to the local clergy immediately. In some cases, it is required that the local officiant be present and participate in the service. In others, there is no such requirement, and the church or synagogue is literally turned over to the visiting officiant. Sometimes, a payment to the local clergy person is requested for his help in making arrangements.

Your obligation? Check what the regulations are before asking the out-of-town officiant to perform the ceremony. Get permission to use the church or synagogue. Coordinate the communication between the out-of-town officiant and his contact person at the church or synagogue where your ceremony is to

THE FABRIC OF LIFE

Jewish brides and grooms can start a family tradition and create an heirloom keepsake by asking friends and family to contribute favorite squares of fabric selected for the occasion from their own sewing kits. Piece the squares together to create a "chuppah" full of memories that represents everyone who is celebrating your marriage with you.

be held. Your officiant may even need a key to the building to have access to a robing room or to set up a Holy Communion.

If the out-of-town clergy is to be the sole officiant, you should get a list from him of any ceremony needs ahead of time.

Finally, it is your responsibility to pay the travel, lodging, and meal expenses of any clergy person you invite from out of town.

RELIGIOUS CEREMONIES

Even with so many different religious rituals and cultural traditions being used in weddings today, there is generally one common thread. Most of the major religions share one mutual belief, and that is that marriage is a joyous occasion worthy of high celebration. Using happiness as the common denominator, today's brides and grooms from different religious and ethnic backgrounds are able to blend the cultural traditions of one with the rituals of the other, by weaving those aspects that matter most to them and their families into the events surrounding their marriage.

Deciding on a ceremony can be a challenge—especially when families and friends have a wide range of practices and beliefs— but there are ways you can foster understanding and help everyone be a part of your wedding. One solution is to provide a wedding program, with the help of your clergy, which explains the symbolic meaning of different parts of the ceremony so that guests can follow along. Programs can also provide translations if parts of the ceremony are in another language.

If your faiths have strictures against interfaith marriage and offer no way for you to incorporate the two faiths in one ceremony, you must either be married in a civil ceremony or hold two separate ceremonies, one right after the other. If you do the latter, you'll need to decide whether guests will be invited to both ceremonies, or if they'll be invited instead to a reception for everyone, held after you've had two private ceremonies.

Whether yours will be a marriage of mixed faiths, one that integrates age-old traditions and rituals into a modern ceremony, or one that follows religious tradition to the letter, let your officiant guide you in choosing the right ceremony rites for you.

THE ROMAN CATHOLIC WEDDING CEREMONY

One of the seven sacraments of the Catholic Church is marriage, and as such it is treated seriously, requiring a proscribed series of religious and personal counseling sessions for both the bride and groom, even if one is not Catholic. Interfaith marriage is accepted as long as the partner of another faith complies with counseling requirements, and most priests will co-officiate with the clergy of the non-Catholic. Divorce is not recognized, however, so the bride or groom whose previous marriage did not end in annulment but rather in divorce is not permitted to be married in the Catholic Church if the ex-partner is still living. It is possible that someone not married in a Catholic ceremony but in a civil service and later divorced may remarry in the Catholic Church, which does not recognize civil marriages in the first place.

Inclusion of a Nuptial Mass is common, although not required. If it is conducted, it lengthens the approximately 20-minute ceremony to about an hour. It was once the case that a Nuptial Mass could be conducted only if both the bride and groom were Catholic, but today this is not a requirement, although the non-Catholic may not receive Holy Communion.

At the beginning of the service, the groom stands by the priest at the altar and the bride walks down the aisle, preceded by her attendants. The bride is met by the groom, and the two remain in front of the altar either kneeling, sitting, or standing throughout the ceremony. Their attendants either flank them or move to front pews in the church. The priest then often welcomes those present and gives a Homily about marriage. After the Homily, he asks if the couple has come freely to marry. They respond and join hands to exchange marriage vows. The priest blesses the rings, the groom puts the bride's ring on her finger, and she puts his ring on his finger; the nuptial blessing is then given, followed by the Mass if one is included. Only Roman Catholic guests are permitted to receive Communion. Throughout the ceremony, personalization and the participation of lay readers may take place, as well as the singing or playing of religious music.

THE EPISCOPAL WEDDING CEREMONY

Like the Catholic Church, the Episcopal Church considers marriage a sacrament and requires that at least one partner must be baptized in the name of the Holy Trinity. Interfaith marriage is accepted, and Episcopal priests are usually willing to co-officiate with other clergy if the couple wishes. If either the bride or groom has been divorced, she or he must receive a dispensation to marry again from the area bishop; if this is not done, the marriage may not take place in the church. Premarital counseling with the priest who will marry you is customary.

The celebration of Holy Eucharist may follow the wedding ceremony if the bride and groom wish. All baptized Christians are welcome to receive Communion.

The Episcopal ceremony is taken from *The Book of Common Prayer* and has five parts, which follow the processional of the bride and her attendants:

1. The priest begins with the call to worship: "Dearly Beloved, we have come together in the presence of God to witness and bless the joining together of this man and this woman in Holy Matrimony."
2. The declaration of consent
3. The ministry of the Word using one or more Scriptural passages
4. The exchange of vows and blessing of the rings
5. The blessing of the marriage

The attendants stand on both sides of the bride and the groom throughout. Personalization is permitted in the form of any number of readings and the inclusion of religious music—usually solos but sometimes hymns sung by the guests. The ceremony, with the celebration of Holy Eucharist, takes about 45 minutes. Without Communion, the service is about 20 minutes long.

BAPTIST, LUTHERAN, METHODIST, AND PRESBYTERIAN WEDDING CEREMONIES

The wedding ceremonies of mainstream Protestant churches are familiar to many; they are the ceremonies most frequently portrayed in movies and television shows. The ceremonies, in general, are very similar. Marriage is not a sacrament, but it is considered holy. Interfaith marriages are permitted and co-officiants welcomed, although the more conservative synods or branches may not permit a co-officiated Christian/non-Christian marriage. Premarital counseling is customary, usually conducted in a series of three or more private meetings with the minister who will conduct the ceremony. Holy Communion may be part of the ceremony if the bride and groom wish.

When the minister enters, followed by the groom and his best man, who stand to the side, the bride and her attendants begin the processional.

The ceremony consists of three parts:

1. The welcome and introduction by the minister
2. The exchange of vows and rings
3. The final blessing

In the charge to the couple, the minister may say to the bride, "Will you have this man to be your wedded husband to live together in holy matrimony? Will you love him, comfort him, honor and keep him in sickness and in health, in sorrow and in joy, and forsaking all others, be faithful to him as long as you both shall live?" He then repeats this charge to the groom.

The bride and groom may add readings and music to the ceremony and may write their own vows to replace the ones included in the church's worship book. The service, without additional readings and music or Communion, can take as little as 15 minutes.

ROMAN CATHOLIC, EPISCOPAL, AND MAINSTREAM PROTESTANT TRADITIONAL PROCESSIONAL, CEREMONY, AND RECESSIONAL

While individual clergy members follow specific procedures and may require a certain processional, order of service, and recessional, most Christian wedding ceremonies follow this order:

1. Guests are ushered to pews.
2. Prelude music is played.
3. Grandparents and other honored guests are ushered to their seats.
4. The parents of the groom are ushered in.
5. The mother of the bride is ushered to her seat.
6. The aisle runner, if used, is rolled out by the ushers.
7. The music selected for the processional of the attendants begins.
8. The clergy member enters the sanctuary.
9. The groom and best man enter and move to the center of the head of the aisle.
10. Attendants enter, ushers first, followed by bridesmaids, the maid of honor, and then the ring bearer and flower girl.

11. If separate processional music accompanies the entrance of the bride, it begins.

12. The bride enters accompanied by her father, her father and mother, her mother, or another escort, or she enters by herself.

13. The ceremony is conducted.

14. The minister pronounces the couple husband and wife.

15. The bride and groom kiss.

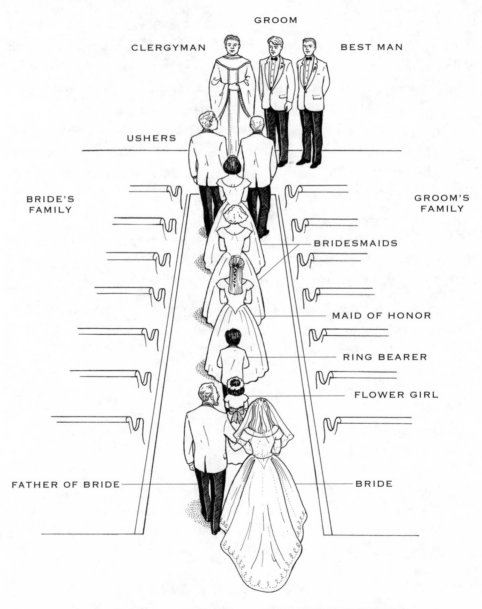

GROOM

CLERGYMAN   BEST MAN

USHERS

BRIDE'S FAMILY   GROOM'S FAMILY

BRIDESMAIDS

MAID OF HONOR

RING BEARER

FLOWER GIRL

FATHER OF BRIDE   BRIDE

TRADITIONAL PROCESSIONAL FOR A CHRISTIAN WEDDING

RING BEARER · GROOM · BRIDE · FLOWER GIRL

USHERS · BEST MAN · FATHER OF BRIDE · MAID OF HONOR · BRIDESMAIDS

CLERGYMAN

CHRISTIAN CEREMONY AT THE ALTAR

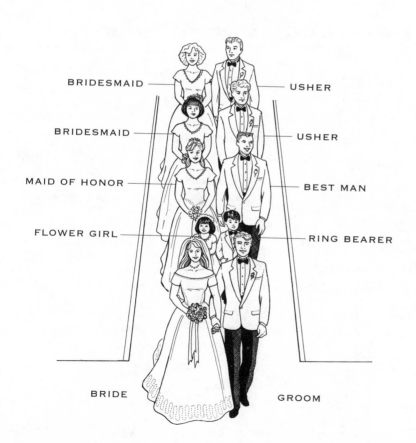

BRIDESMAID · USHER

BRIDESMAID · USHER

MAID OF HONOR · BEST MAN

FLOWER GIRL · RING BEARER

BRIDE · GROOM

TRADITIONAL RECESSIONAL FOR A CHRISTIAN WEDDING

16. The recessional music begins.
17. The bride and groom turn and walk up the aisle followed by their attendants.
18. The ushers return and escort the family members from the front pews.
19. The remaining guests exit beginning from the front.

THE EASTERN ORTHODOX WEDDING CEREMONY

Marriage is a Sacrament in Eastern Orthodox congregations, which can be Greek, Russian, Serbian, Syrian, Polish, and Yugoslavian, among other backgrounds. The ceremony is filled with symbolism, beginning outside the church doors with the Betrothal, when the rings are blessed and exchanged. The couple is then led by the priest into the church to stand on a white cloth in front of a wedding platform. A wedding icon is carried in the processional, and the couple is given lighted candles, which they hold during the service.

Much of the symbolism of the service is represented by threes. During the Betrothal, the priest beseeches God's blessings upon the rings and proceeds to bless the groom and the bride with the rings. He does this three times, in the Name of the Father and of the Son and of the Holy Spirit. He then places the rings on the ring fingers of the right hands of the couples, and the rings are exchanged three times.

The ring blessing is followed by the Sacrament of Holy Matrimony, which is followed by three prayers.

This service, along with the Byzantine Catholic Church service, then uses metal crowns or floral wreaths as a solemn part of the service, called The Crowning. The crowns, often attached to each other with a ribbon as a symbol that the two are now one, are placed on the heads of the bride and groom and exchanged between them. The crowns have several meanings, the two most important being the conformation to Biblical teachings that say God bestows His blessing upon His children in the form of crowns, and the identification of the bride and the groom as the beginning of a new kingdom.

The service, which can last up to one hour, continues with readings, with the presentation of the common cup to the bride and groom to symbolize that from that moment on they will share the same cup of life, and that whatever life has in store for them they will share equally and with the expression of joy. As a symbolic expression of joy, the priest takes the arm of the bridegroom and leads him and the bride around the table three times.

THE JEWISH WEDDING CEREMONY

Jewish weddings may be held anywhere that a canopy, or *chuppah,* can be erected and are most often held where the reception will follow. The *chuppah*

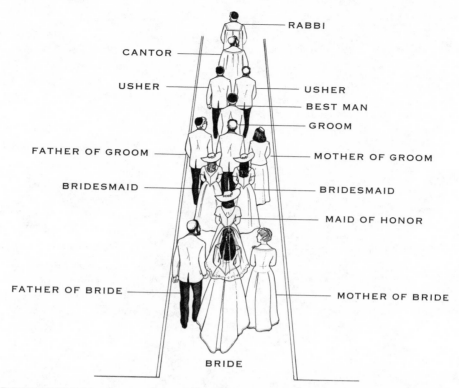

JEWISH PROCESSIONAL FOR CONSERVATIVE OR ORTHODOX CEREMONY

CONSERVATIVE OR ORTHODOX JEWISH CEREMONY, UNDER THE *CHUPPAH*

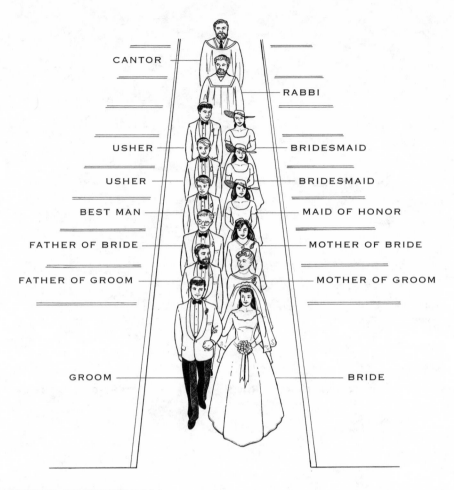

CANTOR

RABBI

USHER — BRIDESMAID

USHER — BRIDESMAID

BEST MAN — MAID OF HONOR

FATHER OF BRIDE — MOTHER OF BRIDE

FATHER OF GROOM — MOTHER OF GROOM

GROOM — BRIDE

JEWISH RECESSIONAL

symbolizes both the tents of ancient ancestors and the formation of the new home of the family being created beneath it. The *chuppah* can be decorated with flowers and may be constructed in a fixed position or held by special attendants. The bride and groom are escorted by their parents in the procession and gather, with their attendants, under the *chuppah*.

Intermarriage is not encouraged but nonetheless occurs, usually with a Reform rabbi presiding. Some Reform rabbis will also permit a co-officiant of another faith, but Orthodox and Conservative rabbis, as a rule, will not. Usually, even in a Reform congregation, a divorced woman cannot be remarried without a *get*, an official rabbinical document of divorce.

To begin the ceremony, which is usually conducted in a combination of Hebrew and English, the bride and groom take a sip of ceremonial wine and are blessed by the rabbi. The bride is given a plain gold wedding ring by the groom, and the marriage contract, or *ketubah,* is read aloud and presented to the couple.

A member of the family or a special guest then reads the Seven Blessings, after which the bride and groom again take a sip of wine, this time symbolizing the commitment of the marriage.

The ceremony ends with the groom stomping a glass wrapped carefully in a cloth to prevent shards flying while guests cry *"Mazel tov!,"* meaning good luck and congratulations. The breaking of the glass represents the destruction of the Temple in Jerusalem and is a reminder that even on such a joyous occasion it is important to remember that others may not be so fortunate.

The ceremony, which lasts about 20 minutes, ends with the recessional, led by the bride and groom and followed by the bride's parents, the groom's parents, the attendants, the rabbi, and the cantor, if one is participating.

Following the recessional, the bride and groom retire to a private room for several minutes before they join the reception. This lovely tradition is known as *yichud*, or "seclusion." These few minutes, which symbolize the couple's right to privacy, give the couple a brief time to be alone before the excitement of the rest of the day. Tradition also says that the couple is to share their first meal together, so they are often brought a small plate of favorite foods.

The reception is often begun with a blessing of the *challah*, a loaf of braided bread that here symbolizes the sharing of families and friends. The meal often concludes with grace and seven special benedictions, sung in Hebrew.

THE MORMON WEDDING CEREMONY

Members of The Church of Jesus Christ of Latter-Day Saints (Mormons) may be married in one of two ways: in a marriage ceremony or a civil ceremony. The marriage ceremony, the "sealing ordinance," is for couples of great faith. This sacred ceremony is always held in one of the church's dedicated temples. Members of the Mormon faith believe that when they are married, or sealed, in a temple by proper priesthood authority, their union may continue forever; they believe that marriage and family relationships can extend beyond the grave. Mormons proclaim that the family is ordained of God and that marriage between man and woman is essential to His eternal plan. Only faithful members may be participants in—and guests at—a temple wedding.

Mormons may also choose to be married in a civil ceremony. These are simple, sacred ceremonies usually held in a church or a home, and they may be attended by anyone. Church bishops, who are part of a lay ministry and receive no pay for conducting civil ceremonies, are nevertheless authorized to perform them.

It is typical after both types of ceremonies that a reception is held (often later in the evening) for any number of guests. Gifts for the couple are usually taken at this time.

THE ISLAMIC (MUSLIM) WEDDING CEREMONY

Marriage is a holy and desirable union under Islamic law. Although marriage is not a sacrament, it is a sacred covenant or contract. There is no objection to interfaith union, but there may be objection to intercultural marriage, which is seen as another issue entirely.

A Muslim marriage ceremony usually takes place in a mosque, at the bride's home, or in an office. When the groom arrives, attended by a *serbala* (the youngest boy in his family, usually the son of a sister), he and his *serbala* are given floral garlands in welcome.

The ceremony is conducted by an imam, who reads from the Koran. The bride, who is heavily veiled, and groom are seated apart during their wedding, often on opposite sides of the room. The bride's father and two witnesses ask the bride if she has agreed to the marriage, and the imam asks the groom if he has agreed. Assuming they have both agreed, the imam completes the marriage certificate.

A meal is served after this ceremony, but the bride and groom are still separated, each sitting with their own families. After the meal, the bride leaves, puts on all the jewelry she has been given for her wedding, and returns to sit next to the groom. Her veil is lifted.

Prior to the religious ceremony, the bride and groom are required to undertake civil preliminaries and may be required to go through a civil ceremony in addition to their religious ceremony. In this case, the main wedding reception does not take place until both ceremonies have been performed.

THE HINDU
WEDDING CEREMONY

Marriage is one of a series of holy sacraments in the Hindu faith, just as it is in the Roman Catholic Church. It is believed that marriage has a purifying quality. The wedding ceremony, which is conducted by a priest, can last all day in India. In the United States, the ceremony has been shortened to about 90 minutes, although cultural traditions surrounding the wedding can last several days. It does not have to be performed in a temple and is often conducted in the bride's home. Interfaith marriages are accepted.

Throughout the ceremony, whether of a duration of 90 minutes or an entire day, the couple is instructed in lessons for married life. There is frequent chanting of mantras, or prayers in Sanskrit, which ask for blessings on the union. A traditional Hindu mantra is "I am the word and you are the melody. I am the melody and you are the word."

The bride usually wears a sari made of a single piece of red fabric embroidered in gold. She is also adorned with 24-carat-gold jewelry, presented to her by the groom's family. The groom wears white trousers, a tunic, and a ceremonial hat.

At the beginning of the ceremony, the bride and groom, usually seated under a decorated canopy called a *mandaps*, may exchange garlands of flowers.

After emphasizing the importance of marriage, the priest ties the couple's right hands together with cord and sprinkles holy water over them. The bride's father then gives his daughter to the groom. A sacred flame is lit, and the bride and groom make an offering of rice to symbolize their hope of fertility.

The most important part of the ceremony is the Seven Steps, which symbolize food, strength, wealth, fortune, children, happy seasons, and friendship. Together, the bride and groom either take seven steps around the sacred flame or walk around it seven times. Until this rite is completed, the couple is not considered married.

Now married, the bride and groom feed each other five times with little bits of sweet food, and the ceremony ends with prayers and readings.

*Planning the
Ceremony*

GREETING GUESTS

Instead of forming a receiving line at the ceremony site or reception, some couples stop at each pew on their way out of the church or synagogue. Guests rise and exit, greeting the bride and groom on their way. The couple should alternate sides rather than going all the way to the back on one side and then returning to the front to greet guests on the other side. A tip: This is best done when the wedding is small. It could be too time-consuming for a large wedding, leaving half the guests outside and half inside, waiting their turn. For a large guest list, the traditional receiving line is faster and more efficient.

It is important for the couple to be aware of the possibility that a civil ceremony may be required by law. Since the requirements for civil and religious ceremonies are separate, the civil ceremony may take place first, but the couple is not deemed married by the community until they have had a religious ceremony.

THE SIKH WEDDING CEREMONY

The Sikh wedding ceremony is called *Arnand Karaj*, which means "the ceremony of bliss." It solemnizes the union of the couple's souls and seals their religious, moral, and legal obligations. It may or may not be performed in a *gurdwara*, the Sikh place of worship. It most often takes place in the bride's home. It almost always is held before noon, because according to Sikh belief, the morning is the happiest time of day. The bride wears a red head scarf and either red trousers and a tunic or a red sari made from a single piece of cloth. She also wears all the jewelry the groom's family has given her. The groom wears a white brocade suit, a scarf, and a turban, or he may wear Western dress.

Wherever the ceremony is performed, a central platform is used, upon which The Holy Book is displayed by the priest who conducts the ceremony. It is not necessary for a priest to be present; actually any Sikh may be in charge of the ceremony as long as both families agree. Guests sit on the floor around the platform with men to the right of The Holy Book and women to the left.

Flower garlands play a role as they do in Muslim and Hindu weddings, beginning when the parents of the bride welcome the groom and his parents by placing garlands around their necks. The bride is brought to greet the groom, and they exchange garlands.

The couple stands before the priest and The Holy Book, and the bride's father hands one end of a sash to the groom and the other end to the bride. This symbolizes giving her away.

The wedding ceremony is composed of four verses from The Holy Book that explain the obligations of married life. Each verse is read, then sung. During the singing, the groom leads the bride around the Holy Book four times, sometimes with the help of guests to symbolize their support. After they have walked around four times, they are married. A prayer and a short hymn follows, and the sharing of a sweet food by all the guests is symbolic of God's blessing on the marriage. Guests place garlands around the necks of the couple or throw flowers petals, a symbol of happiness.

A civil ceremony may be required to legalize the union.

THE UNITARIAN-UNIVERSALIST WEDDING CEREMONY

The roots of this society are Judeo-Christian, making it a pluralistic religion. It is not a church with ecclesiastical rules or rituals, so wedding ceremonies may be personalized and individualized, and couples are encouraged to design their own service from a combination of religious, spiritual, or other traditions that are meaningful to them.

THE QUAKER (SOCIETY OF FRIENDS) WEDDING CEREMONY

A Quaker wedding is the simplest of all Christian marriages, for it has no music, flowers, and decorations, nor any set order of service. Couples who wish to marry in a Quaker meeting house must apply for permission in advance, often two to three months; several levels of approval are required for the marriage to take place. The bride and groom pledge their lifelong love and loyalty to each other but do not exchange rings during the ceremony: it is believed that the words of the pledge are sufficient. A ring, however, may be given to the bride at the end of the ceremony. In some Quaker ceremonies, the elder couples of the society stand before the couple, with each offering words of wisdom from their own experience in creating a happy, successful marriage. A large, scroll-like marriage certificate, to be signed by witnesses as they leave, may also be provided.

WRITING YOUR OWN VOWS

Your wedding vows are the expression of your personal commitment to each other. Most clergy are willing to allow certain adaptations of traditional vows, as long as the basic tenets of those vows are expressed in one form or another. These tenets, in most religions, are promises to be true to each other in good times and in bad and in sickness and in health, and to love and honor one another "until death do you part." They may also include pledges to cherish and respect one another.

If you decide to write your own vows, keep in mind the following tips.

- Make sure your vows express who you are, reflecting your beliefs and sensibilities.
- If you decide to personalize your vows, avoid sweeping generalizations—make your words personally meaningful.
- Keep it brief.
- Simplicity and brevity can be far more eloquent than overblown metaphors.
- Even if you plan to memorize your vows, make sure you or the officiant has a written copy in case you go blank and forget what comes next.
- If you come from two different cultures or two different faiths, vows that commit to building bridges of understanding and honoring each other's traditions are meaningful.

SELECTING READINGS FOR YOUR CEREMONY

Many couples include in their ceremony scriptural passages, poems, and prose pieces, often read by special friends and relatives. Within some religions, readings may be selected from secular as well as scriptural sources. Within others, readings must be confined to the scriptural. Talk to your clergy person about the requirements of your faith.

Readings are generally taken from three categories: those that are scriptural and are about marriage, love, and the nature of joy; those that are classical poetry or prose and similar in theme to the scriptural readings; and original poetry or prose.

Following are a few selections that are popular with brides and grooms.

- Genesis 1:26–28
- Mark 10:6–9
- Isaiah 61:10
- Song of Solomon 8:6

- Ecclesiastes 3:1–8
- Proverbs 31:10–13
- Ephesians 5:1–2, 21–33
- John 15:9–12, 17:22–24
- Hosea 2:19–21
- Sonnets by Elizabeth Barrett Browning
- Sonnets by William Shakespeare

CHILDREN FROM A PREVIOUS MARRIAGE

Children of either divorced or widowed parents should be included in the wedding party as long as they want to be. Including them in the ceremony, whether as attendants or in some other role, will help them adjust to the new family situation more readily and make them feel a part of the creation of that family.

One meaningful way to include children from a previous marriage in the wedding ceremony is by placing a family medallion around their necks after vows have been exchanged. The medallion, sometimes a circle with three intersecting circles inside, represents a promise of family love and inclusion. It is first blessed by the minister, priest, or rabbi, who then shares with those gathered the meaning of the medallion. He then hands it to the parent to give to the children. The children may then stand alongside the attendants or return to their seats for the conclusion of the service.

HONORING THE DECEASED

Increasingly, some couples are finding ways to honor deceased family members, either privately or publicly, in their ceremony. This is a way to remember loved ones, especially parents and grandparents, and to give tribute to the importance of family and tradition. If you decide to include a tribute in your ceremony, be sure that it is neither morbid nor lengthy. A simple declaration of love, a moment of silence, or the lighting of a candle may be the most eloquent way to honor the person who is being remembered. Often, couples find it too difficult to publicly honor the deceased, so they make their memorials private. Some

> ### SAMPLE READING: SACRED
>
> Love is patient and kind;
> it is not jealous or boastful;
> it is not arrogant or rude.
>
> Love does not insist on its own way;
> it is not irritable or resentful;
> it does not rejoice at wrong,
> but rejoices in the right.
>
> Love bears all things, believes all things,
> hopes all things, endures all things.
>
> Love never ends. . . .
>
> So faith, hope, love abide, these three,
> but the greatest of these is love."
>
> **—I Corinthians 13:4–8, 13**

meaningful ways of doing so is to offer a silent prayer, wear something of the person who has died, or lay a bouquet of flowers on the front pew or by the altar.

UNITY CANDLES

With the concurrence of their officiants, some couples include unity candles in the ceremony, as a symbol of the joining of their families. At the start of the wedding service, the bride's parents light a candle on one side of the altar and the groom's parents do the same on the other side. At the conclusion of the wedding, the bride and groom each carry their parents' candles to the center of the altar, where they use them to light a single candle. Once the unity candle is lit, the bride and groom blow out the smaller candles. If the marriage is a blending of two religions, lighting unity candles is a particularly meaningful way to symbolize the merging and acceptance of both traditions.

CEREMONIES OF COMMITMENT

Many religions refuse to be associated with commitment ceremonies for gay and lesbian couples, but there are others that are willing to affirm same-gender unions in one way or another. Within these are choices for the kind of service to be performed. For example, within the Universal Fellowship of Metropolitan Community Churches, a couple may participate in a Rite of Blessing (a simple prayer that acknowledges the relationship and offers it to God) or a Holy Union (a covenant or contract between two people) but not a Rite of Holy Matrimony. The Unitarian-Universalist religion performs a Service of Union; some Episcopalian priests will perform a Commitment Ceremony; and some Presbyterians, a Holy Union. Many other clergy, within the structure of their religion or outside it, will perform a ceremony that acknowledges the commitment of the couple.

Because many churches do not sanction a gay or lesbian union through wedding liturgy, gay couples have more latitude when planning the ceremony. Most write their own vows in some form or another, using both religious and secular sources, as they wish. In thinking about how to structure a ceremony of commitment, couples generally follow the standard guidelines of Jewish or Christian ceremonies. That structure includes:

Whether your ceremony is straight from your book of worship or personalized with vows written by you, many experts recommend that you hold an "emotional rehearsal." If possible, the bride and groom literally walk through the steps of the ceremony and envision who will be there. If there are those who won't be there because of death or estrangement, think about them. Listen to the music you have chosen, and recite your vows to each other. Listen to the words. Doing this in advance accomplishes two things: Having dealt with many emotional issues, you can pay attention to the real moments as they occur, and you can deal ahead of time with those emotions that may overwhelm and stress you on your wedding day.

- **THE INTRODUCTION**: Any activity before the actual service begins, including the processional, a gathering together and welcome, and an invocation. Some gay or lesbian couples want a statement made about being gay, believing that their sexuality is so integral to their relationship that they wouldn't think of not addressing it. Others choose not to address their sexuality, preferring a ceremony that focuses on love and commitment.
- **THE SERVICE**: Consists of prayers, songs, readings, a homily, and an address by the officiant. If readings are included, some gay couples like to read from the Book of Samuel, chapter 18, verses 1–5, and chapter 20, verses 16–17. Lesbian couples often select readings from the Book of Ruth, chapter 1, verses 16–17. Unless the ceremony is taking place in a house of worship that prohibits the use of secular readings and music, the couple also has a wide range of sources from which to choose.
- **THE VOWS**: The expressions of the couple's intent. The couple may borrow vows from any service book ("I, Jane, take you, Beth. . . . I promise to be true to you in good times and bad, in sickness and in health. . . "), write their own vows to be read by the officiant, or declare to each other with no prompting.
- **THE EXCHANGE OF RINGS**: May be preceded by the rings being blessed.
- **THE PRONOUNCEMENT**: The public proclamation by the officiant that the couple is recognized as married. This part of the ceremony can be worded in several ways, such as "Since you have consented to join together in the bond of matrimony, and have pledged yourselves to each other in the presence of this company, I now pronounce you married" or "In the presence of this

company, by the power of your love, because you have pledged to one another your vows of commitment, we recognize you as married."

- THE CLOSING: The kiss, the blessing of the union, the recessional.

MILITARY WEDDINGS

Any enlisted man or woman on active duty or any officer or cadet at a military academy may have a military ceremony. The military wedding is different from other weddings in the following ways:

- Military weddings are formal in attire. Those who are entitled to do so wear full dress uniform—including the bride, if she is a member of the military and so chooses.
- Other attendants wear civilian formal attire.
- Men in uniform do not wear boutonnieres.
- The American flag and the standard of the groom's and/or bride's unit is displayed.
- During the recessional, the bride and groom—if the groom is a commissioned officer—pass under an arch of drawn swords or sabers that is formed outside the church or chapel.
- At the reception, the cake is cut with the groom's sword or saber.

Otherwise, the rest of the ceremony is conducted according to the religion and traditions of the bride and the groom.

DOUBLE WEDDINGS

Double weddings may honor two sisters or brothers, two cousins, or two best friends. If the wedding involves two sisters, the ceremony begins with the two bridegrooms following the clergy person to the altar. Each stands with his best man beside him, with the groom of the older sister standing nearer. As the processional begins, the ushers of both bridegrooms walk up the aisle, keeping to their respective group. Then come the older sister's bridesmaids, followed by her maid of honor. The older sister then follows, holding her father's arm. The order is then repeated for the younger sister and her attendants, with the bride escorted by a brother, uncle, or other male relative.

The first couple ascends the chancel steps and takes their place at the left side of the altar rail, leaving room at the right side for the younger bride and

SAMPLE READINGS: SECULAR

Love is something you and I must have. We must have it because our spirit feeds upon it. We must have it because without it we become weak and faint. Without love our self-esteem weakens. Without it our courage fails. Without love we can no longer look out confidently at the world. We turn inward and begin to feed upon our own personalities, and little by little we destroy ourselves. With it we are creative. With it we march tirelessly. With it, and with it alone, we are able to sacrifice for others."

—Chief Dan George

"Marriage is the union of two divinities that a third might be born on earth. It is the union of two souls in a strong love for the abolishment of separateness. It is that higher unity which fuses the separate unities within the two spirits. It is the golden ring within a chain whose beginning is a glance, and whose ending is Eternity. It is the pure rain that falls from an unblemished sky to fructify and bless the fields of divine Nature."

—From "The Prophet" by Kahlil Gibran

Now you will feel no rain, for each of you will be shelter to each other.
Now you will feel no cold, for each of you will be warmth to the other.
Now there is no more loneliness, for each of you will be companion to the other.
Now you are two bodies, but there is only one life before you.
You will now go to your dwelling place to enter unto the days of your togetherness.
And may your days be good and long upon the earth.

—Apache wedding poem

her bridegroom. The father stands just below his older daughter. The younger daughter's escort takes his place in a pew with his wife or family.

The service is read to both couples, with responses made twice. Generally, if the service includes a father "giving" two daughters away, the older is given away first, then the younger. The father then takes the place saved for him beside his wife in the first pew.

At the end of the ceremony, the older sister and her husband turn and go down the aisle first. The younger couple follows. The bridesmaids and ushers of the first sister pair off and follow. The attendants of the second walk out last.

Each couple should have the same number of attendants, with all ushers dressed alike. The bridesmaids' dresses, while not necessarily all the same, should be complementary.

Planning the Ceremony

One difficulty of a double wedding is the seating of the parents of the two bridegrooms. They must either share the first pew or draw lots to determine who sits in the first row and who sits in the next.

THE BLESSING OF A CIVIL MARRIAGE

Couples who originally missed out on a religious wedding can usually get approval from their church at a later date for a church or chapel ceremony that blesses the marriage. An example of such a service is found in *The Book of Common Prayer*. The widely used Protestant service book follows the traditional marriage service, except that the minister says "Do you *acknowledge* [rather than take] this woman . . ." and makes other similar changes. No one gives the bride away nor does the groom give the bride her ring again.

The service is generally attended only by family and close friends, and there are no attendants. This is, after all, a blessing and not a new celebration of the marriage. The bride wears a street-length dress or suit, and the groom a dark suit. She may carry a bouquet or wear a corsage. There may be music, and the altar is decorated with flowers.

REAFFIRMATION OF VOWS

Traditionally, couples who reaffirm their vows do so on a big anniversary, such as the 25th or an even higher one. This practice is popular today as a way for some couples to celebrate earlier anniversaries. In addition to wanting to recommit to each other publicly, they may want to have the no-holds-barred celebration they missed out on the first time around. A large party will usually suffice—as it may have to, given that some clergy will not perform a duplicate of the first wedding ceremony. Most, however, will conduct a simple reaffirmation of vows. The ceremony can occur during a regular Sabbath service or at a separate time. The form of the service varies, depending on the wishes of the officiant and the tenets of the place of worship. The couple is joined by any members of their original wedding party, plus their children. After the ceremony, there is usually a party.

CHAPTER 11

WEDDING ATTIRE

Before Queen Victoria appeared in her white wedding gown and orange blossoms in 1840 and changed the Western world's thinking about what brides wore to be married, most brides donned their best dress, perhaps pinned a flower to it, and that was that. Even before then, through the 18th century, the poorer bride went to her wedding in a plain white robe, a symbol that she brought nothing to her marriage, and therefore, her husband was not responsible for her debts. Other brides wore colors, often for their symbolism. They wore blue for constancy, green for youth, and red for no particular reason. Never yellow, though, for that meant jealousy. Gradually, white came to symbolize purity rather than poverty. Today white is regarded as the symbolic color of weddings and can be worn by anyone, whether a first- or second- or even third-time bride.

Today, wedding attire runs the gamut from informal to very formal. There are many ways to blend old traditions with new, glamour with simplicity, and fantasy with fun. For the bride, especially, there is a multitude of choices, whether she selects a wedding dress indigenous to her heritage or searches for the most dazzling white gown she can find.

HOW FORMAL IS FORMAL?

When planning your wedding party attire, use the chart on pages 210–11 as a general guide for styles, lengths, and accessories. Remember that these are traditional guidelines only, and that there are many nontraditional choices.

DRESS FOR BRIDAL PARTY AND GUESTS

	MOST FORMAL DAYTIME	MOST FORMAL EVENING	SEMIFORMAL DAYTIME
BRIDE	LONG WHITE DRESS, TRAIN, AND VEIL; GLOVES OPTIONAL	SAME AS MOST FORMAL DAYTIME	LONG WHITE DRESS; SHORT VEIL AND GLOVES OPTIONAL
BRIDE'S ATTENDANTS	LONG DRESSES, MATCHING SHOES; GLOVES ARE BRIDE'S OPTION	SAME AS MOST FORMAL DAYTIME	SAME AS MOST FORMAL DAYTIME
GROOM, HIS ATTENDANTS, BRIDE'S FATHER OR STEPFATHER	CUTAWAY COAT, STRIPED TROUSERS, PEARL GRAY WAISTCOAT, WHITE STIFF SHIRT, TURNDOWN COLLAR WITH GRAY-AND-BLACK-STRIPED FOUR-IN-HAND OR WING COLLAR WITH ASCOT, GRAY GLOVES, BLACK SILK SOCKS, BLACK KID SHOES	BLACK TAILCOAT AND TROUSERS, WHITE PIQUE WAISTCOAT, STARCHED-BOSOM SHIRT, WING COLLAR, WHITE BOW TIE, WHITE GLOVES, BLACK SILK SOCKS, BLACK PATENT-LEATHER SHOES OR PUMPS OR BLACK KID SMOOTH-TOE SHOES	BLACK OR CHARCOAL SACK COAT, DOVE-GRAY WAISTCOAT, WHITE PLEATED SHIRT, STARCHED TURNDOWN COLLAR OR SOFT WHITE SHIRT WITH FOUR-IN-HAND TIE, GRAY GLOVES, BLACK SMOOTH-TOE SHOES
MOTHERS AND STEPMOTHERS OF COUPLE	LONG OR SHORT DRESSES; HAT, VEIL, OR HAIR ORNAMENT; GLOVES	USUALLY LONG EVENING OR DINNER DRESS, DRESSY SHORT COCKTAIL PERMISSIBLE; VEIL OR HAIR ORNAMENT IF LONG DRESS; SMALL HAT, IF SHORT DRESS; GLOVES	LONG OR STREET-LENGTH DRESSES; GLOVES, HEAD COVERING OPTIONAL
FEMALE GUESTS	STREET-LENGTH COCKTAIL OR AFTERNOON DRESSES (COLORS ARE PREFERABLE TO BLACK OR WHITE); GLOVES; HEAD COVERING OPTIONAL	DEPENDING ON LOCAL CUSTOM, LONG OR SHORT DRESSES; IF LONG, VEIL OR ORNAMENT— OTHERWISE, HAT OPTIONAL; GLOVES	SHORT AFTERNOON OR COCKTAIL DRESS; HEAD COVERING FOR CHURCH OPTIONAL
MALE GUESTS	DARK SUITS; CONSERVATIVE SHIRTS AND TIES	IF WOMEN WEAR LONG DRESSES, TUXEDOS; IF SHORT DRESSES, DARK SUITS	DARK SUITS

DRESS FOR BRIDAL PARTY AND GUESTS

	SEMIFORMAL EVENING	INFORMAL DAYTIME	INFORMAL EVENING
BRIDE	SAME AS SEMIFORMAL DAYTIME	SHORT AFTERNOON DRESS, COCKTAIL DRESS, OR SUIT	LONG DINNER DRESS OR SHORT COCKTAIL DRESS OR SUIT
BRIDE'S ATTENDANTS	SAME LENGTH AND DEGREE OF FORMALITY AS BRIDE'S DRESS	SAME STYLE AS BRIDE	SAME STYLE AS BRIDE
GROOM, HIS ATTENDANTS, BRIDE'S FATHER OR STEPFATHER	WINTER, BLACK TUXEDO; SUMMER, WHITE JACKET; PLEATED OR PIQUÉ SOFT SHIRT, BLACK CUMMERBUND, BLACK BOW TIE, NO GLOVES, BLACK PATENT-LEATHER OR KID SHOES	WINTER, DARK SUIT; SUMMER, DARK TROUSERS WITH WHITE LINEN JACKET OR WHITE TROUSERS WITH NAVY OR CHARCOAL JACKET; SOFT SHIRT, CONSERVATIVE FOUR-IN-HAND TIE; HOT CLIMATE, WHITE SUIT	TUXEDO IF BRIDE WEARS DINNER DRESS; DARK SUIT IN WINTER, LIGHTER SUIT IN SUMMER
MOTHERS AND STEPMOTHERS OF COUPLE	SAME AS SEMIFORMAL DAYTIME	SHORT AFTERNOON OR COCKTAIL DRESSES	SAME LENGTH DRESS AS BRIDE
FEMALE GUESTS	COCKTAIL DRESSES, GLOVES, HEAD COVERING FOR CHURCH OPTIONAL	AFTERNOON DRESSES, GLOVES, HEAD COVERING FOR CHURCH OPTIONAL	AFTERNOON OR COCKTAIL DRESSES, GLOVES, HEAD COVERING FOR CHURCH OPTIONAL
MALE GUESTS	DARK SUITS	DARK SUITS; LIGHT TROUSERS AND DARK BLAZERS IN SUMMER	DARK SUITS
GROOM'S FATHER OR STEPFATHER	HE MAY WEAR THE SAME COSTUME AS THE GROOM AND HIS ATTENDANTS, ESPECIALLY IF HE IS TO STAND IN THE RECEIVING LINE. IF HE IS NOT TO TAKE PART, HOWEVER, AND DOES NOT WISH TO DRESS FORMALLY, HE MAY WEAR THE SAME CLOTHES AS THE MALE GUESTS.		

THE BRIDAL GOWN

FABRICS AND LACE

The traditional and most formal bridal fabric is satin, a favorite choice among brides marrying in fall or winter. On a summer day, however, satin is too hot and heavy a material for most brides. Other materials have become popular for the warm seasons. In the spring, lace and tissue taffeta are light and lovely. In midsummer, many brides favor chiffon, organdy, marquisette, cotton, piqué, and linen.

Other suitable fabrics for autumn and midwinter weddings are brocade, taffeta, velvet, and moiré. An infinite variety of synthetic materials give the bride more choices for every season, plus the extra bonus of a gown less likely to wrinkle. You may also want your gown adorned with embellishments, such as pearls, sequins, or laces.

STYLES

Following are some of the more popular and traditional bridal gown styles.

- BALL GOWN. A "Cinderella" style gown with a big, poufy skirt.
- A-LINE. Just as the name implies, the shape of an "A," slimmer at the bodice and widening from the bodice down.
- EMPIRE. Dress with a high waist that is cropped just below the bust, from which the skirt flares.
- BASQUE. The waist in this instance is several inches below the natural waistline and forms a "U" or a "V" shape.

TRAINS

Trains are either sewn onto the dress or come detachable for ease of movement at the reception. Some of the most popular trains for floor-length dresses are these:

- SWEEP TRAIN. Train draping from the waistline to 6 inches on the floor.
- COURT. Train that extends 3 feet from the waistline.
- CHAPEL TRAIN. Train that extends 5 feet from the waistline.
- CATHEDRAL TRAIN. Train that extends 3 yards from the waistline; more often associated with formal weddings.
- WATTEAU TRAIN. Train that drapes from the shoulders.

BALL GOWN

BASQUE ("U" WAISTLINE)

A-LINE

EMPIRE

BASQUE ("V" WAISTLINE)

VEILS

Veils come in a variety of lengths and materials. They are often fashioned from lace or tulle, and may have delicately embroidered edgings and trims.

- **BLUSHER VEIL.**
  Short veil worn over the face that often falls below the neckline.
- **FINGERTIP VEIL.**
  Veil that falls to the tips of the fingers.
- **SWEEP VEIL.**
  Veil that sweeps the ground.
- **CHAPEL VEIL.**
  Long veil that trails one or two feet from the gown.
- **CATHEDRAL VEIL.**
  Long veil that trails from one to three yards from the gown.
- **MANTILLA.**
  A scarf-like veil that drapes over the head and shoulders.

BLUSHER

FINGERTIP

SWEEP

CHAPEL

MANTILLA

CATHEDRAL

HEADDRESSES

Bridal headdresses, or headpieces, may come either attached to a veil, separate but placed over a veil, or without a veil. They may be as simple as a hat, a bow, or a hair comb.

- **HEADBAND.** Worn around the head.
- **WREATH OF FLOWERS.** Worn snugly on the crown of the head or woven into the hair.
- **TIARA.** Crown rests on top of the head.
- **JULIET CAP.** A small cap that hugs the crown.

WREATH OF FLOWERS

JULIET CAP

TIARAS

BOW

SHOPPING FOR A BRIDAL GOWN

You'll probably want to begin looking for a wedding gown as soon as the date is set. If yours is a formal wedding, in particular, where elaborate, custom-made gowns are often the rule, you may need to order your gown as far as a year in advance. Delivery times can be as short as eight weeks and as long as a year. Note: Be sure to make the delivery date a few days before your formal portraits are taken, not the actual wedding day. You can then plan a fitting between the delivery date and the photography date.

Pore over magazines and cut out pictures of looks you like. Clip them in your planner so that when you begin working with a salesperson or wedding consultant, he or she will know the kind of style you are looking for. Take note of a particular brand you like in bridal magazine advertisements; you can call their 800- number to find a salon near you that carries the brand. Some bridal salons carry only a limited number of manufacturers; you might want to call before you visit and inquire about the lines they carry, if you know which ones you prefer.

Consider hiring a seamstress to make your gown. You can find a good one through recommendations by tailors, dry cleaners, or bridal salons. Ask to see samples or photographs of her work.

Here are some ways to go about finding your perfect wedding gown.

- Attend bridal fashion shows, usually held in the spring and fall, to get ideas.
- There are many bridal salons and stores to explore. Ask for recommendations and visit some firsthand.
- Try on various styles before narrowing down your choices: Don't rely on hanger appeal only. You might be pleasantly surprised when you try on styles you hadn't considered.
- Consider alterations costs when buying off the rack. Ask what the store policy is.
- When trying on gowns, wear lingerie similar to the type you plan to wear on your wedding day, and take shoes with a heel the height you think you'll wear.
- Be realistic about your budget. You won't want to skimp, but surely you can find the perfect gown in your price range. Look carefully.

Gown Quality Check

If you are buying in a retail store, investing hundreds and perhaps thousands of dollars in a dress you will probably wear only once, you have the right to expect quality. Check the details:

- SEAMS must be smooth. Fabric must be evenly matched where it meets at the seams. All edges should be finished, and stitches should be tiny and uniform.
- ZIPPERS should be hand-sewn, not done by machine. The zipper should extend to the widest point on your hips, so you can get your gown on and off with no stress to the zipper or seams.

- **FASTENERS** such as cloth-covered buttons, fastening loops, and extra hooks and eyes should be secure and placed at stress points, such as the waist and neck. Buttons should be of the same fabric as the gown.
- **APPLIQUÉS** should be secure with no visible seams. Beads and pearls should be individually stitched in place.
- **LININGS** must be heavy enough to conceal inner construction but light enough to allow draping and shaping.
- **HEMS** should be hand-finished, a layer at a time.

Something Old, Something Borrowed, Something New

You don't *have* to buy a brand-new, custom-fit dress for your wedding, a dress you will likely wear once and put into mothballs. Here are some cost-conscious alternatives to buying new:

- **CONSIGNMENT SHOPS.** Many brides take their wedding gowns to consignment shops, which sell the gown at greatly reduced prices and split the profits with the bride. You can find fantastic bargains in designer gowns, worn once and in perfect shape. Some consignment shops deal with bridal gowns exclusively. Check your Yellow Pages for one near you.
- **CHOOSE VINTAGE.** Many brides are choosing to wear heirloom wedding dresses, whether that of their mother, their grandmother, or another relative or one bought in a vintage clothing store, where it is more than possible to find a beautiful gown at an affordable price. Remember: It's only affordable if it fits and doesn't need a complete refurbishing, because you most likely can't return it—and work on antique clothing can be difficult and costly. Check with a dressmaker or fabric restorer before you buy so that you know what to expect. Ask your dry cleaner to recommend a garment-care shop that works with vintage fabrics. There are amazing processes today that can restore delicate old fabrics to their natural state.
- **BORROWING.** The loan of a wedding dress is a real gift. There is no reason not to accept an offer of a loaned gown, as long as you pledge to take extraordinarily good care of it and return it freshly cleaned and in perfect condition. If you do borrow a gown, you should show your appreciation with a lovely, personal gift. If the gown is not a perfect fit and requires alterations, your friend must be the one to suggest that they be made. If she does not, you must thank her profusely for her willingness to share, and return the dress to her.

- **RENTING.** Many areas now have bridal and evening-wear rental stores, where a bride may rent a dress, just as the groom and ushers rent their costumes. While this can be a practical and satisfactory alternative to buying a one-time-only dress, it is not necessarily an inexpensive alternative. Rentals can be costly; shop around for the best deals.

BRIDAL ACCESSORIES

SHOES AND GLOVES

The bride's shoes are traditionally made of satin (if the gown is satin) or *peau de soie* and dyed to match the gown perfectly. Shoes should be comfortable—not only does the bride walk up the aisle in them, but she also has to stand in them at the reception. Pumps are more appropriate than open sandals.

Some bridal stores offer beautiful beaded ballet shoes or fancy rhinestone-studded tennis-style shoes you can slip into at the reception for comfort.

If the bride chooses to wear short, loose gloves, she merely pulls one glove off at the altar so that her ring can be placed on her hand. But if she wears elbow-length or longer gloves, the underseam of the glove's wedding finger may be ripped open, and she need only to pull the tip off to have the ring put on. This can be cumbersome and wasteful, however, so it is preferable to wear no gloves at all. If the bride's gown is enhanced by long gloves, an alternative to cutting the seam of the ring finger is fingerless gloves.

JEWELRY

The traditional jewelry is classic and neutral-colored, such as a pearl necklace or a pearl and diamond lavaliere. Of course, wearing a piece of heirloom jew-

PRE-WEDDING GOWN CARE

Bringing your bridal gown home means more than just hanging it in a closet. It needs a little extra care to be ready for the big day. Air it out by removing it from the garment bag. Leave in, however, any tissue stuffing in the sleeves or shoulders. Hang in a high point in your house so that the train can be spread on the floor, laid over a white sheet.

elry or jewelry with special meaning (a gift from the bridegroom, perhaps) is a loving gesture, even if it is composed of colored stones.

Makeup

Some brides hire a makeup artist to apply their makeup and that of their attendants on the day of the wedding. If you do, be sure to have a trial run with the makeup artist in the weeks preceding the wedding.

Hair

The bride should experiment with hairstyles to find the one that is the most flattering and natural and that best complements a headdress, if she is wearing one. Plan a trial appointment with your hairdresser to establish the look you want on your wedding day.

THE BRIDAL ATTENDANTS

Since in most cases attendants pay for their dresses and accessories, the bride has an obligation to consider the price of the gowns carefully. Another thing she should consider is figure flattery. When your attendants come in all shapes and sizes, you should look for gowns that will flatter one and all. Get their input and be flexible. You can have each bridesmaid choose a slightly different style to accentuate the positive for everyone. Some brides, respecting attendants' privacy, won't even bother to ask for sizes or body measurements but let the bridesmaids do their own shopping.

If the bride has a "best man" as her honor attendant, he would dress identically to the groom's attendants.

Dresses

There is nothing wrong with variations on a theme. Bridesmaids' dresses may be identical in texture and style, but not necessarily in color—and vice versa.

The trend these days is away from costume-like sameness. You can have each bridesmaid wear a slightly different variation on one color—red, for example, with one attendant in rose, another in soft pink, and another in sunset red.

The number-one rule: Bridesmaids' dresses should match the bride's dress in degree of formality. The material for the bridesmaids' dresses should also complement the material of the dress of the bride. In other words, if the bride chooses to wear satin, the attendants' dresses should not be organdy or ruffled lace.

Consider, too, any religious requirements, such as covered arms and high necks. Check with your officiant to see whether your ceremony site has any restrictions.

The dress of the maid or matron of honor may be different from that of the bridesmaids or her flowers of a different color. For example, for an autumn wedding the bridesmaids might wear deep yellow and carry rust-and-orange chrysanthemums, and the maid of honor might wear rust and carry yellow chrysanthemums.

If dresses are long, the hemline should be short enough to prevent the attendants from tripping on the church or chancel steps.

ACCESSORIES

The bride should ask her attendants to buy their shoes well ahead of time, particularly if their shoes have to be dyed the same color. Also, when bridesmaids' dresses are short or tea length, she needs to make sure all are wearing the same color pantyhose.

The bride selects a headdress for her attendants, if she chooses for them to wear one, but she should never, ever tell her attendants how to wear their hair.

FLOWERS

The bridesmaids almost always carry flowers, most often falling sprays held in front of them or sheaves that they hold in their arms. Those walking on the

WATCH THE LIPSTICK!

If the bride's gown is put on over her head, she should always hold a towel in front of her face if her makeup has already been applied. This is not the time for spot removal, and it is all too easy for foundation or lipstick to rub off on the gown. If the gown is close-fitting, the bride's hair should be styled after the gown is in place. A low stool is a great addition to the dressing room; the bride can sit without wrinkling her dress, her skirts around her over the stool, while she has her hair done and her veil, flowers, or other headpiece put in place.

right side hold them on the right arm with the stems pointing downward to the left, and those on the left hold their flowers on the left arm with stems toward the right.

YOUNG ATTENDANTS

Flower girls are generally dressed in white ballet-length dresses or in gowns similar to those of the bridesmaids but in a style becoming to a child. Flower girls usually wear small wreaths of artificial flowers on their heads or no headdress at all. They may have ribbons or flowers braided into long hair instead. Flower girls traditionally carry small bouquets or baskets of flowers, although they no longer—as a rule—strew them before the bride.

Very small boys—ring bearers, pages, or train bearers—wear white Eton-style jackets with short pants. When they are a little older, they may wear navy-blue suits instead. If a boy's suit is white, his shoes and socks should also be white; if it is navy, he wears navy socks and black shoes.

Junior bridesmaids wear dresses exactly like those of the older bridesmaids, although sometimes of a different color. Their flowers may or may not be different from the others.

Junior ushers dress in the same style of clothing as the other ushers.

THE GROOM AND HIS ATTENDANTS

Attire for the male members of the wedding party is rarely deviated from. In temperate climates, formal evening clothes mean a black tailcoat and matching trousers, a stiff white shirt, a wing collar, a white tie, and a white waistcoat.

Semiformal evening clothes are a black or midnight-blue dinner jacket (tuxedo) and matching trousers, a piqué or pleated-front white shirt with an attached collar, a black bow tie, and a black waistcoat or cummerbund. In hot weather, a white dinner jacket and black cummerbund are used. Evening clothes should never be worn during the daytime.

Formal day clothes are appropriate for daytime weddings and should be worn whenever a wedding is scheduled before six o'clock. The daytime equivalent of the evening tailcoat is a black or Oxford-gray cutaway coat worn with black or gray striped trousers, a pearl gray waistcoat, a stiff white shirt, a stiff fold-down collar, and a four-in-hand black-and-gray tie or a dress ascot tie.

Less-formal daytime clothes are the same except that a suit-style dark gray or black sack coat is substituted for the cutaway; the shirt is soft instead of stiff; and only a four-in-hand tie is worn.

In an informal wedding, although the bride may still wear a simple bridal gown or satiny slip dress, the men switch to lightweight suits or dark gray or navy blue jackets accompanied by white trousers and either white dress socks and white dress shoes or black dress socks and black dress shoes. Shirts are soft white with an attached collar, and ties should be four-in-hand with a dark, small, neat pattern.

The groom may send ushers his own outfit's specifications and ask each to rent similar clothing. Often, however, for the sake of uniformity, he may find it easier to order all the outfits himself from a rental agency. Shoes can be rented, especially when everyone does not own the same dress styles; the groom may delegate this task to his best man. The ushers, in any case, pay the rental fee. Formal-wear rental stores generally stock all accessories, including gloves or cummerbunds. The groom provides his attendants' boutonnieres.

WHY IS IT CALLED A TUXEDO?

In the fall of 1866, Griswold Lorillard, a tobacco heir, shocked guests gathered at the annual autumn ball of the Tuxedo Park Country Club in Tuxedo Park, New York, by wearing a tailless black dinner coat. He explained that the coat was fashioned after a description a friend had given him of a cut-off coat worn by the Prince of Wales. It soon caught on.

TAILCOAT   WAISTCOAT   CUTAWAY

TUXEDO   SUIT

THE BEST WOMAN

When the groom's "best man" is a woman, she may wear a dress in the color family of the bride's attendants, but more often she wears a dress in black or gray or whatever main color the men are wearing. She should not wear a tuxedo, nor should she dress like the groomsmen. She may have a corsage in the same flowers as the boutonnieres but does not carry a bouquet.

HOW TO SHOP

Whether the groom buys or rents his wedding attire, he should consider comfort an important element in making selections. The coat should allow free movement of his arms and lie smoothly across the back. Sleeves should reach to the curl of his fingers when his arms are straight at his sides and should reveal one-half inch of shirt cuff. Pants should be hemmed even with the top of the heel of his shoe in back and have a slight break in front, so the hem rests on the shoes.

THE MOTHERS OF THE BRIDE AND GROOM

The elegance of the mothers' dresses should be keyed to how elaborate the wedding is. Long skirts and dresses are considered appropriate for any wedding from noon on. They may vary greatly in formality—from shirtwaist tops and skirts to brocade evening gowns.

The mothers should try not to wear the same color the bridesmaids or the bride is wearing. Nor should both mothers wear the same color.

At very formal weddings, the mothers should wear gloves, which are kept on while they are in the receiving line. They should also wear something on their heads—whether a small artificial-flower arrangement, a hat, a veil, or a bow.

THE FATHERS OF THE BRIDE AND GROOM

There is no hard-and-fast rule governing the clothes of the bride's father, but since he will be escorting his daughter down the aisle behind the ushers, the party will have a more unified appearance if he wears the same outfit they do. Thus the father of the bride almost invariably dresses like the other men in the wedding party.

At a formal wedding, the bridegroom's father may wear the same type of clothes as those worn by the bride's father. He has, however, no official part in the ceremony and therefore may wear a dark suit if this makes him more comfortable.

CHAPTER 12

PLANNING THE RECEPTION

The wedding celebratory party is your chance to share your good fortune with the family and friends who form the most important relationships in your life. Whether you plan a grand affair with elegant food and service or prefer a barefoot clambake under the stars, the reception should be a reflection of your personality. Combining personal and traditional touches is a homage of sorts to the people and influences who formed you—and an introduction to the person you have become.

CHOOSING THE LOCATION

Finding a reception locale is a top-priority first-level decision, a process that begins once you have determined the size of your guest list—and the size of your budget. Your choice for the reception will affect the style of wedding you have, the food you serve, and the entertainment you choose. Remember that typically the later in the day your wedding is held, the more formal its style, and the more expensive the reception is likely to be.

Choices for reception sites are wide and varied. Don't limit your thinking to hotels, clubs, church fellowship halls, or wedding halls. There is a whole world of reception sites that go well beyond the traditional. How about a country inn, a vineyard, a party cruise boat, or a city loft with soaring ceilings? You might also look into town halls, libraries, aquariums, barges, riverboats, and art galleries.

Prefer something more affordable? Consider historic homes and sites, museums, parks, botanical gardens, greenhouses, and conference retreats. Renting these sites can cost as little as one-tenth—in some regions even one-twentieth—the cost of a traditional wedding facility or hotel party room.

Your reception choices are more clear-cut in special instances. If you are planning a destination wedding on an island or at a resort area, your guest list may be limited only to those family members and close friends who can afford

If your reception is to be held at a hotel, ask whether the hotel offers room rates for group bookings. A club that you are affiliated with may have special rates for members, and you might be eligible and not even know it. Check to see whether there are places that have club affiliations with professional associations, sororities, fraternities, unions, charity organizations, and colleges.

the time and expense to attend. In that case, you may either choose to let a resort facility handle the preparations or decide on a casual celebration at the ceremony site or local restaurant. If you are planning a theme wedding that is not only decorative but throws tradition to the wind, your plans will be different, too. For example, if your passion is country and western music and you want your party to feature square dancing, you will need a space that can comfortably accommodate it. If you choose a beach reception, your theme will be the great outdoors—and the rest of the plans will spring from that.

Do a thorough job of selecting just the right space. Most sites require a hefty deposit the day you reserve it and have equally steep cancellation fees.

There are basically two ways to organize your reception. If you are considering the use of a club, wedding facility, restaurant, or party boat, you can usually count on the services being provided by the site. If you are thinking about a rental facility, your own home, or any other space that is just that—a space—you will need to make arrangements with outside vendors and suppliers.

KEY CONSIDERATIONS

In addition to cost, there are a few other important considerations in selecting a reception site. These include:

Size and Comfort
You may fall in love with a space the first time you see it, but until you determine its comfort capacity—not its standing-room-only capacity—refrain from booking it. No matter how lovely it may be, your guests will be uncomfortable if they have no room to move. On the other hand, if the guest list for your reception is small, don't pick too spacious a site. Otherwise, tables could be miles apart, and the room will feel cavernous and empty.

If you are planning hours of dancing, you will want a dance floor large enough to accommodate dancers. If you plan to have food stations instead of a single buffet line, you don't want guest tables that are so close to the food stations that no one can move.

Other comfort needs: sufficient rest rooms, a place for coats, and plenty of chairs, even if yours is an afternoon tea or cocktail reception where guests will stand more than they sit. You will also want to check the acoustics so that your music is neither too low nor too deafening. And finally, make sure the space offers good air circulation: A church hall may be a perfect space to decorate, but if it has few windows, it may need extra fans to provide better air circulation.

Time Availability

The lag time between the ceremony and reception often depends on several things—including whether formal photographs of the wedding party will be taken after the ceremony and, if so, the time it will take to do so; the distance from the ceremony site to the reception site; whether a receiving line will be held at the ceremony site; and the time availability of both spaces. The ideal lag time is only 30 minutes. While this may not be possible to achieve, you should aim for as short a lag time as possible so that guests aren't kept waiting.

Level of Formality

The degree of your celebration's desired formality is set by both the time of day of your wedding and the environment you choose for the reception. While a morning or afternoon reception can be as informal or formal as you like, an evening reception usually means a formal reception space unless you tell your guests otherwise. Certain spaces, simply by virtue of their casual ambiance, will be unlikely choices for formal weddings. No matter how you decorate, these spaces—such as a backyard garden or a hunting lodge—will never look like a country club or hotel, and would be more appropriate for a morning or afternoon wedding that is informal or semiformal.

Accessibility

When scouting sites, also think about how your guests will get there. If access is difficult, consider hiring minivans or even a bus to transport guests to and from the reception site. If the parking lot of the club is the equivalent of blocks away from the entrance, arrange valet parking (the tab and tips are on you) so that guests don't have to walk far in high heels or in the rain or heat.

Check for access for the disabled. No matter how enchanting, the tower room at the golf club isn't for you if many of your wedding guests are older or have disabilities and the room is up three flights of stairs.

QUESTIONS TO ASK THE RECEPTION SITE MANAGER

- Is a wedding package offered?
- If so, what does it include and what does it cost?
- Are substitutions to the package permissible?
- What policies and restrictions does the site have for food, beverages, music, flowers, decor?
- What are the laws in the state regarding the serving of alcohol? Does the site have a liquor license?
- At what time on our wedding day can vendors have access to the site to prepare for the reception?
- Will the facility provide printed directions to the site for inclusion in the invitations?
- Is there a kitchen for food preparation? Is it fully equipped?
- Are there ample tables and chairs?
- Does the facility use and recommend a particular florist? If we prefer to provide our own decorations, how can this be arranged?
- What flowers, greens, or decorations will already be in place?
- May the reception be extended an extra hour? What would the overtime charges be?
- Are taxes included in the costs?
- Are gratuities included in the costs?
- Is there a room or outdoor space that can be available for group shots to be taken? Is there an additional charge for this room?
- Is there a dressing room available for the bridal party?
- What are the parking arrangements for guests? Is valet parking available?
- How many people can be on the dance floor at one time?
- How large a band or orchestra do you recommend?
- Is there adequate wiring and are there sufficient outlets for a sound system, or would the band or DJ have to bring extra cords and plugs?
- Is electrical power available? Is water available?

- Who assumes liability if a guest becomes inebriated and has an accident?
- What kind of privacy will the party have? (Note that at a wedding reception facility, there can be more than one wedding occurring at a time.)

If the reception site has an in-house catering service, following are some additional questions to ask the site manager:

- What food and drink choices can be offered at the cocktail hour? During the reception?
- What is the price difference between brand-name liquors and house brands?
- What is the price difference between an open bar for the cocktail hour only and an open bar throughout the reception?
- What is the ratio of serving staff to guests?
- What does a sample place setting consist of?
- May we sample food before making selections?
- Is there a special rate for providing food and beverages for the musicians, photographers, and videographers?
- Is insurance against china and crystal breakage included in the costs? If not, what are additional insurance costs?
- What are the choices of table linen colors? Are there choices for china, silver, and crystal?
- Ask to see a book of on-site wedding cakes and whether you can sample a selection. Ask whether you can provide your own wedding cake at no extra cost. If not, what is the extra cost? Can arrangements be made for your baker to finish decorating the cake on-site?
- At what time do servers go on overtime pay? What would the overtime charges be?
- Are gratuities included in the total bill or are they handled separately?
- Who will be on site during the reception to oversee the event? A manager?

MORE DETAILS TO CHECK

Be sure to have all details spelled out before signing a contract. Also, make notes of dates to communicate specific details to the site or restaurant manager, such as the final guest count, arrangements for an outside florist or baker to deliver flowers or the wedding cake, and so on.

You should also see how tables will be set up. If you want a bridal table, determine how many guests the other tables will seat comfortably. Do you require a table where guests may pick up their table assignments and/or a table for gifts in case guests bring them to the reception? Where is a receiving line best placed? Where will speakers be located if music will be amplified?

THE CLUB, HOTEL, OR WEDDING FACILITY RECEPTION

Hotels, private clubs, and catering halls offer wedding packages that vary according to the time and style of your reception. When investigating possibilities, make appointments with facility managers to discuss your needs and hear their suggestions.

Wedding facilities and many hotels and clubs have the capabilities to manage your entire wedding from soup to nuts, from the exchange of vows to your honeymoon departure.

Most facilities have a minimum number of guests they will accept for the larger spaces or main ballrooms. If your guest list is small, consider a smaller secondary room.

One last thing you should do is visit the room where your reception will be held—at the time of day it will take place. Check for cleanliness and the absence of water and food stains. If you can visit during another wedding or party, all the better. That way you can see firsthand how the space looks with lighting, music, and a roomful of people. And be sure that you get the room you looked over, not one that "looks just the same." They never are quite alike.

THE RESTAURANT RECEPTION

Having your reception in a restaurant is a smart idea for the busy couple who has little time to plan. It's all there in one place: food, service, ambiance, and a built-in cleanup crew. Some wedding parties rent out the entire restaurant for a block of time; others celebrate in the restaurant's private party room.

Although some large receptions can be accommodated in a private room of a restaurant, most restaurant receptions are small ones. A restaurant is often chosen for lunch or dinner after a civil ceremony or after a marriage attended only by family and close friends. Unless you are inviting guests to order from the restaurant menu, the food and choice of beverages are ordered ahead of time. Having a set menu, whether served by waiters at a sit-down meal or offered buffet-style, is usually the most economical choice; it also eliminates any complications in paying the check. Many larger restaurants have party-menu choices and even reception consultants to help out. You'll surely want to have a wedding cake, no matter how simple, and toasts to the newlyweds.

THE TENTED RECEPTION

The bride and groom considering the use of an outdoor tent for their reception have a long list of choices. Tents today run the gamut from simple to palatial, outfitted with arches for entryways, bridges and pathways, parquet floors, stained-glass panels, and chandeliers. You can find a colored tent that matches your wedding colors or a climate-controlled tent, with generators for heating or cooling or ceiling fans to keep air circulating.

Because the choices for tents can be mind-boggling, it is a good idea to talk to your caterer or club manager if you are thinking about using one. He may be able to recommend reputable suppliers and offer advice on tent size and the best locations. You will want recommendations; who you rent the tent and supplies from is crucial to your budget, and there is often a big discrepancy in costs from one tent supplier to another. Another tip to remember: Never order a tent over the phone—go in person to see what you are paying for.

In general, you need at least one 60-foot-by-60-foot or 40-foot-by-100-foot tent per 200 people for dinner and dancing. You can include rest rooms, but they're extra footage; if you are having a cocktail hour, that's extra, too. In fact, everything is extra: You'll need to consider sound-system hookups, a generator and a back up generator, ground cover, a dance floor, permits required by local ordinance, and supervisory and other personnel required for tent installation and maintenance.

> ### MARRYING IN THE MAGIC KINGDOM
>
> The number-one wedding/reception/honeymoon destination in the United States? The Walt Disney World Resort, where wedding specialists are on staff to coordinate every detail of your plans.

THE HOME RECEPTION

Pride in home and family—not saving money—is often the overriding reason people choose to have a reception at home. If you do decide to take this route,

WHEELS

While driving to your ceremony and reception in the family station wagon is a fine thing to do, most brides and grooms don't. More than 75 percent of all couples use hired cars for their weddings, and a white limousine is their car of choice 85 percent of the time. Other popular choices are a classic Rolls-Royce, a London taxi, a horse-drawn carriage, and a standard stretch black or navy limo. If hiring limousines is a possibility for you, shop around. Get recommendations from friends. Or call the National Limousine Association for a referral (800–NLA–7707).

keep in mind that if you are hiring an outside caterer, you must give him space to work, where he can do what he was hired to do with little interruption. The space could be as simple as a small pantry with the door closed or as elaborate as the entire kitchen.

RECEPTION FOOD AND DRINK

Once you have located a reception space that meets all of your needs, it's time to brainstorm with vendors on the specific type of menu and services you want.

When choosing the menu for your reception, always keep your guests in mind. You will want a menu to please most everyone, but you don't have to settle for bland or boring. At the same time, you don't want to alienate your reception guests, presumably the people who mean the most to you, by forcing a quirky, trendy, or bizarre menu on them. Choose foods that will excite your guests and that fit perfectly the season and the setting. Your main objective is to have a festive occasion while making your guests feel comfortable.

THE RECEPTION SERVICE

Many of your menu decisions will revolve around the size of your guest list, the season, the time of day, the formality of the occasion, and finally, your budget. Before you think about the types of food and beverages you want to serve, consider the style of service.

SIT-DOWN OR SEATED MEAL

A sit-down meal is one at which reception guests are seated and served by a wait staff. Guests find their way to their tables, usually pre-assigned by you. At a large reception, table numbers are noted on place cards that guests pick up when they arrive. Don't assume that a seated meal is the most expensive kind of reception, because staff costs are often moderated by the fact that guests eat what they are served and can't go back for seconds, as at a buffet.

The types of sit-down services include:

- **PLATED SERVICE.** Guests are served their meal with the full menu already arranged on their plates.
- **RUSSIAN SERVICE.** Plates are already at the guests' places when they sit down. Courses are served from platters by a wait staff. Often, one waiter serves the vegetables, another the meat, and another the salad.
- **FRENCH SERVICE.** Two waiters do what one waiter does in Russian service, with one holding the platter and the other serving.

BUFFET

At a buffet, guests select what they will eat, either from one long table filled with choices or from several stations strategically situated throughout the room. Guests serve themselves or are served by a staff standing behind the buffet table. An advantage of a buffet is serving a varied menu from which most people will find foods they like. You can also have a more informal environment and vary the size of the guest tables. A disadvantage is that buffets often cost more. People tend to eat more, simply because they can return to the serving table as often as they wish.

There are two types of buffets:

- **SINGLE BUFFET TABLE.** A long table is covered with a plain white tablecloth. The centerpiece may revolve around your decorating scheme, but it may also be a simple bowl of white flowers. Stacks of plates, napkins, and cutlery are arranged on the table if guests are to take their plates to chairs or small tables. If they are returning to assigned tables, cutlery, napkins, and beverage glasses are already set.

  At most times, servers stand behind the buffet tables to assist guests; if there are no servers, guests help themselves. Guests pass along the length of the table, going in one direction, and return to their seats or find a place to sit. If there are no assigned tables, very often a waiter will carry beverages on a tray and serve guests wherever they find a seat. If there is a staff, guests (whether seated at assigned or open tables) leave their used plates when they go back for more, then take a clean plate at the buffet table; an ever-alert staff whisks away used plates before guests return to their seats. At a small house reception where there is no professional staff, guests may take their own plates with them when they go back for more.

- **FOOD STATIONS**. Food stations are a variation on buffet service, the difference being that each station is often dedicated to a particular kind of food. Stations set up in strategic locations around the reception room permit excellent mobility, allowing guests to move from one station to another without having to stand in line at one table. A chef may even be placed at a food station, making crepes to order or slicing roast beef.

  Food stations can be theme-oriented: You can have a quesadilla station, a dim-sum station, a pasta station. The stations can also feature a certain type of food; you may, for example, have a seafood station on one side of the room and a salad bar station on the other. The variety and breadth of foods offered will please the majority of palates and the food will be served in a fun, interactive way.

  Food stations may also be set up for dessert after a sit-down dinner. You might want to offer a Viennese coffee station, an Italian pastry station, a make-your-own sundae station, or a cappuccino and cake station.

PASSED-TRAY RECEPTIONS

Ideal for cocktail receptions, passed-tray service is just that—waiters circulate through the room with trays of hors d'oeuvres, stopping to offer them to guests. This is an easy serving solution, but it can be expensive, since most caterers, hotels, and clubs charge a per-person fee for the food. They might figure, for example, on each person eating approximately six or seven servings of hors d'oeuvres. If that is all that is served, guests may leave hungry—and the longer your reception is, the hungrier they will be. One way to supplement passed-tray service is to include a buffet table containing crudités, cheese and fruit, and more substantial fare for guests to munch on between the presentations of the more elegant hors d'oeuvres.

WORKING WITH A CATERER

If you are planning a small reception and have the help of family and friends, you probably don't need professional help in preparing and serving reception food and beverages. By preparing food in advance and freezing it and by keeping the menu and decorations as simple as possible, a small wedding reception can be both inexpensive and, within reason, easy to manage.

Planning a larger reception in your home or anywhere else that provides no services, however, can be a lot of work. Entertaining a large group of guests with any degree of pleasure and relaxation requires the aid of professional catering services. Caterers, in other words, let you be a guest at your own party.

The rule of thumb: Hiring a caterer is recommended for a reception of more than 30 guests. Depending on the size of the company, they can provide only the food or the works: food, beverages, the wedding cake, the serving staff, crystal and china, tables, chairs, and linens. Some even provide tents, dance floors, and party decorations—or can lead you to reliable suppliers and vendors.

The best way to find a reliable caterer is to ask friends for recommendations. Never, ever, use a caterer without checking his references, especially if you have picked him out of the Yellow Pages.

You may choose to use the on-site caterer at your reception location. Banquet facilities often offer wedding packages that include on-site catering. It's a convenient and cost-efficient alternative to renting a space and hiring independent vendors.

If, on the other hand, you have your sights set on an off-site caterer, set up a preliminary meeting with the caterer at his office. Be sure to set a time to meet at your reception site before going too far into your planning. A caterer's experience can be extremely valuable in deciding how well-equipped the site is, where to place tables, how many guests can be accommodated comfortably, how many staff will be required, and any number of other details essential to the perfect reception.

Be sure to look over the caterer's portfolio—usually an album containing photographs of previous receptions. Look for creative touches: fruits and vegetables skillfully cut into beautiful shapes or arranged in eye-catching ways; interesting and complementary color schemes; a variety of dishes; and, if you're considering a buffet, well-organized and attractive presentations. The food should be pretty enough to stand on its own.

Set up a food tasting with caterers you are interviewing. Most will be happy to do so. Ask for a variety of dishes, from hors d'oeuvres to a main course to a dessert.

CATERERS AND COSTS

Caterers generally set prices based on a per-person figure. That figure varies from region to region, state to state, and urban area to rural area. Costs are dependent on other factors as well: the formality of the occasion, the time of day, the day of the week, the number of guests, what kind of food service you choose, how you choose to serve alcohol and other beverages, and the number of service people needed for the job.

Costs can run from $25 per person for a beach clambake to $600 per person for a grand sit-down dinner in a major city. Having an open bar can add more than $10 per person to the total cost.

Don't forget to figure gratuities and taxes into your total costs; they can add up to 25 percent of the total bill.

CATERER CHECKLIST

Once you and your caterer have toured the reception site and agreed on arrangements, be absolutely sure that every service to be provided, and the total itemized costs, are given to you in a contract. Everything down to the last canapé must be specified. Specifically, the following points should be covered:

- Detailed menu and how it will be served
- Beverages—open bar, champagne, soft drinks and other nonalcoholic beverages
- Number of serving staff total, and how many per table for a sit-down reception
- Wedding cake and how it will be served, unless planned elsewhere
- Whether gratuities are included
- Number and setup of tables and chairs
- Delivery charges
- Deadline for guest count
- Overtime charges
- Tents or marquees
- Portable toilets if the site has too few
- Whether glass and china are insured against breakage
- Whether taxes are included in the estimate
- Flowers and decorations (coordinate with florist)

- Table linen choices
- Coat check and valet parking staff provided or not
- Meals for band, DJ, photographers, videographers
- Additional fees for the rental of linens, china, flatware
- Additional fees for setup and cleanup
- Form of last payment (check, credit card, certified check)
- Surcharges for heat or air conditioning

CATERER COST-CUTTERS

- **HAVE A "PACK-UP RECEPTION."** If you're having a small reception, you can provide food that has been "packed up" ahead of time by a caterer. Service takes up a large chunk of your catering bill, with on-site caterers adding as much as 30 to 50 percent to your food costs. Most private and supermarket caterers will pack up food to go and give directions on how to heat and serve it—all you do is pick it up, set it out, and provide your own service.

- **HAVE A HYBRID RECEPTION.** Instead of a costly sit-down dinner, for example, offer cocktail hors d'oeuvres and two or three food stations, featuring crepes, pasta, assorted crudités and dips, cheese, or a carving board. Or have a sit-down first course salad followed by a buffet.

- **CHOOSE LESS EXPENSIVE FOODS AND INGREDIENTS.** Seafood is more expensive than pasta, for example. You can do the same if you're having only hors d'oeuvres—simply forgo the caviar on toast points for miniature quesadillas, for example.

- **AVOID SATURDAY NIGHTS.** Premium charges apply then.

- **CHOOSE A "NON-MEAL" TIME OF DAY.** If your reception is held at midday or anytime between 4 P.M. and 8 P.M., guests expect to be served a full meal. For an early-afternoon or even a late-evening reception, you can get away with lighter fare, and less of it—a cost-cutting way to serve food. The earlier in the day you hold your reception, the more casual (and less expensive) it can be. Alcohol costs also tend to be lower for daytime events.

- **STICK TO YOUR VISION.** Never let a caterer talk you into something that is ultimately not your style or in your price range simply because it's the latest trend. In fact, some caterers suggest reducing your original reception budget by 25 percent to make room for potential cost overruns.

WEDDING CUISINE TRENDS

In choosing the menu, look for food guaranteed to please most everyone, but don't settle for bland or boring. You *can* find foods that will excite your guests, menus that perfectly fit the season and the setting—and choices that are a meaningful expression of your personality.

The following are some of the latest trends in reception food and drink.

- **LIGHTER, HEALTHIER FARE.** Lean meats, pastas, seafood, salads, and vegetables are increasingly popular choices.
- **ETHNIC DISHES.** Some couples are planning their reception menu around an ethnic theme, such as Mexican or Japanese cuisine.
- **REGIONAL SPECIALTIES AND "DOWN-HOME" COMFORT.** This trend reflects the desire by many modern couples to personalize their wedding and show pride in their home environment.
- **FOOD STATIONS.** This is the area where creative caterers are really having fun. Food stations run the gamut, from cappuccino bars to sushi stations.
- **LIGHTER BAR OFFERINGS.** Beer and champagne are being served in place of mixed drinks.
- **COCKTAIL PARTIES.** Cocktail parties and passed-tray hors d'oeuvres are popular choices in place of full meals.

THE WEDDING DRINKS

Your beverage choices are varied. If alcohol is against your religion, don't serve it unless you don't mind if your guests drink. If you do serve alcohol, decide on how much and how it will be served. Some receptions offer champagne and wine only; others hold an open bar during the cocktail hour and serve wine, beer, and champagne during dinner; still others keep the bar open throughout the festivities.

You will be charged in one of two ways: a flat package rate (which is a per-person, per-hour charge) or a per-drink rate (where the bartenders keep a tally of every drink they pour). Find out what the per-person charge covers before deciding. If it is based on an average of five or six drinks per person for the duration of the reception, and you are also serving wine with dinner and champagne for toasting, you might settle on the per-drink rate instead—it is unlikely that each guest will consume that many glasses of liquor along with the wine.

DRINK COST-CUTTERS

Cost-reducing drink and service options include:

- **HAVE A SOFT BAR INSTEAD OF A FULL BAR.** At a soft bar, guests may order champagne; beer; nonalcoholic beer; red and white wine; regular or diet soft drinks, with or without caffeine; iced tea; juices; and coffee, tea, or mineral water. It is a good idea, however, to know your guests' tastes before going this route. If your guests are used to cocktails, it might be wise to have a full bar and fewer guests instead.

- **BUY YOUR OWN LIQUOR.** Some caterers will let you buy your own liquor, whether your reception is at home or at a catering facility. Or they will buy it for you and bill you at cost, plus a small percentage for labor. Often this comes in the form of a cork fee—a per-bottle fee charged by the caterer to open and serve liquor you bring in. Keep in mind that whatever you buy, you bear the responsibility of pickup and delivery. In addition, most liquor stores will refund your money if you return unopened liquor bottles. The unopened bottles of liquor will have to be packed and transported from the reception site.

- **CHOOSE LESS EXPENSIVE HOUSE BRANDS.** If you decide to serve liquor but want to save money, choose house brands rather than name-brand liquors.

- **GLASS INSTEAD OF PLASTIC.** If yours is an outdoor wedding where alcohol is served, it costs roughly the same and may even be cheaper to rent real (and sturdier) glasses than to buy plastic. Another bonus: it is more elegant.

TYPES OF BARS

- **OPEN BAR.** The host pays a flat rate for drinks served for a specific period of time, either during the cocktail hour or for the entire evening.

- **CONSUMPTION BAR.** The per-drink fee discussed above. The same as an open bar, except the host is charged on a running bar tab instead of a flat fee.

- **WHITE BAR.** Only serves "white" alcoholic beverages: vodka, gin, champagne, and white wine.

PLANNING THE DECOR

If you are using the services of a florist, you will be having discussions concerning reception flowers fairly early in the planning process. If you are not using a florist, you should still start thinking about the type of decor you want. Following are some tips on decorating for your reception:

- You can save money by using the ceremony flowers at your reception.
- Rent or borrow potted plants to place at doorways and entranceways.
- Lighting is important. If you can, dim the electrical lighting and use lots of candles, from votive candles to long tapered ones, on all of the tables.
- Consider the little touches. In rest rooms, place small baskets containing soaps, hand lotion, perfume, aspirin, safety pins, and sanitary supplies, tied up nicely with bows or flowers in the wedding colors. Provide a bowl of breath mints and plenty of tissues.

DOLLARS AND DRINKS

If you greet guests with trays of champagne or wine when they enter the reception site or as they leave the receiving line, two-thirds of those who accept will stick to champagne and not switch to mixed drinks. Keep that in mind when ordering liquor and champagne. Allow six to eight glasses per bottle of wine or champagne. Figure two to three drinks per person for the first hour, one per hour after that.

SEATING ARRANGEMENTS

At most sit-down dinners or formal buffet receptions, it is customary for the bride and groom to determine seating arrangements. This takes tact and diplomacy; you will want all your guests to feel they are each seated in a special spot. It's also fun to mix and match guests, trying to find compatible dinner table partners. That's why it's a good idea to start considering seating early in your planning.

SEATING PARENTS

It is customary to have separate parents' tables, one for the bride's family and close friends, and another for the groom's family. It is fine to put both sets together, but this can become unwieldy, since each set generally comes with its own entourage of extended family and close friends.

When the bride and/or groom's parents have been divorced, however, and all are in attendance, it is usually not a good idea to seat them together. Even if relations between the divorced parents are amicable, the extended family and friends of each make it difficult logistically to seat them all at one table.

THE BRIDE'S TABLE

The bridal party table is often a rectangular table set against one side or end of the room. The bride and groom sit at the center of the long side, facing out so that guests can see them. No one is seated opposite them. The bride sits on the groom's right, with the best man on her right; the maid of honor sits on the groom's left, and the bridesmaids and ushers alternate along the same side of the table. If the group is large, the table can be made into a U-shape, with the bride and groom at the center of the center table. The wedding party's husbands, wives, fiancés, and significant others should be seated here, too, if there is room.

When the wedding party is large or when the couple wants to seat the attendants with their spouses and partners, two large round tables may be used to seat the entire group. In this case, the bride and groom would sit with the maid of honor and best man, their respective partners, and possibly some of the attendants' and their partners. Children or siblings of the bride or groom who were not in the wedding party may also sit with them.

NO BRIDAL TABLE

Many couples prefer to wander about and mingle with their guests rather than being seated at a formal table. There should always, however, be a table reserved for the bride and groom and their attendants to sit down and rest.

The newlyweds may go to the buffet table just as the other guests do; in some cases, a waiter fills a plate and brings it to where they are seated. The bridesmaids and ushers need not all sit with the bride and groom at the same time, but all should gather together during the toasts and the cutting of the cake.

PLACE CARDS

If you plan a seated dinner for more than a few guests, you will probably want to use place cards. The tables are numbered, and place cards bearing the name of each guest and the table number of his or her seat are arranged, in alphabetical order, on a side table at the reception entrance. After leaving the receiving line, each guest passes by the table, finds his or her place card, checks the number written on it, then locates the table with the same number.

You can choose to make place cards for the parents' tables and the bridal party tables only. In this instance, you should delegate a friend to take the place cards to the reception site before the ceremony, if possible, and place them in their proper locations.

At some point in your meetings with the site manager or catering director, ask for a diagram of the number of tables and their placement. Make several photocopies of the diagram so that you can experiment with the seating arrangements. Once you've made final decisions, number each table and place card.

PLANNING TRANSPORTATION

In planning your reception, you will need to consider your mode of transport from one site to the next. If you plan to hire limousines, begin looking for a reputable company the minute your ceremony and reception sites are confirmed. The sooner, the better: Rented limos are in high demand at peak times.

Think about the number of cars you need. Considerations are one for the bride and her father to the ceremony and for the bride and groom to the reception; a second car for the bride's mother, any children in the wedding party, and any attendants who will ride with the bride's mother and father to the reception; and a third car for the rest of the bride's attendants. If the sky's the limit and you want to hire additional cars for special guests, grandmothers, or whomever, count them in.

IN DAYS PAST, A RECEPTION MEAL WAS A BREAKFAST

When explaining the details of a "sit-down breakfast" in 1922, Emily Post wrote, "The general sit-down breakfast—except in great houses like a few of those in Newport—is always furnished by a caterer. . . . The feature of the wedding breakfast is always the bride's table. . . . The standing breakfast differs from the sit-down breakfast in service only."

Whatever you do, don't try to cram the entire wedding party in with you on the way to the reception. Even if the car is a huge stretch limo, enjoy the luxury and the romance of having your mate alone with you, if only for a few minutes. This will very likely be the first time you have been alone all day and most probably the last time you will be alone until you leave the reception. Savor the moment.

Drive the route to get the timing down. Unless all sites are in close proximity, allow time for traffic tie-ups. When it comes to weddings, it's far better to be early than to keep everyone waiting.

CAR SERVICES: WHAT TO LOOK FOR, WHAT TO ASK

Begin with phone calls. Ask the following questions:

- How many and what size cars will I need to transport (however many) people?
- What kinds of cars do you have?
- May I select the ones I want to use?
- Do you have a minimum number of hours for a contract?
- How are your rates structured?
- Are any services included in your rates?
- Can gratuities be included in the bill?
- What deposit is required? Is there a cancellation clause available?
- Do you accept credit cards?
- How will the drivers be attired?

With the answers to these questions, you can make some decisions about how many cars you can hire and what your needs are before meeting in person to sign a contract.

When you sign a contract, it is a good idea to ensure that it includes the following:

- Date, time, and place of service
- Number of people to be transported
- Number of vehicles
- Exact vehicles to be used, including vehicle identification numbers of the ones you have selected
- Liability coverage for the company as well as for you, for accidents and damages

Planning the Reception

245

- Rate for each vehicle, with number of hours indicated
- Additional fees, such as taxes and gratuities
- Amount of deposit, cancellation information, date when balance is due, and how to be paid

In return for your business, you should expect to get precisely the cars you hired, and they should arrive on time. You should expect clean, shining cars and mannerly, knowledgeable drivers in appropriate dress. All amenities should be working and available, and the bar stocked as you requested with what you agreed to pay for. Do check local liquor laws to be sure you can sip champagne in transit.

TRANSPORTATION DETAILS

Let your attendants know whether your transportation arrangements include them. This way, they can coordinate with their spouses or dates so that they are not left stranded outside the ceremony site.

If your parents will be traveling by hired car, they will need to make arrangements to have a car remain at the reception site so that they can return home afterward.

Enlist the best man to make sure you and he have transportation ready at the reception site, too, and to help find a way back to the hotel or home for any bridesmaids who do not have dates to transport them.

PARKING SECURITY

One other detail to organize when planning your reception is parking security for your guests' cars. Generally, hotels provide valet parking and security, while clubs, wedding halls, and rental facilities usually do not. Call to confirm.

If your reception is held at a private residence, call the police to find out about local ordinances so that guests' cars won't get ticketed or towed. If the area already has considerable traffic congestion, you will probably need an off-duty police officer or a security guard as well as valet parking attendants.

When hiring parking security, check that the company is fully insured and licensed, and ask that attendants be neatly dressed and courteous. It is better to have experienced drivers and attendants than to hire neighborhood teens to move cars. Ensure that there are enough attendants to patrol the lots or areas where guests will be parking.

CHAPTER 13

FLOWERS

Enduring, fragrant, romantic—flowers are the key decorating elements of the wedding celebration. Flowers not only add visual pleasure and a note of festivity to the proceedings but symbolize the full blooming of new love and a new life. Fresh blooms and greenery—whether cascading from an altar, twined around an arch, scattered from a flower girl's basket, or tucked lovingly into a groom's lapel—represent the full flowering of a couple's love.

Many of the traditions of old retain a place in wedding events, long after their origins have been forgotten. For example, the tradition of flowers strewn along the path the bride walks has its roots in ancient times, when a path of flowers and fragrant herbs was thought to keep evil spirits away. Centuries ago, wedding reception halls were decorated with sweet-smelling jasmine to entice angels to attend and bless the event. In a tradition that began in 12th-century Spain, fresh orange blossoms were fashioned into wreaths to crown the heads of brides. Hundreds of years later, England's Queen Victoria would wear fragrant orange blossoms in her hair in her marriage to Prince Albert. Brides who could neither afford nor find fresh blossoms used wax ones; many a wax bridal wreath has become a treasured family heirloom, passed down from generation to generation of brides.

Modern couples may not know the tradition behind the ritual, but they do appreciate the beauty and purity that flowers bring to a wedding celebration. Today flowers at weddings are used in nearly every aspect of the celebration, from the decoration of church pews to topping the wedding cake. Flowers can be seen everywhere: in the hands of attendants; given to parents, stepparents, and grandparents; in centerpieces and on mantels; wrapped around candles or topping buffet tables—even adorning serving platters. You might even decide to place plants at strategic locations, such as main entryways.

Whether you select flowers for their symbolic meaning, for seasonal fresh-ness, for mix-and-match qualities, for color, size, or fragrance, or simply for aesthetic pleasure, you'll find the process of choosing a delight. Make it a personal quest. Make your wedding flowers an expression of your heart.

GATHERING IDEAS

Do your research before making any decisions. If you plan to use a florist, you'll want to be prepared with lists and concepts before you make an appointment. To start, be on the hunt for good ideas. Scour bridal magazines, interior design and home magazines, floral websites, flower shows, and photography and garden books for inspiration. Visit nurseries and well-known gardens. Anytime you see a picture of something you like—whether a beautiful bouquet, a particular flower, or an interesting color scheme—cut it out and place it into your wedding planner.

When choosing flowers, consider the formality of your wedding, the time of day, the colors you and the bridal party will be wearing, and the season. Consider as well the interior design of the wedding site and reception. A church with a high ceiling, for example, demands taller plants. For an evening wedding, white or brightly colored flowers stand out, especially if the ceremony is held in candlelight. Flowers can also be specifically chosen to complement table linens. Your decor will also be influenced by such factors as the constraints of your budget, and whether the ceremony is indoors or out. But that doesn't mean your choices are limited. On the contrary: they are myriad and wide-ranging.

WEDDING FLOWERS CHECKLIST

The first thing you should do is draw up a list of all your floral needs. A copy of this list should be presented to the florist at your first meeting. Consider any ribbons, greens, candles, vases, pots, or containers you may also need.

The range of floral decorations can go far beyond bridal party bouquets and altar decorations. You may want a plant for each entranceway, flowers to

KEEPING EVIL SPIRITS AWAY

Floral bouquets for brides are pre-dated tens of centuries by aromatic nosegays of fresh herbs carried to ward off evil spirits and to ensure good fortune for the couple. Lavender, rosemary, and rue snippets were strewn at their feet for the same purpose. The mothers of early European brides tucked sprigs of myrtle into bouquets. These sprigs, removed later by the bride, were planted, tended carefully, and watched over, to be clipped and given to the bride's own daughter on her wedding day.

garnish serving platters, flower sprays for candles, bouquets for wedding helpers and grandparents—even a beribboned flower twined around the cake knife. To guide you, the following is a general checklist of floral needs. By no means must you follow this list to the letter: It is simply a guide for you to work from, whether you are collaborating with a florist or floral designer or planning to do the arrangements yourself.

The Bride and Her Attendants

- Bride's Bouquet
- Honor Attendant
- Bridesmaids
- Flower Girl
- Tossing Bouquet
- Floral Hair Decorations

The Groom and His Attendants

- Groom's Boutonniere
- Best Man
- Ushers
- Ring Bearer

Family Flowers

- Parents and Stepparents of the Bride
- Parents and Stepparents of the Groom
- Grandmothers and Grandfathers
- Other Special Guests

For the Ceremony

- Entranceway
- Altar
- *Chuppah*
- Pews
- Candles
- Roses for Parents, if necessary
- Aisle Runner

For the Reception	*As Gifts*
• Centerpieces	• Party Hosts
• Buffet Tables	• Out-of-Town Guests
• Cake-Topper, Cake Knife	• Weekend Hosts
• Cake Table	• Thank-You Notes to Friends and Helpers
• Mantel, Stairway, Entranceways	
• Place Card Table	
• Garnish for Serving Platters	
• Rest Room Arrangements	
• Flower Petals for Tossing	

FLORAL THEMES

Before you meet with a florist, consider the unifying theme of your wedding. Are you planning a country-style wedding with baskets overflowing with wild-flowers and simple bouquets, or do you favor a traditional, formal celebration of understated elegance? Do you have a color scheme in mind or are you considering all white for flowers and decorations? Will you have accessory themes? Are you making floral choices based as much on fragrance as on color and texture? If you are having a *real* theme wedding—Romantic Victorian, for example, Hawaiian Luau, Fifties-style—you'll want to come up with concepts for flowers and decorations that match the theme.

There are many ways to use flowers to personalize your wedding. The following are some ideas to make your celebration special and unique.

THE LANGUAGE OF FLOWERS

As you begin making decisions about flowers, you might incorporate those that have special traditional meaning. In the early 1900s, romance was often communicated with flowers. A young man would present a red rose, which symbolized love, to a young woman. She would return a purple pansy, which silently relayed the message "you are in my thoughts." Traditionally, no words were spoken that would commit either party during this courtship, so knowing the language of flowers was of paramount importance if an accord was to be reached. Today it is a charming idea to select flowers, and even herbs, that convey special floral messages between the bride and the groom.

Flowers

ACACIA—*friendship*

AGRIMONY—*gratitude*

AMBROSIA—*love returned*

ANEMONE—*expectation*

APPLE BLOSSOMS—*hope*

ASTER—*elegance*

AZALEA—*temperance*

BABY'S BREATH—*innocence*

BAY LAUREL—*glory*

CALLA LILY—*beauty*

CAMELLIA—*loveliness*

CARNATION—*devotion*

CHRYSANTHEMUM—*abundance*

DAFFODIL—*regard*

DAISY—*gentleness*

FORGET-ME-NOT—*remembrance*

FREESIA—*innocence*

GARDENIA—*purity*

HEATHER—*future fortune*

HELIOTROPE—*devotion*

IVY—*fidelity*

LARKSPUR—*laughter*

LAUREL—*peace*

LILAC—*humility*

LILY—*majesty*

LILY OF THE VALLEY—*happiness*

MYRTLE—*remembrance*

ORANGE BLOSSOM—*purity*

ORCHID—*rare beauty*

PARSLEY—*beginnings*

PEONY—*bashfulness*

QUEEN ANNE'S LACE—*trust*

ROSE—*love*

ROSEMARY—*remembrance*

SAGE—*immortality*

STEPHANOTIS—*marital happiness*

THYME—*courage*

TULIP—*passion*

VIOLET—*modesty*

ZINNIA—*affection*

THE LANGUAGE OF COLOR

Colors have meaning in many cultures. You may want to develop your floral color scheme around a particular color for its symbolic meaning.

- **RED OR FUSCHIA**. The color of love in China and India.
- **GREEN**. The ancient color of fertility. A color symbolizing luck to modern-day Italians and Irish.
- **RED AND YELLOW**. The marriage colors of Egypt, the Orient, and Russia.
- **BLUE/TURQOISE**. Attached to wedding ceremonies in Western countries ("something borrowed, something blue").
- **PURPLE**. Represented wealth in ancient Greece. The classical color of the soul.
- **BLUE AND GOLD**. Reinforces power, dignity, and rank.

BIRTH MONTH FLOWERS

Another special way to personalize and add meaning to floral choices is to combine the traditional birth month flowers of the bride and groom.

JANUARY	*carnation*
FEBRUARY	*violet*
MARCH	*jonquil*
APRIL	*sweet pea*
MAY	*lily of the valley*
JUNE	*rose*
JULY	*larkspur*
AUGUST	*gladiolus*
SEPTEMBER	*aster*
OCTOBER	*calendula*
NOVEMBER	*chrysanthemum*
DECEMBER	*narcissus*

FRAGRANT FLOWERS AND HERBS

A popular trend is including fragrance in your overall wedding theme, using flowers, herbs, and greenery not just for their visual appeal but for their perfume.

bay laurel	*lily of the valley*
carnation	*magnolia blossoms*
freesia	*mint*
gardenias	*narcissus*
hyacinth	*roses, especially old-fashioned or tea roses*
jasmine	*stephanotis*
lavender	*violets*
lilacs	*wisteria*

FINDING A FLORIST

After doing your research, your next step is to choose a florist. With wedding vision in mind, look for a florist who can embrace your ideas, offer advice and suggestions, show you examples, and agree to your schedule and budgetary limits. Start with recommendations from friends, local caterers, or local nurseries. A florist who is closely affiliated with nurseries or wholesalers can often get good prices on flowers and plants in bulk. If you are holding your celebration in a hotel or reception hall, learn the names of florists who have worked wedding celebrations there.

In the last few years, "floral designers" have become popular. These designers, unlike florists, generally do not work out of a shop and are particularly versed in creative, nontraditional themes. Floral designers can create a unifying look for your entire wedding, integrating not only flowers into the decor but lighting and textiles as well. You'll have to decide whether you want to work with a full-service florist, who can provide soup-to-nuts floral needs in-house, or with a floral designer, who generally creates a design and then executes it by outsourcing jobs. Even though many floral designers do not have a shop, they often have a full staff to handle every aspect of the floral plans.

You should always make an appointment to see a florist or floral designer. It is unrealistic and discourteous to think you can walk in, unexpected, and snare his undivided attention.

At the first meeting, there is nothing wrong with saying up front that you aren't ready to sign a contract, but that you are looking for someone with whom you can work. You should also:

- Ask to see the florist's album or portfolio containing photographs or illustrations of previous weddings for which the florist has provided flowers.
- Ask for references.
- Inquire about wedding packages and what they include.
- Ask about guarantees.

Look for a florist who sees himself as a collaborator, but who also offers creative advice on ways to do things more efficiently. If, for example, your wedding is small but located in a large site, ask the florist to recommend ways to make it intimate. He may do it with greens, flowers, or even decorated screens. The same is true of your reception site and for any other ways you want to personalize your wedding. You'll want a florist you feel comfortable with and one who is experienced in the business of wedding decorating. The florist should also be capable of managing all the details, including the timing and delivery of the arrangements you require.

WHAT TO BRING

Be prepared for your appointment with the florist so that you can both use the time efficiently. The more information you provide and the better your research and planning, the more successful all your meetings with vendors will be.

The following items can be placed or written in your wedding planner.

- A complete wedding flowers checklist, from personal (those that are carried, worn, or given as gifts) to site needs, including the ceremony and reception sites.
- Sketches or photographs of your gown and your attendants' gowns. Include any headpieces.
- Swatches. Include those of your gown, your attendant's gowns, and table linens at the reception. This is an excellent way to match fabrics with complementing flowers. It may be too early to note the color of dress to be worn by mothers, grandmothers, or any other special people to whom you are giving corsages; this information can be delivered, phoned, or faxed later.
- Sizes. If you or any of your attendants are wearing flowers in your hair, you will need to provide head circumferences for wreaths and ask the best way to attach flowers to chignons, twists, or other hairstyles. You will also want to include information on attendants' height and weight so that bouquets will be neither too big nor too small.
- Sketches or photographs of what the groom and his ushers will be wearing.
- Photographs of decorations or color schemes you particularly like.

GETTING DOWN TO WORK

Once you have settled on a florist or floral designer, go over your budget with him. Discuss your wedding-flowers checklist and the range of options for each item. Determine how many of your ideas, large and small, can be accommodated within that budget. Be flexible. The best florists can suggest alternatives that allow you to achieve your vision and stay within cost. If the florist cannot visit your ceremony and reception site, give him a sketch of the layout and describe its existing color schemes. You may also want to consult with the site manager on the types of decor that work well in the space.

You will experience less stress if you remain flexible on floral choices. If on the first pass your wish list results in a budget-busting estimated bill, simply rethink your choices. Ask your florist to recommend inexpensive alternatives.

A SYMBOL OF LOVE

Add a little more romance to your ceremony with a pull-away boutonniere. Concealed inside the bride's bouquet, the boutonniere is pinned by the bride to the groom's lapel after her father or escort steps back, or when she reaches his side if she is walking by herself. It's a touching public display of the bride's love for her groom.

Start over with the basics and make a list of your priorities. What is the most important floral expenditure? The bridal bouquet? The reception centerpiece? Can you splurge on these and rely on simple choices for the less important arrangements? If your choices are made with loving care, it won't matter whether you used an expensive or exotic flower to express your joy. The magic of flowers is that there is beauty and elegance in the simplest of forms.

You will also need to discuss your reception plans with the florist. Check with your caterer and cake-maker to coordinate the overall floral design and ensure that the color schemes match. Often, wedding cakes are decorated with real flowers and greenery, so those will need to be coordinated as well. If the caterer is providing the table linens, you will need to select colors that complement the floral design, or vice versa.

Most florists have some sort of contract or agreement confirming your arrangements and may require a deposit. Make sure you get an item-by-item breakdown of the prices before you sign anything. Check whether the contract includes delivery costs and any gratuities. Arrange for either you or your designer to place a confirmation call to the florist before the orders are to be delivered, then add confirmation-call reminders to your planner.

DELIVERY DETAILS

If you have contracted with the florist to deliver and install the floral decorations, you should provide him with a list of all flower deliveries that need to be made. Discuss the best place and time to deliver each component of the decor. Where, for example, do you want the bride's and her attendant's flowers delivered: the bride's home if everyone will be dressing there, or directly to the ceremony site? If yours is a morning wedding, will the flowers hold up if they are delivered the night before? Include dates, times, instructions for access, and accurate names, telephone numbers, and addresses. Copy the information into your planner as well, and mark your calendar to make a reminder call a day or two before the big day.

LITTLE EXTRAS

Relay all the details of your wedding to your florist so that he can provide you with original ideas to enhance and personalize your plans. Here are some extras that might be included in the contract:

- If you will be lighting a unity candle, it can be decorated in flowers.
- Flower petals to toss can be provided by the florist.
- Special floral gifts for helpers need to be discussed up front. The florist might suggest simple nosegays, corsages, or flower arrangements for later.
- You may include thank-you flowers for bridal showers. If you know friends will be giving you a shower, flowers delivered before or after as a thank-you can be discussed and ordered at the same time you are ordering your wedding flowers.
- Welcome flowers for some out-of-town guests staying in hotels or inns. (Be sure to write the cards beforehand and give them to the florist.)

CUTTING COSTS ON WEDDING FLOWERS

Flowers and decorations are not an insignificant part of a wedding budget—on average, flowers can account for up to 20 percent of total costs. If you need to find ways to cut down on expenditures, it is not difficult to do so. Creative solutions to decorating needs can save money. Following are some smart ways to trim your flower budget.

1. **DO-IT-YOURSELF FLORAL ARRANGEMENTS.** Is it proper to do your own flower arranging? Of course it is! Loose bouquets of seasonal flowers tied with ribbons, arches of freshly blooming dogwood or cherry blossoms, or garlands of ivy draping a staircase are beautiful and easy to create.

If you want your wedding decorated with flowers from your own garden, you'll need a plan of action. Before you decide whether to do the flower arranging yourself, consider the time element. If you are having a small wedding with few arrangements, the task is probably realistic.

If you are having a large wedding with many floral needs, you'll want to think twice about doing the growing, cutting, and arranging yourself, no matter how efficient you are. A fun way to proceed is to get friends and family to help you decorate the ceremony and reception sites on the day of the wedding. You might delegate the delivery.

Another option is to combine your own flowers with those ordered from a florist. Just be sure to carefully coordinate the merging of these two sources. Make two columns in your checklist of needs, one for you and one for the florist. For example, you could order altar flowers from the florist but decorate the ends of the pews yourself with ribbons and lilies of the valley from the garden. You could order reception centerpieces from the florist, but place vases of fresh-cut cherry blossom branches at the entrance.

Still another possibility is to provide your own backyard blooms but give the florist the responsibility of cutting, arranging, and decorating them. That way, you'll enjoy your favorite flowers—and save money doing so—but you won't have to do all the work.

You can make bouquets, corsages, and boutonnieres ahead of time and refrigerate them. Don't leave yourself so little time to pick your flowers that you are dashing to the ceremony straight from the garden. A good way to keep cut flowers fresh overnight is to place them in a bucket of water in a dark, cool room. Cut the stems underwater until you cut them again to arrange; this will help keep them fresh for a couple of days more.

2. USE SEASONAL FLOWERS. Although the advances of modern technology have resulted in the year-round availability of formerly hard-to-get flowers, you can still cut costs by using seasonal flowers that are in bloom locally. They don't need to be shipped, they can be cut close to the time they will be used, and they tend to be hardier than those that are forced in a greenhouse. Following is a list of seasonal flowers.

SPRINGTIME FLOWERS	SUMMERTIME FLOWERS	YEAR-ROUND FLOWERS
apple blossom	aster	Readily available year-round flowers are ones that are grown in greenhouses but that are not rare or difficult to grow.
cherry blossom	calla lily	
daffodil	dahlia	
dogwood	daisy	
forsythia	geranium	
iris	hydrangea	
jonquil	larkspur	baby's breath
larkspur	roses	bachelor button
lilac	stock	carnation
lily		delphinium
lily of the valley	**FALL FLOWERS**	gardenia
peony		ivy
sweet pea	aster	lily
tulip	chrysanthemum	orchid
violet	dahlia	rose
	marigold	stephanotis
	Shasta daisy	
	zinnia	

3. **USE THE "UNWILTABLES."** The hardiest flowers keep fresh and don't wilt after a long day of celebrating. The following are some of the flower kingdom's longest-lasting blooms.

baby's breath	ivy
bachelor button	lily
carnation	orchid
daisy	rose
delpinium	stephanotis
gardenia	

4. **SHARE FLOWERS WITH ANOTHER COUPLE.** Before meeting with a florist, check with your contact at the ceremony site to see whether another wedding is scheduled the same day as yours. It is entirely possible that you can join forces and share the cost of flowers. Offer your telephone number to the ceremony's officiant and ask that the other wedding couple

get in touch with you if they are interested in sharing. Once connected, talk about your individual plans for decorating. Diplomacy is called for here. If the other couple plans multicolored arrangements and you want all white, a joint venture will not work—and you should tactfully say so. If, however, your ideas coincide, then meet to coordinate your plans. Sharing may allow both of you to add more decorations and more expensive flowers. Be clear up front on the fee and the method of payment—whether it will be evenly divided, whether one of you will reimburse the other, or whether you will jointly contract with the florist for ceremony decorations. It is wise to keep in touch, as plans can change.

5. **RENT DECORATIONS.** It is often more cost efficient to rent rather than buy potted plants, trees, and topiaries for your ceremony or reception sites. Renting large palms or ferns for a church ceremony, for example, is a much smarter choice than paying extravagant prices to buy them. Discuss the possibility of renting with your florist. If he or she does not rent, ask for referrals to vendors who do before making any final decisions. Local nurseries often rent big potted plants.

6. **SAVE ON DELIVERY.** One way you can save money is to delegate a friend with a van or a large backseat to pick up your flowers from the florist and deliver them to the wedding and reception sites. Make sure that your friend has all the necessary information to ensure that deliveries are timely and reliable.

7. **DOUBLE YOUR INVESTMENT.** Arrangements at your ceremony site can double as decorations at your reception. Make sure you have allotted sufficient time between the ceremony and reception to make the switch. Delegate the task of transporting the flowers to a friend, or hire a service to whisk them away from the ceremony after guests exit and deliver them promptly to the reception site. Make sure, too, that there is someone at the reception site ready to place them correctly and add water if the arrangements have been emptied out during transport.

8. **HAVE A HOLIDAY WEDDING.** If you are planning your wedding around Christmas or any other holiday season, your ceremony site might already be dressed to the nines in holiday decorations. A church bedecked in poinsettias and greens requires little else from you other than the personal flowers you and your attendants carry and give to family members. Check with your officiant and ask about the types of decorations planned or whether there are photographs from previous seasons you can review to ensure the look is one that works with your plans.

- Combine fresh flowers with silk or dried. Silk is a good choice for two reasons: It is about one-third the cost of fresh—and it lasts forever. Dried flowers can be prepared in advance from your own garden's bounty.
- Have attendants carry a single flower, such as a long-stemmed rose trailing a ribbon.
- Borrow potted plants or topiaries from friends or relatives.
- Make fruit and vegetable centerpieces; use purple eggplant, red, yellow, and green peppers, squash, artichokes, pomegranates, apples, and grapes. Intertwine with vines of fresh-cut nasturtiums.
- Use garlands of fresh greenery, tied with colorful ribbons, in place of flower garlands.
- Use inexpensive filler, such as sprays of greenery or baby's breath, to plump up your flower arrangements.

SITE CHECKS

Before you begin formalizing your floral plans, you must check with your ceremony and reception sites to determine what is permitted and what isn't, and to ensure access for decorating. For example, it is imperative to get clearance to install your floral decorations at the ceremony site. It would be a colossal disappointment and waste of time to finalize your floral plans, only to find that your selections weren't allowed at the site in the first place.

Get the name and number of the contact person at the site and write it down in your planner. Provide the name and number to your florist. Some questions you should ask the site manager are the following:

CEREMONY SITE

- Are there any decorating restrictions or rules?
- At what time may decorations be delivered and how will access be arranged?
- What is the name of the usual florist for church or synagogue weekly flowers?
- Are candles permitted as decorations other than within the sanctuary? Do local fire codes prohibit them?
- If you want to use an aisle runner, does the ceremony site provide one, or do you need to order one from the florist?
- Are any other weddings or ceremonies planned on the same day as your wedding?

- Are centerpieces and other decorations included in your contract, or do you have to provide your own flowers and decorations? If the former, may you exclude it from the contract and use your own florist? What percentage of the contract do flowers represent?
- What, if any, decorations will already be in place?
- At what time may decorations be delivered and what access will the florist be given for putting them in place?
- May flowers be taken by guests after the reception? The answer should be yes, since you are paying for them, unless you are using the facility's own containers or have other plans for the flowers.

FLOWERS FOR THE BRIDE AND HER ATTENDANTS

The formality and style of your celebration determine the wedding attire and the flowers that complement it. It is helpful to know what is traditional for bridal flowers as you plan. Bouquets, by definition, are simply clusters of flowers tied together or anchored in a bouquet holder. The shape of the bouquet generally determines the best flowers to use.

Do all the bride's attendants flowers have to be identical? While they should complement their gowns and echo the style of the bride's bouquet, attendants' bouquets carried in semiformal and informal weddings can be of different flowers, with each bridesmaid carrying a nosegay of her favorite flower in the same hue as those of the other bridesmaids. One difference may be the size of the bouquet, generally determined by the height and size of the attendant. Bridesmaids come in all shapes and sizes, and just as you adapt their gowns to flatter, so can you adapt their flowers. Give their heights and measurements to the florist, who can customize their bouquets. A six-foot bridesmaid holding a tiny nosegay looks as uncomfortable as a petite bridesmaid struggling with a large cascade.

You can also provide a personal touch by asking each bridesmaid what her favorite flowers are and surprising each with specially designed bouquets.

BOUQUETS

- **FORMAL BOUQUETS**. Formal bouquets are traditionally all white, generally one type of flower, or a combination of two or three different flowers, such as roses, gardenias, stephanotis, and lilies of the valley. The flowers can be fashioned into a cascade or a formal bouquet or nosegay and are adorned with satin ribbons, chiffon, or organza.

- **SEMIFORMAL BOUQUETS**. Usually arm bouquets or nosegays, semiformal bouquets often are colorful—either a combination of mixed colors or different flowers of the same hue or color scheme, such as pinks or corals. Semiformal bouquets can also be all-white, but are often touched with color by the addition of softly tinted ribbons.

- **INFORMAL BOUQUETS**. Informal bouquets can be every bit as elegant as formal bouquets but offer greater variety in shape and flower choices. An informal bouquet can be a gathering of flowers taped at the stem and tied with ribbons, or something as simple as a cloud of baby's breath.

- **BOUQUETS TO TOSS**. If the bride decides to keep her wedding bouquet as a keepsake, she may opt for a "breakaway" bouquet, which allows the bride to keep part and separate another part to toss. Or she can order a completely separate "tossing" bouquet, often similar to but not as elaborate as the one she carries. Note: Whether bouquet-tossing is part of the wedding festivities is entirely optional.

BOUQUET SHAPES

Hand-in-hand with the formality of a bouquet is its shape. There are four basic shapes of bouquets:

- **NOSEGAYS**. Nosegays are circular, densely arranged flowers, approximately 18 inches in diameter. The nosegays may be *posies*, which are petite nosegays made of tiny buds, or *tussy-mussies*, another type of small nosegay composed of tiny buds carried in Victorian-period silver, cone-shape holders. Tussy-mussies are often made of flowers that have traditional meanings, true to their Victorian origins. *Biedermeier* nosegays are arranged in rings of flowers, with each ring including only one flower variety. Nosegays can be carried with either long or short gowns.

- **ARM BOUQUETS**. Arm bouquets are crescent-shaped arrangements, curved slightly to fit on the arm. Because they are larger than nosegays, they usually are best suited to long gowns.

- **CASCADES**. A bouquet that cascades is one that gracefully trails blossoms and/or greens from its base. It can be any shape, from nosegay to tear-shape, and it looks best with a long gown.

- **SPRAYS**. Sprays are flowers gathered together in a triangular-shape cluster. They can be carried with either long or short gowns, as they can be of varying sizes.

WAYS TO CARRY BOUQUETS

If you have a wedding consultant, he or she will advise your wedding party on the best way to carry a bouquet; if not, ask the florist or floral designer. You should never have one attendant clutching her bouquet tightly at chest level while another has it dropped below her waist. Usually, a nosegay is held with two hands, centered just below the waist. An arm bouquet is rested along the lower half of one arm. Experiment with loosely tied bouquets and single flowers. Whatever you do, don't press the bouquet against your gown, for it can get crushed and mark the gown with pollen.

ALTERNATIVES AND ADDITIONS TO BOUQUETS

The bride and her attendants are not restricted to carrying bouquets. They may walk down the aisle with a single long-stemmed flower or two or three. They may wear flowers pinned to their dresses, wrist corsages, pomanders (blossom-covered globes held by a loop of ribbon), flower- and ribbon-decorated fans, or flowers attached to a prayer book. Additions to bouquets may be potpourri or tiny bells that sweetly ring as the bridal party walks down the aisle.

Many modern brides are choosing members of the opposite sex as bridal attendants. This is fine, but male attendants should not carry bouquets. They should instead wear the same boutonnieres that the groomsmen wear.

FLOWERS FOR THE HAIR AND VEIL

Fresh or wax orange blossoms were once the flowers that crowned the bride's veil, but today an array of flowers is often used, woven into bandeaux or circlets and Juliet caps with veils, or worn tucked into a chignon, French twist, or French braid. Flowers can wreath the heads of the bride's attendants, too, or be as simple as a small spray attached to the back of upswept hair. If you want to gather your veil into fresh flowers, make sure it is delivered early enough so that the florist can determine the prettiest look and the most secure way of attaching the flowers to the veil.

FLOWERS FOR THE GROOM AND HIS ATTENDANTS

A boutonniere, worn by the groom and his attendants on their left lapels, makes for a festive and understated grace note to the men's attire. Understated and small scale are the key words: The groom and his groomsmen should never appear to be wearing corsages. A boutonniere may be any flower, but it should be a hardy variety that won't wilt or crush easily. Usually, the groom wears a

flower that is also used in his bride's bouquet, and groomsmen wear a boutonniere that complements that of the groom. A small-scale white or ivory rose, lily
of the valley, stephanotis, or freesia is equally elegant and understated and may
or may not be wired with greens.

Wedding party boutonnieres are usually delivered to the ceremony site
where the groomsmen gather, well before the wedding begins. But if all are
dressing in the same location and traveling to the ceremony site together, their
boutonnieres can be delivered there instead.

FLOWERS FOR CHILDREN

If your wedding party includes a flower girl, she may hold a tiny nosegay, a
diminutive bouquet, or a small basket of flower petals. Traditionally, fresh rose
petals from the flower girl's basket are strewn before the bride during the recessional. But fresh petals are notoriously slippery, so many brides choose dried
flowers instead.

Children are also enchanting carrying hoops decorated in satin and fes-
tooned with flowers in the spring and summer or swathed in evergreens in
December. An old English tradition, and popular in France, this custom is also
practiced today in the South.

Children from a previous marriage of either the bride or groom who are
not wedding ceremony participants might receive flowers to wear or hold.

FLOWERS FOR OTHERS

It is traditional for fathers, stepfathers, mothers, and stepmothers to receive
boutonnieres or corsages for the wedding ceremony. In addition, the bride and
groom may want to give flowers to grandmothers, grandfathers, godmothers,
godfathers, or any other significant people in their lives.

If you want to surprise people with flowers and you don't know what they
will be wearing, white or ivory are safe choices. Wrist or purse corsages are also
a smart idea for the women on your list, since they may be wearing something
that they don't want pinned or that a shoulder corsage would not complement.

Additional flowers for others are those you send as thank-you gifts for
hosting parties, housing out-of-town guests, or performing special tasks for
your wedding. A sister who is reading a verse, a friend who is singing a solo, a

bridal consultant, or the person in charge of the guest book should all be considered recipients of a special token of affection from you. Some brides and grooms arrange to have flowers sent to their parents the day after the wedding with personal messages of love and thanks.

When your flower recipient list extends beyond the wedding party and parents' corsages and boutonnieres, make sure you provide a full list to your florist. If they are to be delivered to the person's home, reconfirm those arrangements as well. Or have someone in charge at the ceremony site who can present the flowers to these recipients, on your behalf, when they arrive.

FLOWERS FOR THE CEREMONY

If you are having your ceremony in a church or synagogue, ask the minister or rabbi to advise you on the types of decorations that work best there, whether flowers or greenery for the altar or chancel, *chuppah,* pulpit, or candelabra. The ceremony flowers may be as simple or as elaborate as the setting, your budget, and the formality of the ceremony.

IN A CHURCH OR SYNAGOGUE

Traditionally, an arrangement or two of flowers that blends with the bridal party flowers is all you need to provide for your ceremony. Placed on the altar in a church or the reader's platform in a synagogue, they are lovely to look at when guests arrive and serve as a background for the ceremony. Candelabra and a standing unity candle can be wound with garlands of greens with a few flowers tucked in. When permitted in a synagogue, the *chuppah,* or canopy, can be decorated with garlands of flowers as well. If your budget permits, however, you can add more floral focal points.

PRESERVING MEMORIES

If you want to save your bouquet, talk to your florist about using flowers that dry well, such as roses and baby's breath. Hang your bouquet upside down in a dry, dark place before you depart for your honeymoon and leave it for two weeks. Display it carefully—dried flowers are especially fragile.

Many florists now have the technical capacity to freeze-dry flowers—preserving them for all time in much the same state they were in when fresh. After the wedding, bridal bouquets are taken apart and each component freeze-dried separately. Then the arrangement is put back together and the bouquet is placed in a glass box, frozen in time and there for your children—and even your grandchildren—to see.

Flowers

If a stairway with railings forms the entrance to your ceremony site, you can drape the railings with garlands, leading the way to the door. Double doors at a church entrance could be adorned with floral wreaths, a beautiful welcome to guests.

The ends of pews may be decorated with satin ribbons or ribbons and flowers, marking the path the wedding party will walk. In a very large church or cathedral with soaring ceilings, height can be added to pew decorations with arrangements on standards placed at the ends of every three or four pews, leading to the altar.

At Home, at a Club, or at a Wedding Facility

Ceremonies that take place outside of a church or synagogue can be beautifully decorated. It is a good idea to take photographs of the areas that will be used, thus having a reference when you are planning your decorations. If a sweeping staircase is the site of your processional, you can drape it in floral garlands. If guests are to be seated in rows, facing the altar or *chuppah,* frame the aisle in well-secured standing arrangements, or tie ribbons at the sides of the chairs closest to the aisle.

A backdrop of greens and flowers frames the bride and groom. If a fireplace is the center of the backdrop, it can be filled with greens and the mantel decorated with green roping or an arrangement of greens or flowers.

An altar may easily be made by covering an ordinary table with a white silk, lace, or damask cloth. Whether there is a cross or other religious objects on the altar depends on the service, on your faith, and on the officiating clergy. Often there is simply a kneeling bench for the couple. If there is a railing, it can be covered with greens, and a tall stand holding a flower arrangement at each end of the rail makes a lovely frame for the ceremony. Depending on the size of

FLORAL POETRY

Flowers have long been part of the poetry of love. In 1589 Christopher Marlowe wrote, in "The Passionate Shepherd to His Love":
"... And I will make thee a bed of roses
And a thousand fragrant posies,
A cap of flowers, and a kirtle
Embroidered all with leaves of myrtle. . ."

the room, an aisle runner may be used. If the ceremony site is a club or a historic facility, check to see what elements are available. It is very likely your florist can provide a kneeling bench, stanchions for flowers, and an aisle runner.

If your reception will be held at the same place, you will want to carry over the same floral theme from the chapel to the reception rooms.

OUTDOORS

You may think that because your ceremony is outdoors, you will have little need to embellish nature. That is often not the case. You may want to add such festive ornamentation as potted plants placed at strategic spots, hanging baskets of flowers that match your color scheme, an arched trellis woven with flowers, or colorful ribbons, streamers, and garlands. If the wedding is at night, candles or Japanese lanterns provide a romantic ambiance. In the evening, garden scents are particularly pungent; you may want to marry in the proximity of a sweet bay bush or night-blooming datura.

Don't forget to formulate a backup plan with the florist in case of inclement weather. Unless your wedding is being held under a tent, you will need to consider a floral design for the backup indoors site. Formulate with the florist a set plan of where the floral arrangements will be situated, and if the backup site is located at a different address, make sure delivery instructions are changed.

DESTINATION WEDDINGS

One of the most popular wedding trends is marrying in a romantic, exotic locale far from home. Destination weddings are generally planned and coordinated long-distance. To find a reliable florist, you can take one of several tacks. You can:

- Inquire about coordinating the flowers and decorations through the wedding site or hotel manager. Many popular destination weddings resorts offer complete wedding packages that include floral selections.
- Ask your local florist whether he or she is affiliated with any florists at the wedding location.
- Find a florist through the network of large floral organizations, such as FTD.
- Check on the Internet for lists of florists. One (weddingpages.com) includes a City Directory of florists and other vendors in many cities in the United States.

Flowers

The long-distance florist may send or fax sketches of his plans and photographs of previous weddings. Ask about local blooms; for a Hawaiian wedding, for example, take advantage of the exotic local flowers.

FLOWERS FOR THE RECEPTION

The choice of reception flowers is as unlimited as there are sites. Arrangements can be added to each table, to the place-card table, to serving stations or buffet tables, and even placed in rest rooms. Flowers can encircle the wedding cake, coil around entranceways and archways, and frame the musicians' bandstand. Pots of beribboned topiaries and standards may form a backdrop for the bridal party table.

Centerpieces should be either low enough so that guests can easily see one another when seated or elevated in tall vases so that they are above the diners' heads. Bridesmaids' bouquets can form the floral focus at the bridal party's table or be placed around the cake on a separate table. At an evening wedding, candles or candelabra decorated with greens and simple flowers may serve as centerpieces.

If the reception is held outdoors, you can embellish the setting with the same flowers and plants you used for the outdoor ceremony. Decorations don't have to stop with flowers. An evening wedding outdoors may find lighted Japanese lanterns or glittering Christmas lights strung through the trees or candle luminarias placed on the pathway to the site.

FLOWERS FOR OTHER WEDDING OCCASIONS

Traditionally, the responsibility for holding additional wedding celebrations such as the rehearsal party and a bridesmaids' brunch is borne by someone other than the bride or the bride's family. It's a good idea, however, to suggest that the person giving the party contact the florist selected for the wedding ceremony and reception. The reason? The florist may be able to offer better prices because of the ease of planning and delivery details. He also may be able to reuse some of the same arrangements, particularly any accessorizing greenery.

WHEN THE CELEBRATION IS OVER

If you have no plans to use your ceremony and reception flowers again, recycle them! Arrange to have them delivered to area nursing homes and hospitals, local charities, or public buildings, such as the town hall. Another choice is to offer to leave them for the next worship service in celebration of your marriage. You could also have centerpieces from the reception delivered to a loved one who was unable to attend the wedding, accompanied by a note from you.

CHAPTER 14

MUSIC

From the traditional "Here Comes the Bride" to the oft-used "Daddy's Little Girl," music adds joy, solemnity, fun, and a sense of tradition to a wedding day. Music serves as a ceremony cue, as pleasant background to conversation, as a call to dance the night away. The right music helps make a wonderful day even better. In fact, no other single element of your celebration has the power to engage the emotions the way music does. Fortunately, there are numerous ways for the bride and groom to orchestrate and personalize their wedding music—and few professionals are more enthusiastic than musicians when it comes to talking about what they love.

CEREMONY MUSIC

If you plan to marry in a house of worship, check with your priest, minister, or rabbi on site restrictions. More and more churches and synagogues have established specific rules regarding music selections, and it is wise to know them before making plans. Some houses of worship are so strict that such well-known pieces as the "Bridal Chorus (Here Comes the Bride)" from Wagner's *Lohengrin* and Mendelssohn's "Wedding March" are not allowed at all—the reason being that each is a secular, not sacred, piece of music.

Your officiant may refer you to a house music director, who can then review the range of the musical choices available to you and provide you with acceptable options. But don't immediately accept the music director's recommendations—you need to hear the music before you commit to it. He should play samples of traditional and popular choices to help you decide what to use for the prelude, the processional, and the recessional, and as background for the ceremony. You can also find music CDs that play nothing but wedding favorites. Look for such titles as *The Wedding Album* (RCA/Ariola International) and *Wedding Favourites* (London: Decca Record Co.).

NEED TO FIND A MUSICIAN?

Here's a great tip on finding musicians to play at your ceremony and reception: Try the music departments of local colleges or universities, local orchestras, or even high-school bands. Amateur musicians from local colleges will be less expensive than professional wedding musicians—but don't hire them without hearing them play.

Ask about acoustics and also whether you may have visiting musicians. If you are allowed to bring in your own musicians, you will need to know whether there are any sound limitations and the types of music that work best in the space. The officiant or music director may even be able to provide the names of musicians who have played in and are familiar with the site.

If you are having your ceremony in a house of worship and plan on including hymns to be sung by the entire congregation, keep your guests in mind when making your selections. The more familiar or beloved a hymn, the more participation from your guests—and the more joyful your celebration will be.

THE HOUSE ORGANIST

It makes sense to use the services of the house organist in the church or synagogue where your ceremony will take place. Who knows better than he or she the ins and outs of the organ, the acoustics, and the timing of religious ceremonies? Using the house organist might also save on costs for ceremony music. If you hire an outside organist, you may have to pay a fee, which is standard practice, endorsed by The American Guild of Organists.

THE ORDER OF MUSIC

When working with the music director or organist, organize your choices into the four basic musical components of your ceremony.

The Prelude

It is a happy beginning indeed when guests arrive at a wedding to the joyful sounds of music. The prelude music should begin at least a half hour before the

Music

ceremony starts. It can be played simply by a lone organist or performed by a string quartet; it can showcase the smooth strokes of a harpist or the ethereal trills of a woodwind ensemble.

The Processional

The processional music begins as the mother of the bride is seated, the groom and his best man enter, and the bride and her attendants are ready to begin their walk. The music can be simply that of an organ or, at a home wedding, a piano. A trumpeter can accompany the organ, adding a joyful and almost regal note.

Music played during the entrance of the bride and her attendants should be joyous and formal at the same time. The same piece can be played throughout the processional; sometimes the bride is accompanied by a different piece of music.

Whatever processional music you choose, be sure that it is easy to keep pace with. While a slow, graceful walk has replaced the customary hesitation step, it can be difficult to achieve when there is no audible cadence to help everyone keep time.

CREDIT WHERE CREDIT IS DUE

If you are providing a program for your ceremony, you will want to list the music that is performed during the prelude as well as during the ceremony. Be sure to get the correct names of each piece and add the composer, information that may be of interest to your guests. It is also a good idea to list the names of those performing. Check and double check the spelling of everything you include.

The Ceremony

Many couples prefer that guests participate in the ceremony in the singing of hymns or a favorite song. This brings a communal spirit to the proceedings, especially when the ceremony is a brief one.

In addition to one or two hymns, other musical interludes may be added at appropriate places during the ceremony. These can be a vocal, performed by a soloist or a children's choir, or an instrumental, performed on a harp, a trumpet, or a combination of instruments.

Work with your officiant and, if there is one, the music director or organist to determine where in the service the music should be placed. Make sure, if soloists are to perform, that practice time with the organist or other instrumentalists is scheduled.

The Recessional

The music you choose for your recessional should be the most joyous of all. It is a jubilant time—you are married!—and the music should reflect that jubilation. Often the bell note on the organ or bells in the bell tower are rung to add to the festive ambiance. Look for upbeat, joyful music that has you and your attendants fairly floating down the aisle and out the door.

CEREMONY MUSIC CHECKLIST

Following is a checklist of details you'll need to attend to in working with and hiring musicians for your ceremony.

- Make sure the musicians can attend the wedding rehearsal. They need to be as familiar with the wedding service as all the other participants are.
- If the organist you select is not the house organist, you must coordinate it so that he or she has access to the organ to practice. Find out times that the church or synagogue will be open and when the organist can have practice time. If your ceremony is at another site, you need to make the same arrangements.
- Be sure you understand how and when payment will be made. If a house of worship provides a bill, the fee for the organist is often included and you can write one check. If not, he or she must be paid directly, either in cash or by check, before or directly after the service. This is traditionally the best man's job, so you might suggest he take care of this after he has delivered the groom to the room where he will wait for the ceremony to begin.
- Your musicians will add a great deal to your ceremony. A thank-you note from the bride or groom is not mandatory, but it is very much appreciated.

RECEPTION MUSIC

Music can make a party, and your reception should be just that: a full-tilt celebration of your nuptial vows. Whether you hire a disc jockey playing recorded music or have the house jumping with a full-fledged swing band, music sets the tone. Quality and proficiency count, but so does diversity. Have your musicians mix it up, combining upbeat tunes with tender ones. Don't subject your guests to three hours of waltzes or three hours of blasting rock selections: Remember, your guest list might very well span different generations. Make sure that the musicians you hire are capable of moving from one kind of music to another, especially if your reception includes dancing.

A second element to consider when selecting reception musicians is the space. Do not hire an orchestra unless you are going to be in a large space or you'll risk deafening your guests and making it impossible for them to hear one another. Alternatively, the sound of an unamplified flutist may be lost in a large space, making it appear as if you have no music at all.

Finally, when your ceremony and reception are small or held at the same location, it is entirely possible to have the same musicians play for both. Find a musician with the ability to play both classical and popular music. The benefit to you: being able to work with just one person to coordinate musical selections.

Be creative in planning your music. If your reception is large and long-lasting, you don't necessarily need music going the entire time. You can have tapes or a lone guitarist, pianist, or flutist performing background music during cocktails and dinner, then bring in the band just before dancing will begin. Ask the band representative whether any of the band members would be willing to perform solo during cocktails and dinner—for a fee, of course.

TIME OF DAY

The time of your reception is crucial to what kind of music and musicians you select.

Brunch, Lunch, or Tea Reception

If you are having a brunch, lunch, or afternoon tea reception and no dancing, a single pianist, harpist, or violinist, a string quartet, or taped background music are appropriate choices. The music you select for such an occasion is meant to be in the background, and classical or light romantic selections set the mood for relaxed elegance.

Afternoon Cocktail Reception

Guests are mobile at cocktail receptions, moving from table to table, standing and talking. Let your music move with them. This type of reception is the perfect venue for strolling musicians, instrumental combos and quartets, or a single pianist. The music itself should be livelier than that at a tea reception, but still never showy or obtrusive. This is not the place to have a vocalist—most guests would feel obliged to stop conversing and give the singer their attention.

Dinner Dance Reception

The music for a dinner dance reception may range from a dance band to a full orchestra to a disc jockey. Remember, the smaller the guest list, the smaller the musical group. If the guest list and reception space are large, use this handy rule of thumb to help you decide what kind of group to hire: For an orchestra or band, you will need five or six pieces per 150 guests; seven or eight pieces per 200 guests; and a full orchestra for 300 guests or more. This is just a general guide—some groups can produce a sound that is bigger than they are.

HIRING MUSICIANS

Reception bands can be booked many months in advance, so you'll want to start looking for musicians as soon as you're engaged. Word of mouth is often your best resource, so ask everyone you know for recommendations—but don't book a band before you listen for yourself. You can do this by seeing the musicians in concert or at another wedding; you could also ask to attend a practice session. If the band has made a tape or video of their performances, by all means get it.

Remember to look for a varied repertoire, especially if your guest list includes a wide range of ages and style. You'll want music that everyone can enjoy and dance to—and that may include a musical repertoire encompassing the fox trot *and* Top 40.

NIGHT SPOTS ARE NOT ENOUGH

Make sure that the band you hire is a professional wedding band, not just a nightclub band. There's a difference. A wedding band is comfortable performing music that appeals to the wide range of ages represented at most receptions. Be sure the band wants to know what you don't want as well as what you do want. Love the Electric Slide but hate the Macarena? Let them know.

1. "The Way You Look Tonight"
2. "Just the Way You Are"
3. "I Will Always Love You"
4. "Unforgettable"
5. "Wonderful Tonight"
6. "The First Time Ever I Saw Your Face"
7. "Love Will Keep Us Together"
8. "Endless Love"
9. "We've Only Just Begun"
10. "All I Ask of You"

For an ethnic wedding, you'll need to find musicians who can play traditional ethnic music.

If you find a group you like, make sure it's the group you get. Often a variety of interchangeable instrumentalists and vocalists make up a band, so be sure you get in writing that the group you heard on the tape is the one that will be playing at your wedding.

HIRING A DISC JOCKEY

If you are looking for ways to cut wedding costs, consider hiring a disc jockey (DJ) to play music at your reception. A DJ is typically half the cost of a live band. A DJ often has a standard play list that can be expanded upon at your request. Ask whether he takes requests at the reception as well. Make sure he can balance the selections, offering alternating slow and fast tunes. Again, you will have to see the DJ in action before you make a decision to hire him. Once you do, make sure he visits the reception space and has a trial run there to test his sound system and the space's acoustics.

If you have a DJ on tap for post-dinner reception dancing, you might want to hire a flutist or a string trio to play during the cocktail hour.

Making Requests

If you have hired a DJ or group experienced in weddings, you probably won't need to create a long list of songs for your reception. A seasoned reception band will generally offer a large, wide-ranging repertoire and have a good sense of the audience. It is their job to pace the selections and know when to move from waltz to rumba to rock.

You may, however, want to select songs for special moments, such as music for the bride and groom's first dance, for the bride's dance with her father, and for parents of the couple. In that case, communicate your choices to the musicians in writing.

Some musicians provide a list of the selections they offer. That makes it easy for you; you and your partner simply check off the music you want to hear.

Consider adding personal favorites—experienced wedding musicians can usually get their hands on them. You may also want to be specific about songs you do *not* want played. If you absolutely cannot bear to hear "Endless Love" played at your celebration, by all means let your musicians know ahead of time.

Master of Ceremonies

There is no real reason to have a master of ceremonies at a reception. A good bandleader or DJ knows how to keep things moving and will work around your schedule. The only time the bandleader or DJ needs to speak to guests at all is to ask for their silence to allow an officiant to say grace, for example, or a best man to propose his toast. You certainly don't need to be hailed over the microphone as you enter the reception, nor do you need anyone telling jokes that are amplified. An announcement that a flambéed dessert has just come out of the oven is over the top. To avoid a misunderstanding, be clear with the bandleader or DJ about the behavior you expect from him.

Reception Music Details

Hiring musicians is not just about making a musical selection list. It is also about attending to details, such as the following:

- Coordinate the equipment needs of your musicians with the offerings of the reception site; for example, make sure that amplified musicians will have sufficient outlets and electrical power to play. Ask whether the reception site already has a sound system or piano on the premises.
- Make sure that there is no extra charge demanded by the reception site for bringing in an outside band or DJ. Some sites have house bands that they require you to use or charge you for if you don't.
- If you have hired more than one group, make arrangements for the two to coordinate their performance time. For example, if your reception is five hours long and your band is willing to play for one-and-a-half hours, during which they take two half-hour breaks, the strolling guitarist will need to be on call during those breaks.
- Make arrangements for meals for the musicians. You are expected to feed any members of the band or the DJ at some point during the reception. Talk to your caterer about providing meals not only for the musicians but also for the photographer, videographer, and any other professionals you have hired. A club or caterer will often give service providers a different meal from the one

A SAMPLING OF MUSICAL SELECTIONS
FOR THE CEREMONY

FOR THE PRELUDE

- Air (Handel)
- Rondo (Mozart)
- "Jesu Joy of Man's Desiring" (Bach)
- Largo (Handel)
- Concerto no. 1 (from Vivaldi's "The Four Seasons", "Spring")
- Pavane (Fauré)

FOR THE PROCESSIONAL

- The Bridal Chorus (from Wagner's "Lohengrin")
- Wedding March (from Mendelssohn's "A Midsummer Night's Dream")
- "The Prince of Denmark's March" (Clarke)
- Wedding March (Guilmant)
- Air (Bach)
- Canon in D Major (Pachelbel)
- Arrival of the Queen of Sheba (Handel)
- Trumpet Voluntary (Clarke)
- Trumpet Tune (Purcell)

DURING THE CEREMONY

- "Ave Maria" (Schubert)
- "One Hand, One Heart" (Bernstein and Sondheim)
- "Jesu Joy of Man's Desiring" (Bach)
- "Joyful, Joyful, We Adore Thee" (Beethoven)
- "The King of Love My Shepherd" (Hinsworth)
- "The Lord's Prayer" (Malotte)
- "Biblical Songs" (Dvorák)
- "Liebestraum" (Liszt)
- "In Thee Is Joy" (Bach)

FOR THE RECESSIONAL

- "Ode to Joy" (Beethoven)
- Trumpet Voluntary (Clarke)
- Wedding March (from Mendelssohn's "A Midsummer Night's Dream")
- Trumpet Tune (Purcell)

FOR THE POSTLUDE

- Overture (Handel)
- Rondeau (Mouret)
- "Le Rejouissance" (Handel)

your guests are served, or the same meal at half the price. Don't forget to budget for these meals. Your service providers are not reception guests, so you are not expected to give them alcoholic beverages or seat them with your guests. Give the caterer or club manager a head count of service providers, so that he can provide a separate table for them.

Questions to Ask Musicians

When interviewing musicians or DJs, make a list of questions to ask and provide any pertinent information. Make sure that the songs you definitely want played will be played. Questions you might ask include:

- How many breaks will be taken, how often, and for how long? (The standard is one per hour for five to ten minutes.)
- Will you provide taped or synthesized music during your breaks?
- What will you wear?
- Are there any other costs not included in the quoted fee (travel time, continuous music)?
- Are you willing to go into overtime, and if so, what is the charge? What is your cancellation policy?
- Will the musicians I'm contracting be the ones at my reception?
- Will the band (or DJ) take requests from guests at no extra charge?
- Do you sing in any other languages? (This is important for ethnic weddings.)
- Do you have a play list? (Most bands know from 500 to 700 songs, from swing to Top 40 to oldies to ethnic.)

The Contract

Before you have established the fee for your reception musicians, get everything in writing. Understand precisely what you will be getting in return for the price you are paying. Find out how many hours of playing time are contracted, how many breaks the band will take, how overtime hours will be billed, what the required deposit is, when the balance is due, whether a refund is available if you cancel, and the amount of any taxes or other charges.

CHAPTER 15

PHOTOGRAPHY AND VIDEOGRAPHY

T hink of the times you've lovingly thumbed through your parents' and even your grandparents' wedding albums, seeing the happy faces of old friends and cherished relatives. Consider your own wedding photographs and videotapes as a tangible record of a wonderful time in your lives and a gift for generations hence. That's why choosing the right person for the job is so important.

YOUR WEDDING PHOTOGRAPHY

We've all seen examples of wedding portraits from years gone by: There was the stiff, no-nonsense groom seated in a straight-backed chair, the bride standing, grim-faced, at his side, and family members staring stone-faced into the camera.

Fortunately, wedding portraiture broke free of that narrow mold long ago. Today, the craft of wedding photography knows no bounds, with styles ranging from classical to artistic to journalistic.

When you go looking for the right photographer for your wedding, consider the style that best articulates your vision. Don't be dazzled by special effects or complicated setups. Look for a clean, straightforward style. When you visit a photographer or videographer, always ask to see samples of his or her work; this is the most telling element of a photographer's background. If he is only a so-so photographer, he can't hide behind a résumé filled with school honors and impressive references. He can have the latest lenses and lighting equipment and a bevy of assistants, and it won't make a ripple if the work is second-rate. The picture tells all.

CHOOSING A STYLE

Each photographer has his own, distinct style, which is reflected in the portfolio of his work. Before you choose a photographer, decide on the photographic style you prefer, and then seek out those photographers whose work reflects that style.

TRADITIONAL

A traditional photographer generally treats every image as a posed portrait, even shots you may consider candid. That doesn't mean the photographs will appear forced or posed, but there will likely be few spontaneous "action shots" included in the mix. Traditional wedding photographers look to capture perfect moments with artistry and dignity and generally produce excellent, albeit formulaic, shots of the wedding party, families, and planned events.

CLASSICAL

These photographers specialize in expertly composed, well-lit portraits. They try to keep an unobtrusive presence at the reception in order to set up perfect, classical images. You won't find them mingling or telling the crowd to "look at the camera" to come up with magic moments.

PHOTOJOURNALISTIC

A wedding photographer who takes a photojournalist approach is one who considers it his job to record events, not stage them. This photographer will take the group shots you want but will also include candid and spontaneous images. His are not the formal "grip and grin" roundups of guests smiling for the camera. He prefers capturing close-ups, impromptu reactions to events, and sensitive impressions of a wedding led by the free flow of the affair, not orchestrated by the photographer.

COMMERCIAL

These photographers will perfectly capture shots of the centerpieces, cake, flowers, and decor and could be hired just for this purpose, supplemented by another photographer to handle people pictures. A commercial photographer's

> ## GET A HELPER!
>
> Sometimes gathering members of groups together for ceremony portraits is a near-impossible task, since everyone is most likely having fun and mingling with others. Enlist the support of a good friend: Give him or her a copy of the list of more formal shots you want to take, and ask him or her to round everyone up, a group at a time. That way, you won't spend your entire reception rounding people up for photographs.

EQUIPMENT, EQUIPMENT

A photographer's portfolio may be all you need to get a good sense of the type of work he can do for you. But knowing a little bit about the technical side of photography can help you when discussing equipment options. Photography done with a medium- or large-format camera will be less grainy when enlarged than images shot in 35mm. If you prefer a natural look indoors and out and dislike flash photography, the photographer will use fast film (often that with an ASA of 200 or faster), but faster film also loses sharpness when enlarged. The recommended equipment for shooting videos: Three-chip cameras in Super-VHS or Hi-8 formats.

sense of style may be more formulaic and less spontaneous than a journalistic photographer. Just the same, he is a professional and capable of taking magazine-quality images.

PHOTOGRAPHIC ARTIST

A photographic artist is similar to a photojournalist, in that he rarely takes traditional shots but prefers to find artistic ways to photograph elements, people, and events. The photographic artist is adept in the medium of black and white and in producing beautifully composed photos, so his photographs are likely to be less candid than full of drama and artistic beauty.

CHOOSING THE SHOTS YOU WANT

Once you have studied the different styles of wedding photography, you can decide which photographs you want taken in a formal portrait style and which you'd prefer to be captured in candid, natural shots. You'd be wise to select a photographer who does both types of photos well. In the case of a very large wedding, you may even use two different photographers: one whose specialty is formal portraits and ceremony shots, the other whose candid style you prefer for the reception. Sometimes, one studio will handle both kinds of photography.

Before signing a contract with a photographer, make a list of the photographs you want and how many copies you think you'll need to give to parents and attendants.

ENGAGEMENT PHOTOGRAPHS

In the past, engagement photographs were typically black-and-white head-and-shoulder shots of the bride alone, taken for the medium it would appear in—newsprint. Today, however, the bride and groom frequently appear in engagement portraits together. The portraits are then often framed and given to family members. Whatever you decide on—a photo of you alone or both of you—is fine. It's entirely a personal choice.

Although the pictures are usually taken in color, the photographer will also provide 5" x 7" black-and-white prints for you to submit to the newspaper along with your engagement announcement. Find out whether the newspaper prefers glossy or matte prints.

You will probably have the engagement portrait taken before you have begun the search for a wedding photographer—but try to use someone you might consider booking as your wedding photographer. It's a good introduction to the way he works, as well as an introduction to the quality of the work. If you find he fits the bill, you'll have a head start on your working relationship.

PORTRAIT PHOTOGRAPHS

Any formal portrait of the bride that will be submitted to the newspapers is generally taken one to two months before the wedding. In general, newspapers need to have it in their possession anywhere from 10 days to three weeks before it runs. This means that your gown and accessories need to be ready that far in advance. Because you will want the formal portrait to look as though it were taken on the day of the wedding, you may want to have your hair and makeup done in the style you will wear on your wedding day.

Photographers usually shoot a formal portrait in the studio, against seamless paper, in controlled lighting. You may, however, prefer having your picture taken at home or even at the bridal salon on the day of your final fitting.

To ensure a picture-perfect portrait, make sure that your gown is wrinkle-free, that your headpiece is placed correctly and complements your hairstyle, and that you are wearing the jewelry you will have on at your wedding. You'll want to wear makeup, neatly applied. Most important, sleep well the night before. You want to look and feel well-rested—even the most flattering lighting will not hide fatigue or stress.

> ### FILLING YOUR ALBUM
>
> When you know guests have taken pictures and you would love to see them, give them a call and ask for the loan of the negatives. If they insist on sending you prints instead, offer to pay for them and for the postage it takes to mail them.

Today the formal bridal portrait that appears in the newspaper often includes the groom. Make a decision on whether you want a portrait of the two of you together before the wedding. If so, book the portrait appointment at a time that is convenient for both of you, and make sure the groom's attire has been fitted, if necessary.

The formal bridal portrait can also be a lovely gift for parents and grandparents. Ask the photographer for prices on extra 8" x 10" prints.

CEREMONY PHOTOGRAPHS

Flash attachments have historically been the bane of every wedding officiants' existence. Thankfully, with the advent of high-speed film and high-tech cameras, the flash is no longer necessary to take quality ceremony photographs. But that doesn't mean that cameras are welcome in every church, chapel, or synagogue. Many officiants will not permit the clicking and whirring of cameras during the ceremony, an occasion they consider sacred. Before you contract with a photographer for ceremony shots, be sure to ask the officiant precisely when photographs are permitted and when they aren't.

If photography is not permitted during the ceremony at all, you will have to ask the photographer to take simulated ceremony shots before the wedding or re-create them afterward.

If the ceremony photos are to be staged before the wedding begins, this should be done well before, never as guests are being seated. The photographs should be completed at least an hour before the start of the ceremony.

If you are having photographs taken between the wedding and the reception, don't think you have to rerun the entire wedding ceremony to get the right shots. Simply select specific images you want to re-create instead. Otherwise

FARAWAY FRIENDS

A videotape of your wedding is a great present to give to faraway friends and relatives who couldn't share your special day in person. If your videographer charges a lot for copies of the edited master, check with duplicating services or a local cable television station to compare prices for copies. It can be considerably less.

the process will drag on, and guests will be left with an overload of downtime between the wedding and the reception.

Possible re-created photos might include:

- The bride and her father walking up the aisle.
- The bridesmaids, maid of honor, flower girl, ring bearer, and ushers walking up the aisle.
- The groom and best man turned as they would to watch the bride walk up the aisle.
- The bride and groom standing or kneeling at the altar and/or exchanging vows.
- The bride and groom with their children.
- The entire wedding party as they stand for the ceremony.
- The bride and groom kissing.
- The bride and groom walking down the aisle after the ceremony.

If there are other special moments or people you want photographed at this time, be sure to delegate a friend to ask these people to stay over after the ceremony. Included could be shots of grandmothers being ushered to their seats or the organist or soloist at work.

RECEPTION PHOTOGRAPHS

There are three kinds of reception photographs:

- Posed portraits of the wedding party and family members with the bride and groom.
- Shots of planned events, such as cake-cutting, first dances, and bouquet-tossing.
- Candid photos of everyone at the reception as it progresses.

Portraits

Posing for pictures with your respective families can get a little complicated these days. If your parents are divorced, it is simply not appropriate to ask them to flank you in a photograph in a semblance of a united family. Instead, a portrait of you with each of them individually is fine. If they have remarried, you might have a portrait taken of you with each of them with their spouse. The placing of such photos on your list of wanted portraits can make your parent and stepparent very happy. If enmity toward the new spouse is great, you don't have to do it—just don't try to re-create the family you once were.

Provide, in advance, your list of "must-have" shots to the photographer so that he can be thinking about suitable backdrops. Possible formal shots might be:

- The bride alone.
- The groom alone.
- The bride and groom together.
- The bride and her maid or matron of honor.
- The bride with her parents (or each parent, plus stepparent, as applicable).
- The groom with his parents (or each parent, plus stepparent, as applicable).
- The groom with his best man.
- The bride with her mother.
- The bride with her father.
- The groom with his mother.
- The groom with his father.
- The bride and groom with all their attendants.
- The bride with her attendants.
- The groom with his attendants.
- The bride and groom with the bride's family (parents, siblings, aunts, uncles, cousins).
- The bride and groom with the groom's family (parents, siblings, aunts, uncles, cousins).
- The bride and groom with their siblings, if they are not all in the wedding party.
- The bride with "generations"—her parents and grandparents.
- The groom with his parents and grandparents.

Planned Events

For planned events—both the traditional ones, such as the cake-cutting, and those that personalize your wedding—ask an attendant, close friend, or even the catering manager to direct the photographer to the site of each so that he can be thinking in advance about the best way to take the picture. Provide the photographer with a list of events and approximate times they will occur. These can include:

- The bride and groom arriving at the reception.
- Guests going through the receiving line.
- Close-ups of the cake table, centerpieces, and other special decorations.
- The best man toasting the bride and groom.
- The bride and groom cutting the cake.
- The bride and groom feeding each other cake.
- The groom toasting the bride.
- The bride and groom's first dance.
- The bride dancing with her father.
- The groom dancing with his mother.
- The bride tossing her bouquet.
- The groom tossing the bride's garter.
- The bride and groom leaving the reception.

Candid Photographs

Let your photographer know up front the kinds of candid photographs that mean the most to you. If you want shots of every table, let him know so that no one is left out. If you don't want table shots but prefer shots of people in action, say so. If you love capturing totally spontaneous moments, again just let your photographer know in advance. Good candid shots can be breathtaking.

"GETTING READY" PICTURES

If you want work-in-progress shots, you might book the photographer to start before the wedding begins, taking pictures as you get ready. These shots could include:

- The bride putting on the finishing touches—a necklace or a garter.
- The bride's mother helping her with her veil.
- The bride kissing her mother good-bye as she prepares to leave for the ceremony.
- The bride and her father arriving at the ceremony site.

SELECTING A PHOTOGRAPHER

Once you have agreed on what type and style of photographs will make you the happiest, you can begin seeking a wedding photographer in earnest. While your first consideration is your ability to relate to the work he has done in the past, you will need to incorporate price and service comparisons into your decision-making process. If you like the photographer's work but don't like the photographer, look elsewhere; your annoyance will show up in your photos. If in a visit to a professional studio you are shown the work of several photographers but prefer the work of one, ask for that person—and only that person—to be assigned to your wedding.

QUESTIONS TO ASK PHOTOGRAPHERS

Be prepared. Take a list of questions with you when interviewing photographers. Following are some sample questions.

- If you are planning formal portraits ahead of time, does the photographer have a dressing room in the studio? Is there a "prop" bouquet for you to hold, or do you need to provide one?
- Is a wedding package offered? If so, what does it consist of? For example, does the photographer provide an album for the bride and groom and smaller albums for their parents and perhaps grandparents? Is the package mandatory, or are there options, such as a greater number of prints or additional 8" x 10" prints?
- What is the number of photographs in the standard album?
- What is the size and cost of extra albums?
- What does it cost for additions to a package?
- What is the number of pictures to be taken at, before, and during the ceremony and at the reception?
- May the proofs be purchased? Can the negatives be kept? How long does the photographer hold onto negatives after the wedding (in the event that something happens to the bride and groom's wedding album)?
- How long will the photographer stay at the reception? What is the per-hour fee for overtime?
- Is the photographer familiar with the ceremony and reception sites?
- Are there extra charges for site visitation and/or travel time?

WHAT TO LOOK FOR

When reviewing a photographer's portfolio, look for clean, sharp images that convey emotion and feeling. Keep in mind that you are being shown the photographer's showcase work. It won't get any better than what you are looking at, so be sure you like what you see.

The one factor that makes the difference between two equally competent professionals is their wedding philosophy. Ask the people you interview how they feel about weddings to try to ascertain if they are truly enthusiastic and dedicated—or if this is just another job.

VIDEOGRAPHY

A wedding video can be a wonderful addition to your collection of memories. It will be there on your first anniversary and it will be there on your twentieth. It provides a wonderful record for your children, capturing like no other medium the mood and the moments of your wedding day.

While the costs of videotaping a wedding have gone up in the past few years, so have the credentials and professionalism of dedicated, full-time professionals, as well as the quality of the equipment they use. Standard video packages include your entire wedding story, from the time you arrive at the ceremony (or even before, if you wish) until you depart from the reception. Finished tapes are usually one-and-a-half to two hours long, edited from three to five hours of raw footage.

WHAT TO EXPECT

A wedding video usually includes the entire service and all or part of the reception. The final product you receive is generally an edited, color videocassette tape with sound. The editing is done in a studio, and the edited tape can con-

Photography and Videography

tain not only scenes from your ceremony and reception but old family photographs, an image of your invitation, interviews with guests, reflections by your parents, and messages for each other. Naturally, the more special effects, music, extra photography, and other elements that are added, the more your tape will cost. To produce this tape, the videographer leaves the camera running throughout the ceremony and reception so that he has plenty of raw footage from which to select highlights.

A less-expensive option: a tape edited in-camera. This makes for a choppier video that lacks continuity and transition from scene to scene, nor will the video include special effects, interviews, or still photography.

A third option, and the least expensive, is a wedding highlights tape. Usually lasting only about 15 minutes, this is a fast-paced clip-to-clip view of special moments of the day. It makes an ideal gift to send to those who were not present. Sometimes a videographer will provide a highlights tape as an extra to couples who contract for a full tape.

CHOOSING A VIDEOGRAPHER

Because video cameras and their locomotive-like high beams can be even more obtrusive than 35mm cameras, you will want to look for a videographer who has the kind of commercial-grade equipment that requires less lighting.

When reviewing a videographer's past work, look for artistic quality. If the less-expensive videographer produces a dull video, you might want to splurge a little for the more expensive studio—else why bother videotaping in the first place?

Also, look for credentials. Talk to more than one professional, and view any previously made wedding tapes. It's a big investment of your time to preview tapes, but it is worth it to make sure your money is well spent. Seeing the videographer's work will give you the opportunity to see his or her training, experience, talent, and style.

Look for the following, too:

- Steady, not shaky images.
- Clean, crisp focus.
- Continuity and clarity of sound.
- Mix of distant and close-up images.
- Seamless editing from one scene to the next.

BLACK-AND-WHITE OR COLOR?

There is a decided trend toward black-and-white wedding photography, particularly among the burgeoning school of brides and grooms who prefer a more candid, photojournalistic approach. Although black-and-white film is less expensive, it is more expensive to process and print than color. If you want some black-and-white photos, make sure your photographer is skilled in this area. Many brides and grooms hire photographers who are willing to switch back and forth, capturing, for example, the processional in color and the recessional in black-and-white; this can be the best of both worlds, particularly when it is negotiated as part of the package. If the timeless romance of black-and-white appeals to you, be sure to find out your parents' preferences, and discuss in detail with your photographer any events and moments you want to be captured in color and which ones you really want in black-and-white. Be mindful that black-and-white won't preserve the day's colors.

Other options are prints in sepia tones, or black-and-white prints with various details hand-tinted—rosy cheeks or flower buds, for example.

QUESTIONS TO ASK A VIDEOGRAPHER

Be prepared. Take a list of questions with you when interviewing videographers. Following are some sample questions.

- Will background music be dubbed on the tape? If so, who selects the music?
- Can credits be added so that the names of the wedding party and others can be listed on the tape?
- Will you be involved in editing our final tape?
- What special effects are usually used, and when can we decide whether we want them?
- What do additional copies cost?
- Are there additional costs for a video portrait of the wedding party and other groupings?
- Who keeps original video footage?
- What happens to them if they are the property of the videographer?
- How long is the master tape kept on file, in case we want to order extra copies?
- Can we buy the master tape, and if so, for how much?
- How soon will we be able to view original footage?

VIDEOTAPING YOUR WEDDING

Both your preferences and your budget can determine what you arrange to have taped. Do you want the videographer recording the wedding party getting ready for the ceremony? The bride and her father arriving at the ceremony? The mothers being seated? Guests arriving? Do you want the ceremony taped, if your officiant permits it, or just the reception? Do you want your guests "interviewed" by the videographer, or do you think this will only be an unwelcome intrusion? Looking at the tapes of friends or those provided by the videographer may help you decide exactly what elements of your day you want recorded.

THE CEREMONY

The videotaping of your ceremony must be cleared with your minister, priest, or rabbi before you sign any contracts with videographers. Any specific guidelines should be discussed with the videographer, including the placement of equipment, lighting restrictions, and whether events can be restaged later.

Most churches and synagogues allow videographers to tape from a specific location—the side of the altar, for example, or the rear of the balcony—to prevent disruption. Lights are generally not allowed, so newer equipment that requires little or no extra lighting is essential. Often a wireless microphone is attached to the groom's lapel so that vows can be recorded clearly.

If your ceremony will be taped, meet with your videographer in advance to describe the ceremony plans: Will you and your intended face each other? Is there a soloist? How many members of your bridal party will there be? Will you have a receiving line at the ceremony site? Will guests shower you with rose petals, bubbles, or birdseed as you leave the ceremony?

First decide what video memories and planned events you want recorded at your reception. Then give the videographer you hire a specific list of events planned for the reception. He will need to know whether there is a receiving line, whether guests will be seated at assigned tables or mingling through the room, whether there will be dancing, and the timing of the cake-cutting.

CONTRACT NEGOTIATIONS

When you find the photographer or videographer you want and agree to the date and terms, have him write up an itemized cost breakdown. He should include in the contract the date, the agreed-upon arrival time, the length of shooting period, how many photos/hours of video will be taken, a breakdown of package cost and inclusions, any extra charges, and the schedule for reviewing proofs and delivery of the finished album or edited video.

Make sure that price guarantees for additional prints, enlargements, and extra album pages/prints and upgrades are included in your agreement. Ask whether he offers a package discount when you buy extra albums for parents and other relatives. All packages are negotiable to a point. If you'd prefer not to have a finished album from the photographer, choosing to purchase loose photographs instead, discuss your options.

Finally, provide your photographer or videographer with a copy of the sites' photography regulations and restrictions regarding the use of cameras, flash photography, lights, and tripods—and sound equipment for videotaping.

TAKE CARE OF YOUR TAPE

Having planned and purchased a video of your wedding, you'll want to take excellent care of the tape. Always rewind after a viewing to keep it clean and evenly wound and to prevent stretching. Make sure the little tab on the back of the case is removed so that you don't accidentally tape over your wedding. Store the tape in a cardboard sleeve or plastic case to keep it dust free. Keep it out of dusty, damp, or too-warm places.

Photography
and
Videography

You will also need to give him the names and phone numbers of the site managers so that he can scout out the wedding locations. Otherwise, you can show him the sites yourself.

Once your decisions are made and a contract is written, be sure to ask the photographer or videographer to cover all options in full detail, so you both will have a record of what is available and of what you want. If you haven't discussed these points during the interview process, this is your last chance. You should have a record of the number of hours to be spent photographing or filming, the number of staff involved at the sites (assistants may be needed for a very large wedding), the delivery and payment schedules, and an outline of the final product, such as albums, the number of prints, or the edited video.

INSURANCE

What happens if your photographs or videotapes don't turn out? Are the professionals expected to pay a damage fee or will they offer to re-create portions of the day? While nothing will replace lost photos or footage, you shouldn't have to pay for someone else's errors or accidents. Make sure your contract clearly delineates not only your right not to pay if work is not delivered, but also the return of your deposit and the professionals' financial responsibility to pay *you* if they don't deliver. If they will not agree to the latter, check on wedding insurance with your insurance agent to see what coverage is available and at what cost.

In addition, your ceremony and reception sites may require liability insurance for any vendor or service you bring in from the outside. Check early on to see whether it is required and, if so, make sure the professionals you hire have liability insurance and proof of it to be sent to those who require it.

CHAPTER 16

THE WEDDING CAKE

Wedding feasts through the centuries have evolved in much the same ways as many traditions and rituals have, with simple dinners developing into more elaborate displays of celebration as customs changed. Throughout, the wedding cake has always been a focal point of the nuptial festivity, from being a symbol of fertility for the ancient Romans to the cake of meal that Native American brides offered their grooms to the storybook confections of modern times.

As the customs have evolved and become more elaborate, so have the expenses. In modern times, the wedding cake is not an insignificant part of the wedding budget. For example, wedding cakes that serve 200 guests and more can cost anywhere from $200 up to several thousand dollars. Costs can be determined as a flat fee or on a per-slice basis, ranging anywhere from $1 to $10 a serving. Thus, wedding-cake planning deserves the same thoughtful attention you give to the other aspects of your wedding celebration.

WHO'LL MAKE THE WEDDING CAKE?

Your wedding cake may be ordered from the caterer, a restaurant, the reception site, a professional bakery, a grocery bakery, or a master baker. If the wedding is small, a close friend or relative who is a skillful baker may offer to make your wedding cake. On the other end of the spectrum are individual tiered cakes made and decorated for each guest. Your cake can even be a convincing fake for display only; guests are served from a separate iced sheet cake that is cut and served from the kitchen.

The factors to take into consideration when choosing a wedding cake are your budget, the formality of your wedding, and whether the reception site requires that you use an in-house cake or pay an additional fee to bring one from the outside. You will also need to decide whether the cake will be the only dessert; if not, perhaps a simpler cake will suffice. If the wedding cake is all the dessert you're having, a nice accompaniment may be a light, refreshing sorbet.

Make an appointment to meet and review any baker's portfolio, whether he is the baker at the club, the one used by the caterer, or one you find and interview yourself. Ask to see photographs of the baker's work. You'll want your cake to look good, but looks aren't everything—you'll want it to taste as good as it looks. Most reputable bakers offer tastings of cakes, fillings, and icing. Sample a baker's work before signing a contract.

You can choose a cake with a traditional look and an adventurous taste. Inside a classic tiered façade, for example, may be a carrot cake filling. A good baker will help you choose a texture and icing that marry nicely. You may even want to mix textures—combining a tender cake with a smooth filling or using a hard-finish royal icing over a smooth-finish fondant.

THE BAKER NEEDS TO KNOW

When choosing a wedding cake, give the baker the specifics for the size and type of wedding you are planning. Include the particulars of the reception site, such as:

- Room decor.
- Ceiling height.
- General temperature.
- Linen colors.
- Wedding party colors.
- Floral scheme (flower types and colors).

MESSENGER CAKES

In China, the good news of a wedding is sometimes shared by the presentation of cakes by the groom's family to the bride's family to send to relatives and friends. The cakes, a sign that wedding festivities are under way, traditionally are given in round, lacquered boxes inscribed in gold with a Chinese character meaning "double happiness." The recipient of such a box is expected to send a gift in return. The more elaborate the box, the more expensive the gift.

You'll want to provide the baker with the names and numbers of your other vendors, including the caterer, florist, and wedding planner. Also make sure the baker has the name and number of the site location manager to coordinate details and delivery as well as clear directions to the reception site. If necessary, drive the route between the bakery and the reception site yourself to ensure that your directions make sense.

MULTIPLE FLAVORS

Provide guests with a variety of tastes by giving each tier or layer a different filling. Some popular flavors to mix and match: devil's food with hazelnut; German chocolate with French creme; Amaretto with chocolate mousse; fudge truffle with strawberry creme.

QUESTIONS TO ASK THE BAKER

In addition to viewing a baker's portfolio of cakes and tasting various combinations, make sure that any contract you sign—whether with an outside baker or with a caterer—spells out all the details of your arrangements, including flavors, ingredients, decorations, and of course, date and time. Some reception sites charge an extra cake-cutting fee if your cake is not ordered through them; be sure to ask. Other questions to ask the baker include:

- Will this be a fresh-baked cake, or will it be a previously frozen cake?
- What size cake is right for the number of guests you expect?
- What combinations of flavors of cake, filling, and icing do most people request?
- Can we have a smaller cake than we need and supplement it with a less expensive sheet cake in the kitchen?
- Will there be an additional charge for delivery?
- Is there a charge or deposit required for cake stands and pillars?
- Is a deposit required for the cake?
- Are deposits refundable?
- When is the final payment due?
- What determines the cost, and what are your options?

If your cake is to be baked at another site and transported, it is a good idea to follow up yourself and tell the site caterer or club manager when the cake will be delivered. A cake consisting of more than three tiers is generally transported unassembled and put together and decorated on site. Find out from the location manager if there is space for the baker to work and the best time to do so.

The Wedding Cake

WHEN TO ORDER THE CAKE

Order your wedding cake at least six to eight weeks in advance. If yours is a limited engagement period or a last-minute nuptial, you can get good-quality cakes at short notice from professional bakeries and grocery-store deli bakeries.

CAKE VOCABULARY

Don't know the difference between a marzipan paste and a fondant finish? Here's a primer on some of the terms you will be discussing with your baker.

BUTTERCREAM

Cakes iced in buttercream are the best value in terms of price per slice. Buttercream is smooth and creamy—but not too sweet. It takes flavors well, remains soft so that it is easy to cut, and is perfect for finishes such as basketweaves, swags and swirls, fleur-de-lis, and rosettes. Genuine buttercream is made with real butter, so cakes iced with it need to be kept in a cool place; heat and humidity make it bead, run, and drip. Some bakers counter this effect by adding shortening to the icing to give it a measure of stability. If your cake will be kept cool in an air-conditioned reception room, the added shortening is unnecessary. If you demand true, all-butter icing, ask the baker to forgo shortening altogether.

WHIPPED CREAM

Whipped cream is a light, soft icing that, as with buttercream, becomes temperamental in heat and humidity. A whipped-cream cake must be kept refrigerated until just before it is served. Bakers may also use stabilizers when working with whipped cream. If you don't want stabilizers used, discuss with your baker whether this will affect the appearance of the cake.

FONDANT

Rolled fondant icing is a combination of sugar, corn syrup, gelatin, and usually glycerin. It can be rolled out in sheets and wrapped around each tier of the cake, presenting a smooth frosting with a porcelain-like sheen. It serves as the perfect base for flowers and decorations piped in royal icing (see below) because of its smoothness. A cake iced in fondant, however, is usually not refrigerated. While this is not a problem for the cake, it may be for a filling that requires refrigeration.

ROYAL ICING

Soft when it is piped onto a cake, royal icing then dries to a hard finish. It is what bakers use for creating latticework, flowers, and beading around the edges of the cake. It is used for decorative touches only, not to ice an entire cake.

SPUN SUGAR, PASTILLAGE, AND MARZIPAN

THERE GOES THE HAIR

The symbolism was well-meant but misguided: Hours spent arranging the perfect bridal coiffure were undone by ancient Romans, who broke a cake made of salted meal over the bride's head to ensure abundance or fertility. Other ancients often dropped wheat, flour, or cake on the bride's head and then ate what they dropped so that they could share in her good luck.

Finishing touches can be made of any of these decorative icings, all of which are edible. Spun sugar is caramelized sugar that is pulled into strands and quickly formed into bows and other shapes. It melts into a gooey mess in heat and humidity, so it isn't a good choice for a room without air-conditioning. Pastillage is a paste of sugar, cornstarch, and gelatin that hardens as it dries to a porcelain-like finish. It is used to create realistic-looking flowers and decorations. Marzipan is also a paste, made of ground almonds, sugar, and egg whites. It is sometimes rolled in sheets, as with fondant, but it is usually molded into flowers and other decorative shapes and painted with food coloring.

CAKE TOPPERS

The little plastic bride and groom figurines of old may be the quintessential wedding cake topper, but times—and trends—change. Cake toppers are an art form all their own these days, with pieces created from ceramic, porcelain, hand-blown glass, clay—even crocheted from yarn. The fashion nowadays in nuptial cake toppers is a delicate cascade, from the highest tier down, of fresh, silk, buttercream, or pastillage flowers and ivy or ribbons—or some combination thereof.

Consider the entire design when planning the cake topper. A tiny plastic model of the car you drove on your first date, for example, may detract from an elegant-looking cake. Inform your baker of your preferences in advance.

The Wedding Cake

If you decide to use confectionery flowers as a cake topper, be sure to discuss your idea with your florist. You'll want your edible flowers to complement the wedding's floral scheme. Give your baker photographs or drawings of the flowers and decor you plan for the reception or suggest setting up a meeting between the florist and baker so that they can coordinate their design work.

Speaking of flowers, you should avoid the use of fresh non-edible flowers on or near the cake. Some flowers are poisonous or have been sprayed with chemical insecticide.

DISPLAYING THE CAKE

The wedding cake is generally in place and on display when guests enter the reception location. It is sometimes placed on the bridal party table or in the center of a buffet table, but most often it is put on a small table or cart of its own. If this is the case, you can personalize the display by using a favorite family tablecloth or your mother's wedding veil over an undercloth. You can use a cloth from the caterer with swags caught up by fresh flowers, a design that may be repeated on the cake with similar-looking flowers made of edible icing. You might want to wrap the handle of the cake knife with a ribbon or flowers and place it on the table next to the cake. Or perhaps you have a special cake knife to use, such as a family heirloom.

Sometimes the presentation of the cake is an event in itself. The cake is kept hidden in the kitchen until it is time for you to cut it. The lights are low-

ERIN GO BRAGH

If there is a little Irish in your heritage, you'll probably like to know that the customary wedding cake in Ireland is a rich, brandy- or bourbon-soaked fruitcake filled with cherries, spices, raisins, and almonds. Along with the cake comes a special toast, something along the lines of "As you slide down the banister of life, may the splinters never face the wrong way." Before this cake became popular, small, dry crackers were the tradition in Ireland and England. Every guest took one home, probably the origin of sending a slice of groom's cake home with guests "to dream on."

ered, the music stops, and the room becomes hushed. The cake is wheeled into the middle of the room and spotlighted. Then everyone gathers around to witness the cutting of the cake.

THE CUTTING OF THE CAKE

No matter what the presentation, the cutting of the wedding cake continues to be a traditional part of the reception. At a sit-down reception, the cake is cut just before dessert is served. At a luncheon, tea, or cocktail reception, it is cut closer to the end of the reception. If the cake has been on display throughout, the bridesmaids simply gather around the bride and groom at the appointed time. Notify the caterer or club manager the approximate time you plan to cut your cake so that he can alert the kitchen staff to remove the cake for serving after the cutting. The photographer should be alerted in advance in order to set up the shot.

To start, the bride puts her right hand on the handle of the cake knife and the groom puts his hand over hers. It is easiest if they pierce the bottom tier of the cake with the point of the knife and then carefully make two cuts, removing a small wedge onto a plate provided by the caterer in advance, along with two forks.

The groom gently feeds the bride the first bite, and she feeds him the second. This tradition is meant to symbolize their commitment to share with and support one another, and as such, it is inappropriate for either to stuff the cake into the other's face or comically offer up too large a bite. The couple generally share a kiss, and the caterer then has the cake whisked away and cut so that guests may be served. A lovely gesture before the cake is taken away is for the bride and groom to cut cake slices for their parents. Tradition has it that the bride serves her groom's parents, and he serves hers. If the top layer is to be saved, be sure to tell the caterer in advance so that it isn't cut and served to guests.

CUTTING THE ENTIRE CAKE

If the wedding is small or at home, you'll want someone to be in charge of cake-cutting once the two of you have made the traditional first cuts.

Here, then, is a review of the art of cake-cutting:

1. Start by cutting the bottom layer. Run a knife all the way around the base of the second layer; the cut runs in a circle parallel to the outside of the bottom layer.
2. Cut individual slices from the bottom layer. Slices are lifted onto cake plates to be served to guests.
3. Next, cut the second layer into individual slices the same way by running the knife all the way around the base of the next layer.
4. Cut individual slices and serve.
5. Next, cut the bottom layer again by running the knife all the way around the base of the second layer; the cut runs in a circle parallel to the outside of the bottom layer.
6. Cut and serve individual slices.
7. Remove the top layer to either cut and serve or freeze and save.

Finally, separate remaining layers to cut and serve.

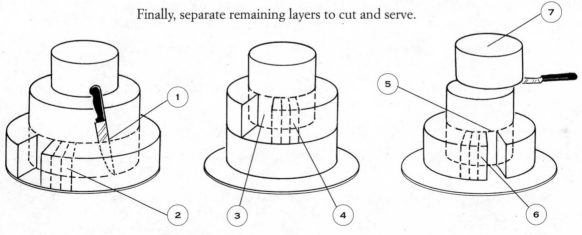

WEDDING CAKE COST-CUTTERS

- WASTE NOT. People like big wedding cakes, but often much of the cake at a reception goes uneaten. Because cake is generally bought on a per-serving basis, many caterers suggest that you do not order a piece of wedding cake for each of the guests at the reception; unless yours is a sit-down dinner, buy less. Consider, say, for 300 reception guests, ordering a cake that will feed 225. It will save you quite a bit of money, and you will probably still have leftover cake.
- FAKE CAKE. A good budget-extender is a fake wedding cake with Styrofoam layers. It can be as large as a real cake but cost only a fraction what the real cake would cost. Make the top layer real to freeze for your first anniversary. The whole "cake," frosted beautifully and decorated with fresh flowers, is then carted to the kitchen after you make the first slice into the top layer. Waiters then serve a less-expensive frosted sheet cake to the reception guests.
- FAKE TIERS. If you love the look of a multi-tiered cake, you can have the bottom tiers made of Styrofoam and the top tiers real cake.
- DISPLAY CAKE. Have your baker make a small, elegant cake for display and serve guests slices of a less-expensive sheet cake. The sheet cake should be cut discreetly by the staff in the kitchen and served individually or placed on the cake table for guests to pick up.

GROOM'S CAKE

The groom's cake has its origins in early Southern tradition, when a single female guest would place under her bed pillow a slice of cake given as a wedding favor. Then, it is said, she would dream of her future husband. Since the wedding cake was eaten at the wedding, the slice to take home came from a second cake, called the groom's cake. The groom's cake was also part of pioneer tradition, when cakes were baked by the groom's parents for traveling guests to enjoy on long trips home.

The tradition of sending guests home with a piece of cake has all but disappeared, primarily because ordering a second cake and having it boxed and tied with ribbons is another added expense. But having a second cake to serve to guests at the reception is fun. The groom's cake traditionally was a dark fruitcake, contrasting with the white fruitcake wedding cake. Today the groom's cake is often a chocolate cake, iced in chocolate, or baked in a shape, such as a football or a book, that reflects an interest of the groom. If it is to be used as a second dessert, it is placed on a separate table from the wedding cake and cut and served by the wait staff. At a small, at-home wedding, it may be cut and served when the wedding cake is served.

Having a special groom's cake is a charming touch. Some couples even ask to have it packaged in small boxes to send home with departing guests. It makes a wonderful wedding gift as well, festively wrapped and tied with a ribbon.

CHAPTER 17

AT THE CEREMONY

This is the moment when all your careful planning and organizing crystallize, when time-honored customs embroidered with fine detail combine to create magic. As the hour approaches, take a deep breath and relax. The day is yours to savor.

GETTING READY

THE BRIDE PREPARES

The bride generally dresses at home. If room permits, her attendants will arrive at least an hour before all are scheduled to leave for the ceremony and dress there as well. The bride's mother and honor attendant help her with the finishing touches.

It is the duty of the maid of honor and bridesmaids to check that the bride is wearing something old, something new, something borrowed, something blue. The maid of honor makes sure that an emergency kit of pins, makeup, tape, and other essentials is nearby and ready to go. Any bags for an immediate honeymoon departure should be packed and put in the car.

If the bride's attendants will all be present, their bouquets should be delivered to the house, as should the flower girl's nosegay or basket, the bride's mother's corsage, and the bride's father's boutonniere.

Pictures of the bride and her attendants getting ready are taken, if desired. The photographer then leaves for the ceremony site to take other pictures as the guests arrive and to set up for ceremony shots.

The bridesmaids travel together; the bride's mother accompanies them with any children who are in the wedding party and/or the bride's children from a previous marriage. The bride rides with her father. If the groom has children from a previous marriage, they would be taken care of by the groom's parents or other family members.

Forbidden to marry in early 19th-century America, slaves began to show their commitment to each other by crossing staff-like sticks that symbolized the strength and vitality of trees. The custom, intended to honor and bless their new life together, drew no objection from the slave masters, who permitted a couple to stand before witnesses, pledge their devotion to each other, then jump over a broom—a symbol of the start of the couple's homemaking. Forging a cultural link, many modern African-American brides and grooms include the rituals of the crossing of sticks and "jumping the broom" in their ceremonies. If you so choose, ask your officiant how you can incorporate these symbols into your own service.

The flower girl and ring bearer will ride to the ceremony with the bride's mother, if they are not delivered directly to the ceremony by their parents before the ceremony takes place.

THE GROOM GETS READY

The groom usually spends the hour or so before he is to leave for the ceremony with his best man, who makes sure that all the necessary papers are together and that the bride's wedding ring rests securely in his pocket. If the groom will be leaving directly from the reception for his honeymoon, the best man checks that all bags are packed and readies the clothes to change into after the reception. The best man also traditionally arranges for the newlyweds' transportation from the reception.

The groom and his best man should arrive at the ceremony site about 15 minutes before the hour of the ceremony. Once there, the best man drops the groom off in a private room, such as the vestry or officiant's study, and returns to the sanctuary to retrieve his and the groom's boutonnieres from the head usher. Returning to the groom, he helps him pin on his boutonniere and waits with him until the signal comes that the ceremony is about to begin.

THE USHERS ARRIVE

If a head usher is appointed, it is his duty to make sure that the other ushers have transportation to and from the ceremony. The ushers should arrive at the ceremony site about an hour before the ceremony is to begin.

Boutonnieres delivered to the ushers are pinned on. Any other boutonnieres—for the groom's father or, perhaps, his grandfather—are distributed. Ushers are also responsible for presenting corsages to those designated to receive them, such as mothers, grandmothers, and any special friend helping out. The bride has provided a list to the head usher, who then parcels out the tasks among his ushers.

If a ceremony program has been printed, the ushers are usually responsible for handing them to guests as they seat them; however, this job can also be given to children who are relatives of the bride and groom and do not have another part in the ceremony.

If pew cards have been issued, the ushers should not ask for them but should wait for guests to present them. They determine who will escort special guests, such as grandmothers and godmothers, a determination often based on kinship. If the groom's brother is an usher, for example, he would escort his grandmother and mother, just as the bride's brother would escort his own grandmother and mother. The head usher designates which ushers will be responsible for rolling out the aisle carpet and which ones will place and later remove any ribbons along the ends of the pews.

A last-minute check is made by the ushers. If the room is stuffy or hot, they can open windows. They can make sure that pews are clear of papers or other debris. They familiarize themselves with where a telephone is located, in case of emergency, and where the rest rooms are, should a guest ask.

As for the ushers' demeanor, they needn't walk in stony silence when escorting guests but may indeed smile warmly and exchange a few quiet remarks. The seating of guests is not a time when absolute silence and somberness is expected.

THE GUESTS ARRIVE

The ushers show all guests to their places. They ask any guests they do not immediately recognize whether they wish to sit on the bride's side (the left) or the groom's (the right). Just as the reserved pews are divided more or less evenly, so should the rest of the church be divided.

In taking guests to their seats, ushers should offer a crooked arm for the female guests to hold onto, with their escorts walking behind them. Or the usher may lead the way as the couple follows him to their seat. If a male guest is escorted by himself to a seat, the usher walks on his left.

If the day is warm and the weather good, the parents of the couple may want to greet arriving guests for a while outside the ceremony site. Their presence is a welcoming one for guests, but they should keep conversations brief, warm, and welcoming, so as not to detain everyone.

SEATING FAMILY

The parents of the bride always sit in the first pew on the left, facing the chancel; the groom's parents sit in the first pew on the right. If the church has two aisles, the bride's parents sit on the right of the left aisle (as they enter the church), and his parents sit on the left of the right aisle. This way, they are both seated in the center section of the house of worship.

Behind these front pews, several pews on either side of the center aisle are reserved for the immediate families of the couple. The people who are to sit there may have been given or sent pew cards to show their usher, or the usher may have a list of guests to be seated in the first few pews.

SEATING WIDOWED PARENTS

Widowed parents of either the bride or groom should not necessarily be expected to sit in lonely splendor at their child's wedding. If they prefer having someone by their side during the ceremony, it is perfectly correct to do so. They may choose a relative, a good friend, or perhaps a fiancé or companion. The guest of the widowed parent does not participate in any way, however, such as standing in the receiving line—unless he or she is engaged to the widowed parent or so close as to be family. In any case, every effort should be made to treat the companion as an honored guest.

SEATING PARENTS WHO ARE DIVORCED

When either the bride or groom's parents are divorced, there may be specific instructions for seating, in the interest of amicability. But they most likely would not sit together.

Unless the bride is estranged from her mother, her mother (and stepfather, if her mother has remarried) is seated in the front pew. Members of the mother's immediate family—the bride's maternal grandparents, aunts, and uncles—sit immediately behind her. The bride's father, after escorting his daughter up the

One of the greatest difficulties for brides today is choosing between a father and a stepfather as the person to "give her away"—that is, walk her down the aisle. It is no easy choice, especially when she is close to both. The most diplomatic decision may be to fall back on tradition and ask her biological father to escort her up the aisle. If she is closer to her stepfather, she would choose him; if her father has stepped forward to pay for the wedding, the decision again becomes cloudy. Some brides take a different route and have their mothers escort them. Others choose to walk alone or to have a brother or uncle do the honors.

It is rare that both fathers escort their daughter, but it's not unheard of—as long as they are friendly and share affection for the bride. Under no circumstances, however, would a bride have her mother and father escort her up the aisle if either has remarried. This would be inappropriate and artificial, not to mention potentially painful or threatening to the new spouses. If they are divorced but have not remarried, both could escort her, but again it might present problems. It is better for the bride to walk with her father and let her mother be seated before the ceremony.

aisle and presenting her to her groom, sits in the next pew back, behind the bride's mother's family, with his wife and their family members.

If there is bitterness between divorced parents but the bride has remained close to both, the situation is much more difficult. Unless she has lived with her father since the divorce, her mother may host the wedding, either entirely or with the bride's father. The usual procedure is followed, with her father giving her away and then sitting in the pew behind his ex-wife's family. His second wife may sit there, too, if the bride wishes, unless her mother strongly resents the new wife. In that case, it would be more tactful for the new wife to sit farther back in the church, preferably with a friend. In these circumstances, the father might not even attend the reception. Paternal grandparents and other relatives on his side might be excluded entirely, unless the bride has remained close to them.

Even if the wedding is given by the bride's father, the seating arrangements remain the same. The bride's mother (and her present husband, if the bride is

At the Ceremony

comfortable about his being there) sits in the first pew. The bride's father and stepmother sit in the front pew only when the bride is estranged from or not close to her mother or is closer to her stepmother. Ordinarily, the father's family sits in the third or fourth pew, where he joins them after escorting the bride.

When the groom's parents are divorced, they are seated in the same manner. The groom's mother, accompanied by close members of her family, sits in the first pew (or pews) on the right side of the aisle. The groom's father and family sit in the next pew behind the groom's mother's family.

Naturally, if the divorce is an amicable one and all are great friends, there is no reason that all the bride or groom's divorced parents cannot share the first pew. It is only when relations are strained or sensitivities great that the etiquette of careful seating need be employed.

GETTING READY FOR THE PROCESSIONAL

Once the mothers are seated, it is time to place the aisle runner, if one is being used. Two ushers or the junior ushers pick up the runner, place it at the foot of the chancel steps, and carefully draw it back down the length of the aisle. A broad white ribbon may be put in place on either side of the aisle. The ribbons have been folded at the ends of the last reserved pews. The ushers walk with the ribbons to the back of the church, laying them over the end of each row. The ribbons are not removed until the guests in the reserved pews leave. After they are escorted out, the ushers will indicate that the remaining guests should exit, starting at the front.

SHARING THE PEACE

When communion is offered at a Christian wedding, the minister or priest will often ask everyone to reach out and share a message of peace with one another, at the point in the service where he says "peace be with you." At this time, and especially if the guests are few in number, the wedding party may move out into the congregation, offering handshakes, hugs, and kisses to guests. It is but a small break in the ceremony and it gives the bride and groom the opportunity to connect with their guests.

After the bride's mother is taken to her place, no guest may be seated from the center aisle. If guests arrive after the bride's mother is seated, they must stand in the vestibule, go to the balcony, or slip into a pew from the side aisles. The ushers may assist them.

The bride and her father arrive at the precise moment for the wedding to start, and the procession forms in the vestibule at the back of the sanctuary. As soon as the attendants have taken their places, a signal is given, and the officiant, followed in order by the groom and the best man, enters the church. Many churches have a buzzer system in the vestry or study to announce to the groom and best man that all is ready. In others, the sexton or wedding coordinator goes to the vestry with the message; sometimes the opening bars of the wedding march or another specific piece of music give the signal. In any case, the groom and the best man enter and take their places at the right side of the head of the aisle or, in some churches, at the top of the steps to the chancel. The best man stands to the groom's left and slightly behind him, and they both face the congregation. As soon as they reach their places, the procession begins.

AN ARCH OF UMBRELLAS

On your exit from the ceremony, take a page from the military honor guard and run through an arch not of swords or sabers but of, say, golf clubs, if time on the links together began your romance. Try oars if you love canoeing, umbrellas if you love the rain, or baseball bats if you can't get enough of America's favorite pastime. The choices, as you can see, are limitless.

THE PROCESSIONAL

The ushers lead the procession, walking two by two, the shortest men first. Junior ushers follow the adults. Junior bridesmaids come next. The bridesmaids follow, walking in pairs or singly. (See Chapter 10, Planning the Ceremony, for more details and a diagram of processionals for both Christian and Jewish weddings.)

The spaces between each couple or individual should be even and approximately four paces long. The hesitation step, which used to be very popular, is actually considered awkward and difficult these days. A slow, natural walk is the more graceful.

The arrangement of the attendants at the front of the church varies. The ushers may divide and stand on either side, as may the bridesmaids, or the ushers may line up on one side and the bridesmaids on the other. Your minister or priest will help determine what looks best during the rehearsal. In a Jewish ceremony, the rabbi helps determine how many of the wedding party fit under the *chuppah*.

The maid of honor stands to the bride's left or behind her. If there is a flower girl, she stands on the other side of the maid of honor. The best man stands in his original position, but because he turned to face the altar as the bride and her father arrived at the altar, he is now on the groom's right. If there is a ring bearer, he stands next to the best man.

THE CEREMONY BEGINS

When the bride reaches the groom's side, she lets go of her father's arm, transfers her flowers to her left arm, and gives her right hand to her groom. He puts it through his left arm, and her hand rests near his elbow. If the bride is not comfortable this way, they may stand hand in hand or merely side by side. The minister faces them from the front of the chancel.

In a Christian ceremony, the bride's father remains by her side or a step or two behind until the minister says, "Who will support and bless this marriage?" or "Who represents the families in blessing this marriage?" The bride's father reaches in front of her and puts her right hand into that of the minister and says, "Her mother and I do." He then turns and takes his seat in the assigned pew.

In a Jewish ceremony, the groom and his parents walk in the processional before the bride and her parents. When they all arrive at the *chuppah*, the bride joins the groom by standing on his right. Each set of parents remains with the bride and groom during the ceremony.

If there are children from the bride or groom's previous marriages, the officiant could ask, "Who will support this new family with their love and prayers?" In this instance, the bride, groom, children, and often the guests may answer together.

THE RECESSIONAL: I NOW PRONOUNCE YOU. . .

At the conclusion of the ceremony, the officiant may say, "I now pronounce you husband and wife." Some of the clergy are still saying "man and wife." If you prefer, ask to be pronounced as "husband and wife."

The bride and groom kiss, and the recessional begins. The maid of honor hands the bride her bouquet back and straightens her gown and train for her as the bride starts down the aisle. The flower girl and ring bearer walk together behind the bride and the groom, followed by the maid of honor and the best man. The other attendants step forward and exit behind the couple either singly or side by side, depending on their number. They may walk together as they entered, groomsmen with one another and bridesmaids together, or a bridesmaid may walk with an usher. Each member of the wedding party knows how to fall in line, since this recessional will have been practiced during the rehearsal.

YOU MAY KISS THE BRIDE

Why does a wedding ceremony end with a kiss? A kiss was long believed to be the medium for the exchange of spirits where a part of the bride's soul joined the groom's soul, and vice versa, truly uniting the couple as one. In some cultures, a kiss literally seals the wedding contract, while in others a kiss is not required. Most people just think of it as an expression of love.

THE PHOTOGRAPHER REAPPEARS

The photographer, who has remained at the back of the sanctuary after taking pictures of the bride's arrival, may now catch the radiant couple as they come down the aisle. The videographer, who may have been taping from the back of the balcony, quickly descends and joins the photographer in documenting the wedding party's recessional.

At the Ceremony

At this point, any number of things can happen. The bride and groom, their mothers, and the maid of honor and bridesmaids may form a receiving line and greet guests as they exit. If either the bride or groom has children, they may want to have them stand in the receiving line, too, as a part of the family.

If a receiving line is planned for the reception instead, the wedding party may wait out of sight to the side as guests exit. They may then gather at the top of the steps for a wedding-party portrait. While they are posing, the person delegated to distribute rose petals or bubble-bottles to the lingering guests begins to hand them out. When the photography is completed, the wedding party heads to their waiting cars and is showered by the guests.

If certain aspects of the ceremony are to be re-created for the photographer, the wedding party waits to the side and re-enters the building for pictures to be taken as quickly as possible. The guests either wait, taking their cue from the parents, or depart for the reception if it is suggested they do so.

Regardless of which exit procedure is followed, the bride and groom must at some point sign their wedding papers, witnessed by the maid of honor and best man. If this has not been taken care of before the ceremony, then it should be done before they leave for the reception.

IN THE MEXICAN TRADITION

Brides and grooms of Mexican descent who are removed from their heritage by time and distance can reconnect by adding long-standing cultural traditions to their nuptials. In addition to the common customs of decorating the church with white roses and holding the mass at nine o'clock in the evening, they can ask those closest to them to be "godparents," giving a responsibility to each. One responsibility is to make three bouquets—one to place on the altar; one to keep as a memento; and one for the bride to toss at the reception. Another godparent holds a dish with 13 gold coins ("arras") and rings: The groom takes the coins from the disk and hands them to the bride as a sign of giving her all he possesses; he also promises he will use all he possesses for her support. Two more godparents carry a very long rosary rope ("lazo"), which they drape around the bride and groom as the couple kneels at the altar. Besides the appointing of godparents, musical tradition may also be included: At the reception, the band can play music for La Vibora, a line dance the single women perform.

LEAVING FOR THE RECEPTION

Cars taking the wedding party to the reception should be waiting at the entrance of the ceremony site. The bride and groom are helped into the first car by the best man and are the first to leave for the reception. The bride's parents ride together, and the maid of honor and bridesmaids depart in the same cars in which they arrived. The flower girl and ring bearer may travel with their parents or they may ride with either the bride's parents or the bridal attendants.

CHAPTER 18

AT THE RECEPTION

No matter how large or how small, your reception is a celebration, and you and your family are the hosts. You are there to welcome guests, feed them, enjoy their company, and thank them. Let them know how happy and pleased you are that they are there to celebrate with you.

THE RECEIVING LINE

A receiving line is a traditional way for the wedding party to greet guests at the ceremony before leaving for the reception or upon their arrival there. Having a receiving line or not is simply a matter of choice. Its purpose makes sense at a large wedding, where it is unlikely that the bride, the groom, and their parents will get a chance to speak to everyone. If you choose to eliminate a receiving line, make sure that you greet every guest at your reception.

Usually, the wedding party completes the formal photographs at the ceremony site before leaving for the reception. If you choose to do so, take the pictures quickly so that guests won't have to wait a long time for you, your parents, and your attendants at the reception. Ideally, you will have discussed the best place to form a receiving line with the club manager or caterer, one that permits guests to have a refreshment while they are waiting their turn and one that flows into the open area where the festivities will take place. Because guests should not go through the receiving line either eating or drinking, a table should be placed near the beginning of the line for them to deposit glasses and plates or napkins.

WHO STANDS WHERE?

The traditional order, based on the custom of the wedding being hosted by the bride's parents, is for the bride's mother to stand first in line to greet guests.

MOTHER OF BRIDE   FATHER OF BRIDE   MOTHER OF GROOM   FATHER OF GROOM   BRIDE   GROOM   MAID OF HONOR   BRIDESMAIDS

The bride's father is next, followed by the groom's mother and father, followed by the bride, the groom, the maid of honor, and sometimes, the bridesmaids.

It is not required that fathers stand in the receiving line, but it gives them an opportunity to greet all the guests— something they might not otherwise be able to do at a large reception. It is a general guideline that if one father stands in the line, the other father does as well.

Divorced Parents

Divorced parents do not stand in the line together. The parent and stepparent who are giving the reception, or with whom the bride or groom has spent the most time, are the ones who should normally be in the line. If neither parent has remarried and both are helping give the reception, it is easier to go by the rule of thumb that fathers needn't stand in the line, leaving only the bride or groom's mother to do so.

When divorced parents are friendly and accept each other's new spouses, or when both couples are giving the wedding, they may all stand in the receiving line—separated, however, by the groom's parents to avoid creating confusion. If the groom's parents, too, are divorced and remarried, and you absolutely want everyone in the receiving line, then each set of parents would alternate: bride's family, groom's family, bride's family, and groom's family. Or for the sake of not confusing guests with so many parents—and in the interest of having a line that isn't too long—the sets of parents may take turns standing in line.

The lineup would then look something like this:

- bride's mother
- bride's stepfather
- groom's mother
- groom's stepfather
- bride's stepmother
- bride's father
- groom's stepmother
- groom's father
- bride
- groom
- maid of honor
- set the bridesmaids free—the line is long enough!

There are almost unlimited variables in the case of divorced and remarried parents. It is best that the bride and groom plan early with their parents to determine who stands where. Usually the traditional guideline—the hosts stand first in line—comes in handy for helping to diffuse any hurt feelings and questions. And sometimes the fathers circulate among the guests simply to make things easier.

Bridesmaids and Children

Although it is quite correct for bridesmaids to stand in the receiving line, they don't have to, especially if the line is long. Doing so only prolongs the line and stretches the imaginations of guests who think it necessary to come up with a polite, clever comment for everyone. Young children—flower girls, ring bearers, pages, and train bearers—do not stand in the line; the children of the bride and groom, however, may be in line if they are old enough and want to do so.

Disabled Parents

A disabled parent or a parent in ill health may be in the line seated on a high stool, if possible, or in a chair or wheelchair.

PASSING THROUGH THE LINE

Guests should pass through the line as quickly as possible, pausing only long enough to be greeted by the hostess, to wish the bride happiness, and to congratulate the groom. Close friends and family often accompany a congratulations with a kiss. Otherwise, each person extends a hand to the person in line, who turns to introduce him or her to the next person in line before greeting the next guest. This eliminates the need for the guest to have to introduce himself over and over again, and it also makes the process more personal.

No one should tie up the line with extended conversation. If a guest is garrulous, it is up to the parents or the bride and groom to gently break in and say, "We're so glad you're here. . . let me introduce you to . . ." to help move that person along.

At the end of the line, there may be a waiter with a tray of champagne or other beverages offered to guests as they pass on their way to the reception area.

THE GUEST BOOK

It is not obligatory to have a guest book at the reception. But as a memento of the occasion and a record of all present, a guest book is a nice touch. Place the book on a table near the reception entrance or at the end of the receiving line. Delegate a friend, a member of the family, or an attendant to stand by the book and remind each guest to sign. Very rarely, a guest book is placed at the entrance to the ceremony, and one of the ushers asks guests to sign it before entering the sanctuary. This is done when there are more guests attending the ceremony than the reception—for example, when an officiant extends to church members an open invitation to the nuptials.

If a female member of the family or a close friend is supervising the guest book, present her with a corsage or nosegay to show that she is an honored person in your heart. A male friend might be given a small book or other token.

> ## CASH BARS: A NO-NO
>
> You wouldn't think of asking someone to pay for a cocktail in your home, so don't even consider a cash bar at your reception. When you invite guests to your reception they are just that—your guests. If a bar is not in your budget, serve soft drinks, but do not let the hotel or club or reception site manager talk you into selling tickets for drinks or having guests pay their way.

TOASTS

At a sit-down reception, champagne is poured as soon as everyone is seated. At a cocktail reception where guests are either seated at small tables or standing, it is poured after everyone has gone through the receiving line. (If champagne is not being served, toasts are made with whatever beverage guests have in front of them, whether water, soft drinks, punch, or juice.)

The best man attracts the attention of the guests, either from his table or from the microphone, and proposes a toast to the bride and groom. The toast can be the only one offered; often, however, both fathers offer toasts welcoming each other's families and guests or simply expressing their delight in their children's happiness. Other members of the bridal party may propose toasts, and the groom often toasts his bride and new parents-in-law. If any telegrams or messages have been sent, they are read by the best man at this time.

Everyone should rise for the toasts to the newlyweds except the bride and groom, who remain seated. If a toast is directed to the bride only, the groom rises; if it is directed to their parents, both the bride and groom rise. If there is no seating and everyone is standing, including the bride and groom,

---

HERE'S TO THE HAPPY COUPLE!

Short and sweet—that's what the best man's toast to the newlyweds should be. This is not the time for anecdotes or jokes. Two that fit the bill are as follows:

- Quoting from William Shakespeare's "The Tempest":

  "Please join me in a toast to Mark and Cindy, first written by William Shakespeare: 'Look down you gods and on this couple drop a blessed crown. May all your days be blessed and crowned with joy and happiness.' To Mark and Cindy!"

- A favorite Irish blessing:

  > May the wind be always at your back.
  > May the road rise up to meet you.
  > May the sun shine warm on your face,
  > The rains fall soft on your fields.
  > Until we meet again, may the Lord
  > Hold you in the hollow of his hand.

then the newlyweds simply smile as toasts are made. They do not drink a toast to themselves.

When making a toast together, the bride and groom do not make a joint speech, but rather stand together while one speaks or take turns speaking.

THE BLESSING

If a meal is included in your reception, you might want to say grace before guests begin moving through a buffet line or before waiters begin serving. This is a good time to have a relative, a friend, or your officiant participate. No matter who gives the blessing, you should be sure to ask him or her at least a few minutes beforehand, so that a little thought can go into the prayer.

If you have a DJ or bandleader, you might ask him to request everyone's attention, at which point the person giving the blessing goes to the microphone. If there is no microphone, the best man may call for quiet and introduce the person saying the blessing. The blessing complete, the best man would then thank that person, signaling to all that guests can begin eating.

DANCING

At a seated dinner, dancing should not start until after dessert has been eaten. If, however, the reception follows an afternoon wedding and the meal won't be served until later, guests may dance before the bridal party goes to its table. At a buffet reception, the newlyweds may start the dancing as soon as they have left the receiving line or after any group photographs have been taken.

The bride and groom dance the first dance, while guests watch and applaud. When the second song begins, the bride's father-in-law asks the bride for the second dance, and then the bride's father cuts in. The groom, meanwhile, dances with his mother-in-law and then with his mother. Next, the bride's father may ask the groom's mother to dance, and the groom's father asks the bride's mother. As the groom dances with the maid of honor and the ushers with the bridesmaids, guests may begin dancing.

When the family makeup is such that it complicates the order of dances—more than one father and mother, stepparents—then the dancing becomes general as soon as the newlyweds have danced the first dance. The bridal party joins the bride and groom on the dance floor—a signal to the guests that everyone else may join in. The bride and groom should make a point to dance with all of their parents during the reception.

At some point during the dancing, perhaps a half-hour or so before the bride and groom leave the reception, the bride and her father may have a special dance of their own. The bride may want to select the song ahead of time. They may either dance the entire song alone or be joined by the bride's mother and the groom. If the latter, they may change partners halfway through the song and join their respective spouses; the other guests may then join them on the dance floor.

CUTTING THE WEDDING CAKE

At a seated meal, the cake is cut just before dessert is to be served. Slices can then be passed with the other dessert. If the reception is a buffet or cocktail reception, the cake is cut later, often shortly before the couple departs.

YOU'RE OFF!

You probably have formulated a general time to leave the reception. Stick to it. You may be having so much fun that you want to stay forever, but because guests don't generally leave until you do, courtesy demands that you depart.

THEY'RE OFF!: WHY IS IT CALLED A HONEYMOON?

Wherever you spend your honeymoon, tradition says that you should stay a month! In the Middle Ages mead (a fermented drink made with honey, the symbol of fertility, health, and life) was drunk by the bride and groom for 30 days (the cycle of the moon). During this period the couple stayed hidden from their parents and friends, the mead no doubt loosening their inhibitions and getting the marriage off to an auspicious start.

TOSSING THE BOUQUET

Traditionally, just before the couple leaves the reception, the bride or her maid of honor gathers the bridesmaids and all single female guests together, often at the foot of a stairs, in the center of the dance floor, or by the door. The bride then turns her back and over her shoulder throws her bouquet or a facsimile of it, called a tossing bouquet, if she wants to keep and preserve her original one. Tradition has it that whoever catches the bouquet—who gets to keep it, by the way—will be the next one married.

THROWING A GARTER

In some communities, it is traditional for the bride to wear an ornamental garter just below her knee, so the groom can remove it easily and tastefully with no fanfare. For this event, the best man and the ushers gather, and the groom throws the garter over his shoulder. According to tradition, the man who catches the garter will be the next to marry. The throwing of the garter should never be done in a tasteless manner—the groom fondling the bride's leg for all to see, for example, or the man who caught it suggestively putting it on the leg of the woman who caught the bouquet. These are embarrassing actions, for both the participants and the guests.

THE DEPARTURE

The bride and groom may leave in their bridal finery or change into "going away" clothes. If they decide to change clothes, the maid of honor and the best man generally attend the bride and groom in their separate changing rooms and collect the wedding finery. At some point, parents and relatives join them for a good-bye.

When the newlyweds are ready to go, the attendants form a farewell line and are joined by the guests. The couple is often showered with rose petals, confetti, or the like as they dash to their departure vehicle, which may have been decorated by the ushers with "Just Married" written in shaving cream or something similar that is (preferably) biodegradable and easy to clean.

Many couples believe in making a grand departure from the reception (and even the ceremony), whether by horse-drawn carriage, on horseback, or on a boat in water strewn with rose petals. Whatever you do, whether simple or grand, make sure to have someone recording the moment, in photographs or videotape, when you make the great leap into your new life.

INDEX